DB2® Version 8:
The Official Guide

IBM Press Series—Information Management

***DB2 Universal Database v8 for Linux, UNIX, and Windows Database
Administration Certification Guide, Fifth Edition***
Baklarz and Wong

***Advanced DBA Certification Guide and Reference for DB2 Universal Database
v8 for Linux, UNIX, and Windows***
Snow and Phan

***DB2 Universal Database v8 Application Development Certification Guide,
Second Edition***
Martineau, Sanyal, Gashyna, and Kyprianou

DB2 Version 8: The Official Guide
Zikopoulos, Baklarz, deRoos, and Melnyk

DB2 Universal Database v8 Certification Test 700 Study Guide
Sanders

Teach Yourself DB2 Universal Database in 21 Days
Visser and Wong

DB2 UDB for OS/390 v7.1 Application Certification Guide
Lawson

DB2 SQL Procedural Language for Linux, UNIX, and Windows
Yip, Bradstock, Curtis, Gao, Janmohamed, Liu, and McArthur

Business Intelligence for the Enterprise
Biere

DB2 Universal Database v8 Handbook for Windows, UNIX, and Linux
Gunning

Other Complementary DB2 Titles

DB2 Universal Database for OS/390 Version 7.1 Certification Guide
Lawson and Yevich

***DB2 Universal Database v7.1 for UNIX, Linux, Windows and OS/2—Database
Administration Certification Guide, Fourth Edition***
Baklarz and Wong

DB2 Universal Database v7.1 Application Development Certification Guide
Sanyal, Martineau, Gashyna, and Kyprianou

DB2 UDB for OS/390: An Introduction to DB2 OS/390
Sloan and Hernandez

IBM Press™

DB2 Version 8: The Official Guide

DB2® Information Management Software

Paul C. Zikopoulos   George Baklarz
Dirk deRoos   Roman B. Melnyk

PRENTICE HALL
Professional Technical Reference
Upper Saddle River, New Jersey 07458
www.phptr.com

Note to U.S. Government Users — Documentation related to restricted rights — Use, duplication, or disclosure is subject to restrictions set forth in GSA ADP Schedule Contract with IBM Corp.

Editorial/production supervision: *MetroVoice Publishing Services*
Cover design director: *Jerry Votta*
Cover design: *IBM Corporation*
Manufacturing manager: *Alexis Heydt-Long*
Publisher: *Jeffrey Pepper*
Editorial assistant: *Linda Ramagnano*
Marketing manager: *Debby vanDijk*
IBM Consulting Editor: *Susan Visser*

Published by Pearson Education, Inc.
Publishing as Prentice Hall Professional Technical Reference
Upper Saddle River, NJ 07458

Prentice Hall PTR offers excellent discounts on this book when ordered in quantity for bulk purchases or special sales. For more information, please contact: U.S. Corporate and Government Sales, 1-800-382-3419, corpsales@pearsontechgroup.com. For sales outside of the U.S., please contact: International Sales, 1-317-581-3793, international@pearsontechgroup.com.

Printed in the United States of America

First Printing

ISBN   0-13-140158-0

Pearson Education LTD.
Pearson Education Australia PTY, Limited
Pearson Education Singapore, Pte. Ltd.
Pearson Education North Asia Ltd.
Pearson Education Canada, Ltd.
Pearson Educación de Mexico, S.A. de C.V.
Pearson Education — Japan
Pearson Education Malaysia, Pte. Ltd.

Contents

Foreword   xvii

Dedications and Acknowledgments   xix

Part 1   Packaging and Licensing   1

CHAPTER 1   Changes to DB2 Universal Database
and DB2 Connect Packaging and Licensing   3

DB2 Universal Database and DB2 Connect Supported Operating Systems   3
Changes to DB2 Universal Database Licensing and Packaging   5
DB2 UDB Personal Edition   5
DB2 UDB Express   5
    DB2 UDB Workgroup Server and Workgroup Server Unlimited Editions   7
    DB2 UDB Enterprise Server Edition and the Database Partitioning Feature 8
    DB2 UDB Data Warehouse Edition   8
Changes to DB2 Connect Licensing and Packaging   12
    DB2 Connect Application Server Edition   12
    Integrated DB2 Connect Component in DB2 Universal Database Enterprise Edition 12
    Miscellaneous Changes   13
    Changes to Related DB2 Universal Database Products   14

Part 2   Performance   19

CHAPTER 2   Multidimensional Clustering Tables   21

MDC 101: A Simple Contrast between Traditional and Multidimensional Tables   22
Terminology Required to Understand MDC Tables   26
    MDC Table   26
    Dimension   26
    Slice   26
    Cell   28
    Block   29
    Block Size or Blocking Factor   29
    Block Index   29
    Block ID   30
    Generated Column   30
    Monotonicity   31
How MDC Tables Work   31
    Creating an MDC Table   33
    Indexes and MDC Tables   34
    MDC and Query SELECT, INSERT, UPDATE, and DELETE Operations   42
Picking a Dimension for an MDC Table   47
Summary   48

CHAPTER 3   Declared Global Temporary Tables   51

Index Support for DGTTs   52
    Index Restrictions on a DGTT   52
    Creating an Index on a DGTT   53
Minimal Undo Logging to Support the Rollback of Data Changes to DGTTs   54
Statistics Support on DGTTs   55

CHAPTER 4   System Default Value and NULL Compression   57

How Data Compression Works in DB2 UDB   57
    The New Row Record Format   59
Compression Example   60

Supported Data Types for Compression 64
How Do I Know if Compression Is Turned On? 65
Estimating Compression Savings 66

CHAPTER 5   **Informational Constraints** **67**

Why Informational Constraints? 67
Using Informational Constraints 70
  Informational Constraints Example 70
  Usage Considerations 73

CHAPTER 6   **Connection Concentrator** **75**

Connection Management Improvements 75
Activating the Connection Concentrator 76
Connection Concentrator Operation 76

CHAPTER 7   **User-Maintained Materialized Query Tables** **79**

Restrictions 79
Creating Materialized Query Tables 80
Populating Materialized Query Tables 80
Leveraging Materialized Query Tables for Improved Query Performance 81

CHAPTER 8   **Database System Monitoring Enhancements** **83**

Preventing the Collection of Timestamps 83
Enhanced Deadlock Monitoring 84
SQL Access to Event Monitor Data 84
SQL Access to Snapshot Monitor Data 86
  SNAPSHOT_FILEW Snapshot Request Types 86
  Capturing a Snapshot to a File with SNAPSHOT_FILEW 87
  Capturing a Snapshot From a File 88
DB2_SNAPSHOT_NOAUTH Registry Variable 88
Performance Monitor Control Center Tool Has Been Deprecated 89

CHAPTER 9   **Miscellaneous Performance Enhancements**   **91**

Distributed Catalog Cache   91
Prefetching Enhancements with Block-Based Buffer Pools   92
Page Cleaner I/O Improvements   93
Multithreading of Java-Based Routines   93
64-Bit Support   94
Automatic Relationship and Association Management (ARAM)   94
New Join Variations   95
Increased Opportunity for Selection of Bit-Filters   95

Part 3   Manageability   **97**

CHAPTER 10   **Logging**   **99**

Transactional Logging Improvements   99
    Increased Log Space   99
    Infinite Active Log Space   99
    Controlling the Consumption of Log Space   100
    Transactional Logging Performance Improvements   100
    Log Mirroring   101
    Blocking Transactions When the Logs Are Full   101
Diagnostic Logging Improvements   102

CHAPTER 11   **Load Enhancements**   **103**

Online Load   103
Locking Behavior   105
New Table States   105
Loading Data into Partitioned Databases   106
Loading Data from a Cursor   109
Load Wizard   109

CHAPTER 12   **DB2 Tools**   **115**

Configuration Assistant   115
Health Center   118

Memory Visualizer   124
    Memory Tracker   127
Storage Management   128
    Storage Management View Columns   133
Indoubt Transaction Manager   135
Fault Monitor   138

CHAPTER 13   **Container Operations**   **141**

Table Space Maps   141
Dropping Containers from a DMS Table Space   143
Reducing the Size of Containers in a DMS Table Space   144
Adding Containers to a DMS Table Space without Rebalancing   145

CHAPTER 14   **Dynamic Memory Allocation and**
    Online Reconfiguration   **147**

CHAPTER 15   **Online Utilities**   **151**

Online Reorganization   151
    Table Reorganization   151
    Index Reorganization   153
Online Database Inspection Tool   153
Incremental Maintenance of Materialized Query Tables   156

CHAPTER 16   **Miscellaneous Manageability Enhancements** **161**

Throttling Utilities   161
New Administration Notification Log   163
Table Space Change History File   164
QUIESCE Command   166
RUNSTATS Command Enhancements   167
Point-in-Time Rollforward Recovery to Local Time   168
XBSA Support   168
Data Movement Enhancements for Original Equipment Manufacturer Databases 169

Trace Facility Enhancements   169
Multiple Service Level Install for UNIX   170
New Tivoli-focused Options   171
LDAP Support on Linux   171
Dynamic LPAR Support for AIX5.2B   172
Dynamic System Domain Support   172
Transaction Log Space Usage   173
ALTER TABLE VARGRAPHIC   173
Command History Support and CLP Roundtrip Editing   173

Part 4   Development   175

CHAPTER 17   SQL Enhancements   177

SQL Insert through UNION ALL   177
Using Table Spaces with UNION ALL   180
INSTEAD OF Triggers   183
ORDER BY Enhancements   186
        FETCH FIRST Clause   186
        ORDER BY ORDER OF   186
FETCH FIRST   187
SQL Functions   188
        VARCHAR_FORMAT and TIMESTAMP_FORMAT   188
        XML Publishing   190
        Snapshot API   191
        Health Snaphots   194
Identity Column Support   196
        Identity Column   196
        Sequences   198
        Additional IDENTITY Column Considerations   199
CALL Statement   200
MERGE SQL   201
        MERGE Syntax   203
        Additional WHEN MATCHED Logic   205
        IGNORING Records   206
        Raising Error Conditions   207
        Authorization   208

SQL Sampling   209
    BERNOULLI Sampling   209
    SYSTEM Sampling   211
    REPEATABLE Sampling   214
    Additional Considerations   215
Summary   215

CHAPTER 18   **Application Development Enhancements** **217**

Development Center   217
    Starting the Development Center   218
    Project View   219
    Creating a UDF   224
    Creating a Stored Procedure   231
    Development Center   234
    Debugging and Testing   236
Debugging Java and SQL PL   239
    SQL PL Debugger   239
    Debugging Java Stored Procedures   239
SQL Assist   240
    Starting SQL Assist   240
    SQL Assist Structure   241
    Outline View   242
    Details Area   243
    SQL Code   245
    Panel Buttons   246
    Sample SQL Assist Session   246
    Summary   257
Java Enhancements   257
    Type 4 Driver Platform Support   258
    Type 2 Platform Support   258
    Additional Features   258
Package Version Identifiers   259
    Package Overview   259
    VERSION Example   260
    Package Privileges   260
Flush Package Cache   261
Summary   261

CHAPTER 19   **DB2 in the Microsoft Environment**   **263**

Windows 2003 Support   264
DB2 Development Add-Ins for Visual Studio .NET   265
   Product Availability   266
   Registering the Visual Studio .NET Add-Ins   266
   Development Overview   267
   Solution Explorer   268
   Server Explorer   270
   SQL Editor   273
   Dynamic Help   274
   Output Views   274
   Customizing the DB2 Development Tools   275
   Launching DB2 Development and Administration Tools   276
   Summary   278
Native Managed .NET Providers   278
   DB2 Managed Provider ADO.NET Objects   278
   DB2 Objects in the Visual Studio .NET Data Toolbox   278
   Sample DB2 ADO.NET Code   279
   Managed Provider Tools   280
DB2 Database Project for Visual Studio .NET   282
   Adding a DB2 Database Project   283
   Choosing a DB2 Database Reference for Projects   283
   DB2 Project Scripts   284
   Advanced Scripting and Script Options   290
   Advanced Script Options   290
   Project Configurations and Properties   292
   Project Dependencies and Build Order   295
   Summary   296
Loosely Coupled Transaction Support   297
Windows Management Instrumentation (WMI)   298
OLE DB Provider   301
   Enhancements   301
   Restrictions   302
Summary   303

Part 5   Information Integration   305

CHAPTER 20   Federated Systems   307

DB2 Information Integrator   307
Federated Systems Enhancements   308
    Manipulating Data on Data Sources   308
    Manipulating Tables on Data Sources   308
    MQTs for Data Sources   310
    DB2 Control Center Administration of Federated Objects   310
    More Supported Federated Server Platforms   311
    Data Sources Available in DB2 Information Integrator   311
WebSphere MQ Integration Enhancements   312
    Asynchronous MQ Listener   312
    Transactional Support for Websphere MQ Message Queues   313

CHAPTER 21   Web Services   315

DB2 as a Web Services Consumer   315
    Installing the SOAP UDFs   316
    Signatures of the SOAP UDFs   316
    Using the SOAP UDFs   317
DB2 as a Web Service Provider   319
    DB2 Web Services Architecture   319
    DADX Files   320
    Installing and Configuring WORF   322
DB2 Web Tools and the Application Server for DB2   322
XML Enhancements   322
    Migrating XML-Enabled Databases to v8   323
    Automatically Validating XML Documents against Schemas   323
    Manually Validating XML Documents   323
    New XML UDFs   324
    Normalization of Timestamp Data   325
    XML Extender Functionality in Partitioned Database Environments   325
    New XML MQ UDFs and Stored Procedures   326

CHAPTER 22 **Replication Enhancements** **329**

Replication Center 329

Starting the Replication Center 329

Replication Center Launchpad 330

Replication Definitions Folder 330

Operations Folder 331

Replication Monitoring 332

Replication Alert Monitor 332

Checking the Current Status of Replication Programs 333

Analyze Historical Data of Replication Programs 334

General Enhancements 335

Windows Process Model for Replication Programs 335

Password Encryption for Replication Programs 336

Replicating Data Links Values 336

Longer Table Names and Column Names 336

Migration Utility 336

New Trace Facility 336

64-Bit Support for Replication Programs 336

Capture Enhancements 337

Controlling the Capture Program 337

Changing the Capture Program's Operational Parameters 337

New Start Modes for Capture 338

Capture and Apply Programs Can Be Started in Any Order 338

Dynamically Updatable Replication Definitions 338

Dynamic Addition of Columns to Replication Source Tables 338

Enabling Row Capture for Individual Replication Sources 339

Control over Recapturing Data from Replicas 339

Concurrent Capturing and Pruning of Data 340

Multiple Capture Instances 340

Apply Enhancements 342

Transaction Commit Frequency 342

Replicating Changes to Target-Key Columns 342

Replication Performance 343

Fewer Joins between Replication Tables 343

Faster Full Refreshes of Target Tables 343

Improved ASNLOAD Exit Routine 343

Apply Program Optimization for One Subscription Set 343

Fewer Updates for Subscription Sets with Multiple Members 344

APPENDIX A   **CD-ROM Installation**   **345**

DB2 Installation   345
Documentation   345
DB2DEMO   346
    Installation File   347
    Setup and Installation of the Program   347
    Advanced Installation   351
    Special Notes for Windows 98/Me Users   351
    Uninstalling the Demonstration   352
    Support   353

     Index   **355**

Foreword

I t has been a banner year for DB2 UDB version 8, and we are still months away from celebrating the first anniversary of our general availability. Shortly after being introduced into the market, DB2 UDB v8 has amassed a distinguished list of accomplishments.

Within the first few weeks, we captured the ultimate TPC-H data warehousing crown by becoming the first database ever to succeed and publish at the challenging 10TB scale factor. At the time of this writing, we have captured the TPC-C "world cup" with the industry's leading OLTP performance and price-performance. Along the way, we delivered many other firsts and leadership accomplishments including gaining .Net Connected certification; Windows 2003 certification; delivering support for emerging 64-bit platforms such as IA-64 and AMD Opteron; publishing leadership results for other important industry standard benchmarks such as SPECjAppServer2002 and SAP, and the list goes on and on. One could easily say that DB2 UDB v8 has captured the "grand slam" for information management technology.

But our trophy case is only one small part of our growing success story. In today's environment, everyone is being asked to do more with less. Whether you are working within a small company or large enterprise, the number of tasks that you are undoubtedly juggling has increased, effectively giving you less time to concentrate on each. Today, senior executives and business owners demand return on investment and business agility be measured in months. And at the same time that resource allocations are more scrutinized and in less supply, businesses are accumulating more data than ever before. Beyond the expanding management scope of traditional and non-traditional data loads that are growing into the petabytes, we are also are being asked to analyze this data on demand, in real time, at any time, in order to crystallize I/T mission statements into measurable business results.

We absolutely recognize and embrace these trends, so complimenting all the great new core technologies are new breakthrough interface externals that make DB2 UDB the leader for manageability and ease of development.

Manageability benefits from intelligent and dynamic innovations like the delivery of our SMART (Self Managing and Resource Tuning) features. These capabilities enable quicker up and running time, quicker configuration and tuning, better diagnostics and event monitoring, and more. DB2 UDB was already a market leader in terms of ease of use, and with these new features, DBAs and system administrators can now enjoy a new level of manageability and intelligent advice from the database itself.

For application development, DB2 UDB v8 added new integration and support features for Java and J2EE and for Windows development in Visual Studio and Visual Studio.net (including a native .net managed provider). We also increased integration with WebSphere. Utilizing DB2 UDB as a persistence store or Web Services engine becomes a snap as our features are integrated right into the leading application development environments. DB2 UDB's federated capabilities also allow you to leverage these applications across diverse sets of data types, databases, text files, email, presentations, packaged applications, etc. These capabilities help you achieve true economies of scale in developing new applications that work across your entire information infrastructure.

So what specifically are those features in DB2 UDB v8 that have allowed it to become such a powerhouse offering in such a short period of time? What set of industry leading capabilities have the engineers at IBM conceived in this version that has given DB2 UDB the competitive edge in so many areas? How can you take advantage of these new features and innovations to improve the productivity within your own I/T environment, regardless of whether it is small, large or enterprise-sized? I'll assert that you've come to the exact right place to start to answer those questions. Paul, George, Roman, and Dirk have compiled a very concise and well organized tour of the new capabilities within DB2 UDB and as all great communicators do, they demonstrate a distinctive competency for keeping the reader involved through a veritable plethora of material. By the time you finish the book you will possess knowledge for the arsenal of leading capabilities that you can begin to exploit to take your applications and systems to the next level of database technology, a level that we call Information on Demand.

I want to take one last opportunity to thank, no honor, the hundreds of talented individuals that contributed over the multi-year effort to bring DB2 UDB v8 to the market. DB2 UDB v8 is the result of their tireless passion to address the challenging requirements of our customers and partners. We spent many long hours laboring to deliver breakthrough technologies such as multidimensional clustering (MDC), SMART, in-place online table reorganization (a new revolutionary approach to online table reorganizations while providing true continuous availability), just to name a few. I think you will agree that we have achieved a milestone for the industry in DB2 UDB v8.

—Bob Picciano
Director of Database Technology
IBM Toronto Software Lab

Dedications and Acknowledgments

FROM PAUL C. ZIKOPOULOS

To my great uncle Harry Gotziaman (Gotziamanis), who grew from a young immigrant boy shining shoes for a nickel to a kind, generous, and successful businessman. He told me that he could never understand why everyone kept looking up at the tall buildings in the big cities because all the loose change was on the ground. There wasn't a person that my Uncle Harry wouldn't help—truly, he isn't just great because he's my mother's uncle.

Each book I write represents months of personal sacrifice and extra work. I can only say thanks to my wife Kelly, my family (mom, dad, twin Nicolette and husband John Knoteck, and brother Steve), my uncle John Gotziaman, and friends Mike Godfrey and Jeff Jacobs for their continued support and their willingness to schedule their lives around the few days that I am actually in the country (and for picking up the long-distance bills).

I also want to say thanks to Fred Gandolfi. He was my hiring manager at IBM who took a chance on me. I hope he feels it was the right decision.

Finally, special thanks goes to Leslie Cranston, senior software engineer at the IBM Toronto Lab, who helped write Chapter 2 and for spending her precious time making sure I got my part right.

FROM GEORGE BAKLARZ

I'd like to thank Katrina, Geoff, Andrew, Ellie (dog), and Tristan (cat) for their patience and understanding while I was working on this book. Their support and words of encouragement ("Get it done!") were much appreciated.

Special thanks goes to Abdul H. Al-Azzawe, senior software engineer at the IBM Silicon Valley Lab in San Jose, California. The Microsoft Visual Studio .NET integration material in Chapter 19 incorporates many ideas and examples from his papers on the DB2 Developer Domain Web site (*www7b.software.ibm.com/dmdd/*).

FROM DIRK deROOS

Many thanks to Paul, Roman, and George for including me in this project. And to my ever-understanding wife, Sandra, thank you for your support and encouragement.

FROM ROMAN B. MELNYK

The enduring support of my wife, Teresa, and of my wonderful daughters, Rosemary and Joanna, has been essential to my successful completion of this project.

FROM ALL OF US

Collectively, we want to thank the following for reviewing the book along the way: Brenda Winter, Sandra Magill, Robert Platek, Rakesh Goenka, Karl Rempel, Gene Kligerman, Sue Monje, Tyronne Mayadunne, Jesse Lee, Cathy Wong, Jessica Escott, John J. Rubin, Yiying Zhang, John P. Kennedy, Abdul Al-Azzawe, and Leslie Cransten. These are just a few of the people that really make our products shine!

We also want to thank Susan Visser for leading the charge to get more DB2 UDB books into the market, and John Botsford for helping us with the CDs. As well, this book would not be possible without our editing team (led by Scott Suckling) and our Aquisitions Editor (Jeffrey Pepper)—so a big thank you to both of you, too.

Finally, thanks to Bob Picciano for not only taking the time to personally write the foreword, but for his leadership and inspiration at the Toronto development lab that helps create the market for books like this.

Packaging and Licensing

- Changes to DB2 Universal Database and DB2 Connect Packaging and Licensing

Changes to DB2 Universal Database and DB2 Connect Packaging and Licensing

D B2 UDB v8.1 (and the extensions in v8.1.2) for Linux, UNIX, and Windows (referred to as DB2 UDB v8.1 unless otherwise noted) marks yet another stage in the evolution of relational databases. DB2 UDB v8 is *the* database of choice for the development and deployment of critical solutions such as e-business, business intelligence (BI), content management, enterprise resource planning (ERP), customer relationship management (CRM), planning and logistics management (PLM), and so on.

Highlights of the DB2 UDB v8.1 and v8.1.2 releases include new innovative management features, new levels of integration across traditional and nontraditional data types and storage engines, performance and availability enhancements, online management features, enhanced developer productivity, and more. For purposes of this chapter, all references to v8.1 also refer to v8.1.2 unless otherwise noted.

Along with a rich new set of features that cuts the time to value when deploying enterprise applications, the packaging and licensing terms of DB2 UDB (and its associated products) have been changed to deliver greater flexibility and value to its customer base. This chapter details the major packaging and licensing changes to the DB2 UDB product portfolio in the version 8.1 and version 8.1.2 releases. Complete details are available at *www.ibm.com/software/data/db2/*.

DB2 UNIVERSAL DATABASE AND DB2 CONNECT SUPPORTED OPERATING SYSTEMS

DB2 UDB v8.1 became generally available in late 2002 and was delivered for Linux (z/OS and Intel/AMD-based systems), Windows™, and UNIX®-based (AIX®, Solaris®, and HP-UX®) systems. DB2 UDB v8.1.2 became generally available in mid-2003.

In DB2 UDB v8.1, support for OS/2® and NUMA-Q/PTX® have been stabilized at the DB2 UDB v7.2 level. In a direction consistent with Microsoft's support schedule for the personal versions of their desktop operating systems, Windows 95 and Windows 98 (for DB2 Personal Edition) are no longer supported (DB2 clients are still available for Windows 98, however).

Details for end-of-service dates for all DB2 UDB releases and supported operating systems are available at *www.ibm.com/cgi-bin/db2www/data/db2/udb/winos2unix/support/index.d2w/report*. This Web site also contains release-specific product documentation, maintenance FixPaks, maintenance updates, technical hints and tips, and more.

DB2 UDB v8.1 also delivered full function support for 64-bit operating systems running on AIX, Solaris, and HP-UX. DB2 UDB v8.1.2 (delivered by applying the v8.1.2 update, formerly known as Fix Pack 2) adds 64-bit support for Intel Itanium 64 workstations that run Windows and Linux, as well as Linux-based AMD installation too. DB2 UDB on AIX, Solaris, and HP-UX can run in both 32-bit and 64-bit modes (on an instance-by-instance basis) on the same workstation. Mixed-bit versions of DB2 UDB in 64-bit mode *cannot* coexist in a Windows IA-64 or Linux IA-64 environment, as they support 64-bit DB2 UDB only. For example, a 32-bit version of DB2 UDB for Windows cannot be installed on a 64-bit machine.

Completing IBM's commitment to Linux across the world's most used hardware, DB2 UDB v8.1.2 also delivers a 32-bit version of its engine on iSeries and pSeries hardware. DB2 UDB customers on these platforms can now leverage the advantage of IBM's POWER processors using a lower cost and more flexible Linux environment. Today, customers can leverage the advantages of Linux on any IBM e-server: iSeries, pSeries, ZSeries, and xSeries.

As of the general availability date of v8.1.2, DB2 UDB and DB2 Connect are supported on the operating systems listed in Table 1.1.

Table 1.1   Operating Systems Supported by DB2 UDB and DB2 Connect in v8.1 and v8.1.2

Operating System	Supported Versions for DB2 UDB PE, WSE, WSUE, and ESE, and DB2 Connect
AIX	• Version 4.3.3 (no 64-bit instance support) • Version 5.1 • Version 5.2 (DB2 UDB v7.2 supports AIX 5.2 with FixPak 4 or higher.)
Solaris	• Solaris 7 • Solaris 8 • Solaris 9 (DB2 UDB support for Solaris is only for the SPARC distribution.)
HP-UX	• HP-UX 11i (11.11)

Table 1.1   Operating Systems Supported by DB2 UDB and DB2 Connect in v8.1 and v8.1.2

Operating System	Supported Versions for DB2 UDB PE, WSE, WSUE, and ESE, and DB2 Connect
Linux	Due to the ever-changing nature of Linux, DB2 UDB only supports those distributions that have passed DB2 UDB's Linux validation test package. A list of all validated Linux distributions for DB2 UDB is available at *www.ibm.com/software/data/db2/linux/validate/*.
Windows	• Windows 98 and Windows Me (support for DB2 UDB Personal Edition and DB2 Connect Personal Edition only; DB2 UDB clients are supported on Windows 98 however) • Windows XP (support for DB2 UDB Workgroup Server Edition, DB2 UDB Workgroup Server Unlimited Edition, and DB2 Universal Developer Edition only; this is in line with Microsoft's set direction for Windows XP). We recommend you at least be at Service Pack 1. • Windows NT v4 with ServicePack6a+ • Windows 2000 (ServicePack 2 is required for Windows Terminal Server; we recommend you at least be at Service Pack 1) • Windows Server 2003

Always refer to your DB2 UDB product documentation and support Web sites for any APAR or PTFs that are required to support your operating system.

CHANGES TO DB2 UNIVERSAL DATABASE LICENSING AND PACKAGING

DB2 UDB v8.1 delivers changes to its licensing and packaging that allows users to derive more value than ever before. Along with some minor naming revisions, there are new editions that are covered in this section. The DB2 UDB v8.1.2 offering delivers solutions from Palmtop to Teraflop. Figure 1.1 shows the DB2 UDB v8.1.2 for Multiplatform family.

DB2 UDB PERSONAL EDITION

Although there are no packaging changes to DB2 UDB Personal Edition (DB2 UDB PE) in the version 8.1 release, DB2 UDB Satellite version 6.1 has been merged into DB2 UDB PE. Customers who wish to implement occasionally connected solutions can now choose DB2 Everyplace (which also supports Cloudscape and J2ME clients as data stores) or DB2 UDB PE. The Control Server feature associated with the remote management of satellite systems has been extended so that any DB2 UDB server can be managed the same way as a satellite.

DB2 UDB EXPRESS

DB2 UDB Express is a new innovative DB2 UDB v8.1.2 time frame offering that delivers convenience and hideaway value for small to midmarket and embedded implementations. DB2 UDB Express is a specially tailored, full-featured, industrial-strength, open industry-standards-based relational database for small and medium business and Independent software vendors that accelerates their time to value.

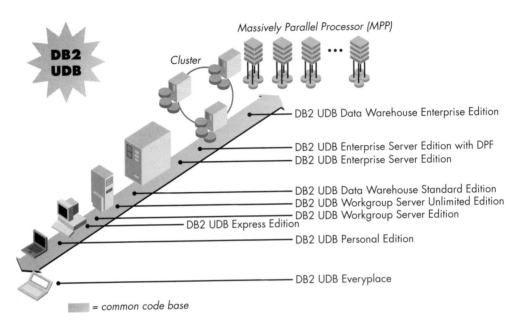

Figure 1.1
The DB2 UDB v8 for multiplatform family.

DB2 UDB Express provides a very attractive entry price for customers who choose to leverage the benefits of Linux or Windows. It also provides a wide selection of business partner applications, services, and support. It has built-in autonomic manageability features such as IBM's self-tuning optimizer, the Configuration Advisor, and the Health Center. These tools help improve the performance and reliability of a DB2 UDB solution, while at the same time minimize administration complexity, required skills, and overall total cost of ownership. This edition of DB2 UDB is fully compatible with the rest of the scalable DB2 UDB family of relational databases for Linux, Windows, and UNIX platforms. Business partners can preconfigure DB2 UDB Express to transparently install within their application for easy deployment in customer engagements.

DB2 UDB Express supports the following key capabilities and benefits:

- Easy to install and deploy. The database can install silently within your application, and has autonomic features that minimize required complexity, skills, and resources for installation and management. DB2 UDB Express unobtrusively installs itself within an application and can be easily preconfigured in offerings for key vertical markets such as finance, insurance, and retail, etc.

- Faster time to value. DB2 UDB Express easily integrates with your applications, comes with a PartnerWorld support structure, and results in faster time to market for chosen solutions.

- Affordable. This software is very competitively priced to meet market needs. In fact, a 5-user solution on DB2 UDB Express (remember, this is every bit a DB2 UDB server, there are no compromises here), costs under $1,000 (retail prices are in U.S. currency, prices in your geographies may vary).
- Avoids customer lock-in with a vendor. DB2 UDB is based on open industry standards and it is portable across prevalent industry platforms.
- Protects your existing investment. There is no need to "rip and replace" with DB2 UDB's open standards and federation capabilities, which give you faster, more effective insight into your data across multiple platforms and data stores.
- Scalable on demand. As your business grows, so can the underlying database.

DB2 UDB Express can only be installed on Windows or Intel/AMD Linux-based workstations that run on no larger than two-way Symmetrical Multiprocessor (SMP) hardware boxes. Web access to this version of DB2 UDB is only licensed for use in intranet (behind a company's fire-wall) or extranet (where the user can be identified; for example, an online banking scenario) enviroments and is limited to a 32-bit run-time memory model.

For more information on DB2 UDB Express, see *www-3.ibm.com/software/data/info/db2express/*.

DB2 UDB Workgroup Server and Workgroup Server Unlimited Editions

In DB2 UDB v8.1, DB2 UDB Workgroup Edition (DB2 UDB WE) v7.2 and DB2 UDB Work-group Unlimited Edition (DB2 UDB WUE) v7.2 were renamed to DB2 UDB Workgroup Server Edition (DB2 UDB WSE) and DB2 Workgroup Server Unlimited Edition (DB2 UDB WSUE), respectively. There are no significant packaging changes to these products, but, there are licens-ing changes that you should be aware of.

In DB2 UDB v7.2, an Internet processor license was available for DB2 UDB WE. In DB2 UDB v8.1, DB2 UDB WSE can only be licensed using registered and concurrent users. DB2 UDB WSE v8.1 cannot be licensed for internet connectivity (access from outside a company's fire-wall); however, it can be licensed for Intranet connectivity (within a company's firewall) using registered user or concurrent licenses.

DB2 UDB WE and DB2 UDB WUE v7.2 also had restrictions with respect to the maximum number of processors that the underlying hardware could have. On UNIX-based workstations, DB2 UDB WE v7.2 could only be installed on SMP machines that had no more than two proces-sors; for Windows and Linux installations, four processors were the maximum allowed. For DB2 UDB WUE v7.2, the limits were four processors on UNIX-based workstations and eight proces-sors on Linux-based or Windows-based workstations. In DB2 UDB v8.1, both of these offerings can now be installed on SMP hardware that has up to four processors for any operating system.

For details on the differences between DB2 UDB's Workgroup and Enterprise server offerings, read "Differences Between DB2 UDB's Workgroup and Enterprise Edition Offerings" by Paul Zikopou-los at *www7b.boulder.ibm.com/dmdd/library/techarticle/0301zikopoulos/0301zikopoulos1.html*.

DB2 UDB Enterprise Server Edition and the Database Partitioning Feature

There were some significant packaging changes to DB2 UDB's enterprise offerings in the new version of DB2 UDB. In DB2 UDB v8.1, DB2 UDB Enterprise Edition v7.2 (DB2 UDB EE) was renamed to DB2 UDB Enterprise Server Edition (DB2 UDB ESE). DB2 UDB v7.2 delivered DB2's database partitioning function as a separate edition called DB2 UDB Enterprise-Extended Edition (DB2 UDB EEE). From a functional perspective, DB2 UDB EE and DB2 UDB EEE have shared the same code base for more than 6 years: DB2 UDB EEE just offered the ability to partition a database as a single image over multiple database servers. In DB2 UDB v8.1, the additional functionality delivered in DB2 UDB EEE is now a chargeable component of DB2 UDB ESE called the *database partitioning feature* (DPF). The DPF simply needs to be licensed to use it; there is no separate installation process required for the ability to partition a DB2 UDB database. This means that customers that make a commitment to the DB2 UDB platform can seamlessly scale to handle their workloads and business demands. What's more, DB2 UDB v8's GUI tools fully support partitioned database environments. It was a natural progression for these packages to merge because they have always been the same product.

DB2 UDB v8.1 changes the licensing terms for failover configurations. For *active standby* systems, you are required to license all the processors on the standby server. For *idle standby* server, you only have to license one processor. For information on how to license a DB2 UDB server for failover, read "Licensing Distributed DB2 UDB Version 8 Servers in a High-Availability Configuration" by Paul Zikopoulos at *http://www7b.boulder.ibm.com/dmdd/library/techarticle/ 0301zikopoulos/0301zikopoulos.html.*

DB2 UDB Data Warehouse Edition

DB2 UDB Data Warehouse Edition (DB2 UDB DWE) combines a carefully selected set of IBM BI products to provide a comprehensive BI platform with everything needed by customers to deploy and partners to build the next generation of analytic solutions. This edition hardens to IBM's BI mantra: Build BI function into the database, as part of an integrated BI platform exposed solely through open standard interfaces; collaborating with partners for other layers of the architecture.

DB2 UDB has a strong tradition in providing a rich framework for BI applications and off-the-shelf analytical solutions that help customers gain greater insight into their corporate data. In fact, analytical functions have long been a strong component of DB2 UDB's standard SQL application programming interface (API). Functions include:

- Rank, Denserank, Rownumber, AVG, MIN, MAX, CNT, SUM
- Covariance, correlation, standard deviation
- Order by rows for the definition of a smoothing moving average over a period of time
- Grouping expressions: Cube, Rollup, Group by (global), Partition by (local to window)
- Regression: slope, intercepts, diagnostic statistics, coefficient of determination
- Sampling: RAND function as SQL clause

Underlying database objects in DB2 UDB, such as multidimensional clustering (MDC) tables, materialized query tables (MQTs), and the DPF feature, provide a scalable environment that makes for a leveragable engine for fast query execution.

The DB2 UDB infrastructure for data warehousing and analytics is shown in Figure 1.2.

In Figure 1.2 you see that the infrastructure technologies driven deep into the DB2 UDB engine are exposed solely through open standard interfaces. The advantage of this is that they inherit attributes from DB2 UDB such as parallelism, high availability, security, distributed processing, and any new innovations.

Multidimensional online analytical processing (MOLAP) databases have been favored to derive business insight because they are generally thought to be a faster OLAP approach for answering analytical questions, ultimately delivering "speed-of-thought" response times. The drawback to MOLAP is that it requires a separate engine for the data store, a separate administration approach, a separate query language, and a separate API.

DB2 UDB OLAP Server (which is IBM's original equipment manufacturer offering of Hyperion's Essbase server) and Microsoft's Analysis Services engines are examples of MOLAP engines. Proponents of relational OLAP (ROLAP) feel that learning how to manage a new database engine and write a new query language is a burden, and they prefer to leverage existing

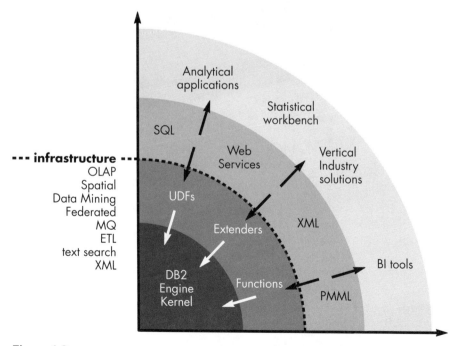

Figure 1.2
The BI infrastructure driven deep into the DB2 UDB engine.

SQL skills to do OLAP. There is also a lot of data redundancy in the MOLAP approach in that the single version of the truth is duplicated across cube servers. The debate over the speed or cost of owning a totally different database and using a different query language is a hot topic.

What if there was another approach that could yield the speed-of-thought response times for the relational engine, with a unification of administration tasks, cube modeling, ETL, and API, and could seamlessly fit into the most popular analytic front-end tools like Cognos, Business Objects, BRIO, etc.?

DB2 UDB DWE adds a new framework called Cube Views. DB2 UDB's Cube Views enhances analytical productivity in the relational engine. Cube Views allows database administrators (DBAs) to model cubes in the database once and reuse them everywhere. With its open frame-work, you can alternatively model cubes in a chosen design tool (e.g., ERwin) and import that model into DB2 UDB. This framework eliminates the need for cube-modeling skills for each and every BI tool as they are simply imported into their respective tools to provide fast and quick analytics. It also eliminates duplication of effort across tools. The DB2 UDB Cube Views topol-ogy is shown in Figure 1.3.

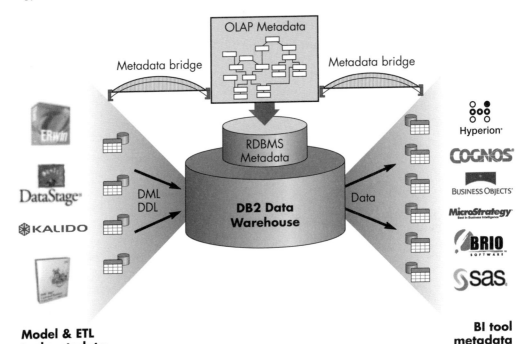

Figure 1.3
Cube Views in DB2 UDB.

The Cube Views framework gives the ability to model virtual cubes based on underlying DB2 UDB objects that can deliver speed-of-thought response times. An advisor is included to suggest DB2 UDB objects that should be created for the virtual cube. The benefits of this framework are that it provides freedom from proprietary and separate APIs for quick analytics, improved consistency of information (everybody views the same detail and aggregations), a consistent set of metrics (because all applications will use the same measures and formulas), incredible speed-up in the cube building phase of the analytical software, and higher performing SQL-accessible OLAP in the database.

The Cube Views framework also works with Office Connect Analytics, a Microsoft Excel plug-in, to display and navigate cube views in DB2 UDB, turning the spreadsheet into an OLAP tool. You can learn more about Cube Views at *www-3.ibm.com/software/data/db2/db2md/features.html.*

DB2 UDB DWE is available in two editions—DB2 UDB DW Enterprise Edition (EE) and DB2 UDB DW Standard Edition (SE)—and it is licensed on a per-processor basis.

DB2 UDB DW EE includes the following:

- DB2 UDB Enterprise Server Edition
- DPF
- Cube Views
- Intelligent Miner Modeling, Visualization, and Scoring
- Information Integrator Standard Edition (limited-use license for relational wrappers support for ETL operations)
- Office Connect Web Enterprise Edition
- DB2 Query Patroller (available as of the DB2 UDB 8.1.2 update)
- Warehouse Manager Standard Edition

All of the DB2 UDB DW products are also available as separately licensed stand-alone products.

The DPF, Warehouse Manager, Office Connect, Information Integrator, and Query Patroller products are not part of the DB2 UDB DW SE package. (The focus of this book is on the core features of DB2 UDB for Multiplatforms up to v8.1.2, so a detailed discussion of Cube Views is not included in this book.)

In short, DB2 UDB DW EE and DB2 UDB DW SE deliver fundamental architectural advantages in an open, platform-neutral model with proven linear scaling, and a real-time data warehouse with a unified engine, wrapped in a comprehensive BI platform that includes OLAP, mining, spatial, statistical, transformation, and federation support. What's more, their packaged retail price is up to 80% off of the retail price of buying each component separately: truly BI for the masses.

CHANGES TO DB2 CONNECT LICENSING AND PACKAGING

DB2 Connect v8.1 delivers a brand new DB2 Connect offering that makes it a more cost-effective solution and some changes to its licensing terms.

DB2 Connect Application Server Edition

DB2 Connect v8.1 introduced a new edition called DB2 Connect Application Server Edition (DB2 Connect ASE). DB2 Connect ASE offers different licensing terms that are meant to address the specific needs of customers who need to deploy multitier client–server or Web server applications that require access to DB2 UDB data on the zSeries or iSeries platforms. These types of applications are characterized by the use of midtier application servers where the majority of the application logic is running. Examples of these applications include PeopleSoft, Siebel, WebSphere, BEA Weblogic, i2, Microsoft IIS, CICS, Microsoft MTS, Microsoft COM+, Ascential DataStage, Brio, Business Objects, COGNOS, Microstrategies, and others.

DB2 Connect ASE license charges are based on the number of processors available to Web or application servers that use DB2 Connect to access host-based data. DB2 Connect ASE license charges are not based on the number of processors available to DB2 Connect itself, the size of the back-end database to which it is connecting, or the amount of applications running on the application server. For example, DB2 Connect ASE license charges are the same regardless of whether DB2 Connect ASE is colocated on the same box as the application server or installed on a separate server.

You might implement an environment where you place the presentation and business logic of your solution on different application server tiers. In these complex environments, the easiest way to understand how you must license a DB2 Connect ASE server is to ask yourself "Where is the SQL generated?" The processors that aid in the generation of the SQL must be licensed.

For example, consider the topology illustrated by Figure 1.4.

In this implementation, the three two-way SMP servers handle the presentation logic and have Hypertext Transfer Protocol (HTTP) application servers installed on them. Clients connect to this tier as a front end to the Web solution. The eight-way SMP server contains the application server where the business logic and the SQL are generated. The SQL requests are routed through another tier that houses DB2 Connect ASE that has six processors. In this environment, you would need to purchase eight DB2 Connect ASE licenses.

Integrated DB2 Connect Component in DB2 Universal Database Enterprise Edition

DB2 UDB ESE v8.1 includes a DB2 Connect component that is provided for occasional midrange or mainframe connectivity for data replication and server administration. The DB2 Connect component of DB2 ESE server licenses (at no extra charge) five registered users to

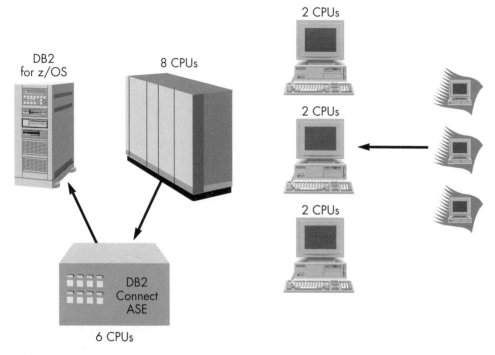

Figure 1.4
A traditional multitier topology that is well suited for DB2 Connect ASE.

access zSeries- and iSeries-based DB2 UDB servers. This number of licensed users cannot be increased without licensing an edition of DB2 Connect.

If additional users need access to these servers, an appropriate DB2 Connect product needs to be purchased and installed; however, you are entitled to the five complimentary registered users. For example, if you needed 11 registered user licenses and you have licensed a four-way DB2 UDB ESE server, you would be required to purchase a DB2 Connect server license with six additional registered user licenses (assuming you wanted to remain with the registered user model). If you required 11 concurrent licenses, you would be required to purchase a DB2 Connect server license with 10 concurrent licenses (because a DB2 Connect EE server license comes with one registered or concurrent user license).

Miscellaneous Changes

The DB2 UDB v8.1 announcement notice restricts users from installing a DB2 Connect server on a DB2 UDB WSE or DB2 UDB WSUE server. These terms have been officially changed in the DB2 UDB v8.1.2 announcement letter. You are entitled to install a DB2 Connect server on a DB2 UDB WSE v8.1 or DB2 UDB WSUE v8.1 server.

A JDBC Type 4 drive was shipped in DB2 UDB and DB2 Connect v8.1 to enable direct connections to Distributed Relational Database Architecture (DRDA) servers. Connectivity to DB2 on iSeries or zSeries servers must be licensed through DB2 Connect even if you choose to use this driver.

Finally, the DB2 Connect Web Starter Kit is no longer available. You can learn more about the DB2 Connect packages and how to license DB2 Connect by reading "Which Edition of DB2 Connect is Right for You?" by Paul Zikopoulos, Leon Katsnelson, and Roman Melnyk at *www7b.boulder.ibm.com/dmdd/library/techarticle/0303zikopoulos1/0303zikopoulos1/html*.

Changes to Related DB2 Universal Database Products

The DB2 UDB v8.1 release also includes changes to some of the extensibility features available with DB2 UDB.

DB2 UDB XML Extender

In DB2 UDB v7.2, the DB2 UDB XML Extender was a free-of-charge add-on product that required a separate installation to deliver Extensible Markup Language (XML) function to a DB2 UDB server. In the DB2 UDB v8.1 release, the XML extensions have been componentized and are part of a typical installation for all DB2 UDB servers. A separate DB2 UDB XML Extender installation is no longer required.

Text Searching Extenders

In DB2 UDB v7.2, there were three separate text searching engines available:

- DB2 UDB Text Information Extender (DB2 UDB TIE).
- DB2 UDB Net Search Extender (DB2 UDB NSE).
- DB2 UDB Text Extender (DB2 UDB TE).

In DB2 UDB v8.1, the DB2 UDB TIE and the DB2 UDB NSE now ship in the same box.

A complimentary copy of the DB2 UDB NSE is provided and can be installed on DB2 UDB PE and DB2 UDB WSE for up to five named users. If you need to support more than five users of this technology, you must license DB2 UDB NSE and install it on either a DB2 UDB WSUE or a DB2 UDB ESE server. This product is licensed on a per-processor basis. If you purchased a copy of DB2 UDB NSE v7.2, you are entitled to a free copy of DB2 UDB NSE v8.1.

When DB2 UDB v8.1 became generally available, the DB2 UDB TE was only available at the v7.2 level. The TE is used for multilinguistic searches. In DB2 UDB v8.1.2, the TE is now shipped as part of the DB2 UDB NSE and provides full linguistic searching, based on language-specific dictionaries, to DB2 UDB. The DB2 UDB NSE is licensed on a per-processor basis.

In v8.1.2, the DB2 UDB NSE is now available on Linux (for Intel and AMD servers) and HP-UX in addition to the normal supported platforms. In addition, DB2 UDB NSE for AIX can be run in a partitioned database environment.

DB2 UDB Spatial Extender

In DB2 UDB v7.2, the DB2 UDB Spatial Extender (DB2 UDB SE) could only be purchased and installed on DB2 UDB EE and DB2 UDB EEE systems. In DB2 UDB v8.1, a complimentary copy of the DB2 UDB SE is provided and can be installed on DB2 UDB PE and DB2 UDB WSE with up to five named users. If you need to support more than five users of this technology, you must license DB2 UDB SE and install it on either a DB2 UDB WSUE or a DB2 UDB ESE server. This product is licensed on a per-processor basis.

The v8.1 release also includes support for Linux, Solaris, and zLinux—platforms that were previously unsupported for spatial analysis with DB2 UDB.

DB2 UDB DataJoiner, DB2 UDB Relational Connect, and DB2 Information Integrator

In DB2 UDB v7.2, read and write access to heterogeneous data stores that managed traditional and nontraditional data were supported from a single product or combination of products that included (but were not limited to) DB2 UDB DataJoiner, DB2 UDB Relational Connect, DB2 DataPropagator (DPropR), Life Sciences Data Connect, and more. In DB2 UDB v8.1, these products were removed as orderable offerings. This left a temporary gap in DB2 UDB v8.1's features, as these products helped businesses leverage disparate data stores in a cost-effective manner, via a single standard SQL API, with included optimization and function compensation. (However, DB2 UDB v8.1 could federate to any member of the DB2 family and Informix databases; this is part of the core engine capabilities.)

A new offering, DB2 Information Integrator (DB2 II), was made available within the DB2 UDB v8.1.2 time frame to provide customers with read and write access to structured and unstructured data, as shown in Figure 1.5.

Specific integration functions delivered by DB2 II include the federation of caching for improved federated query performance (through MQTs), full support for DB2's SQL API, content and life sciences federation, XML and materialized query integration, IBM Lotus Extended Search, .net, ODBC, OLE DB, DB2 UDB NSE, heterogeneous relational replication, and more.

DB2 UDB II is available in four editions:

- **DB2 Information Integrator Replication Edition.** This package includes a limited-use data store (for use as a replication control server) as well as connectors that are priced on a per-connection basis.
- **DB2 Information Integrator Standard Edition.** This package includes a limited-use data store (for use as a local cache), the DB2 UDB NSE, and connectors priced on a per-connection basis. DB2 UDB v7.2 customers that purchased DB2 DataJoiner, DB2 Relational Connect, and DB2 Life Sciences Data Connect are entitled to an upgrade to DB2 II Standard Edition.

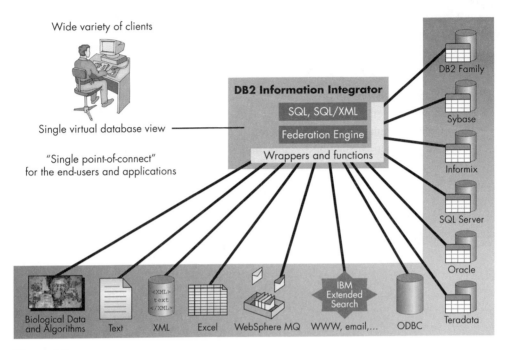

Figure 1.5
Access to any data through the an open standard SQL API and DB2 II.

- **DB2 Information Integrator Advanced Edition.** This package includes a full function data store, the DB2 UDB NSE, and connectors priced on a per-connection basis.
- **DB2 Information Integrator Advanced Unlimited Edition.** This package includes a full-function data store, the DB2 UDB NSE, and an unlimited number of connectors to heterogeneous data stores.

DB2 II charge metrics include per-processor charges and per-connector charges. The upgrade path for customers that purchased DB2 UDB DataJoiner, DB2 UDB Relational Connect, or Life Science Data Connect is DB2 II Standard Edition.

Another offering, called DB2 II for Content, is also available. This product is the follow-up product for Enterprise Information Portal (EIP) and it retains the same packaging as its predecessor.

You can learn more about DB2 II at *www-3.ibm.com/software/data/integration/*.

DB2 UDB Query Patroller

As of DB2 UDB v8.1.2, DB2 UDB Query Patroller can be ordered as its own product, an option not previously available to users of this software. Due to a complete rearchitecture of the product, DB2 UDB Query Patroller v8 can only be used to manage DB2 UDB v8 servers.

DB2 UDB Query Patroller's workload management features give administrators control of the data warehouse, allowing them to:

- Prioritize query response time and throughput discretely for users and groups
- Limit the impact of large and complex queries on the system
- Share cached query results
- Report on warehouse usage
- Eliminate the "runaway query" syndrome
- Improve end-user satisfaction by allocating warehouse resources according to defined service levels

DB2 Query Patroller v8 provides enhanced functions to manage and control all aspects of query submission and execution. These enhancements include a server-based SQL intercept from all sources; better SQL statement costing; additional options for result set storage; and simplified installation, configuration, and administration.

Deprecated Packages

Other packaging changes in the DB2 UDB v8.1 server release include the removal of the DB2 UDB OLAP Starter Kit, the DB2 Warehouse Manager connectors for i2TradeMatrix and ETI*Extract, and the DB2 Connect Web Starter Kit. DB2 Net.Data has been stabilized at the DB2 UDB v7.2 level.

Performance

- Multidimensional Clustering Tables
- Declared Global Temporary Tables
- System Default Value and NULL Compression
- Informational Constraints
- Connection Concentrator
- User-Maintained Materialized Query Tables
- Database System Monitoring Enhancements
- Miscellaneous Performance Enhancements

Multidimensional Clustering Tables

When analysts ask questions about their business, they are typically along the lines of dimensions: "What were my sales in the east region in the year 2000? What were the sales of blue widgets in Mexico in the fourth quarter of year 2001?"

A challenge facing today's relational database vendors is that their technologies only support ordered data storage and access of data across a single interest (or dimension). The alternative is to investigate Multidimensional OnLine Analytical Processing (MOLAP) engines. MOLAP offers proprietary vendor storage engines designed for multidimensional analysis. However, MOLAP comes at a cost of proprietary access application programming interfaces (APIs), a proprietary query language, a separate database engine, transformation costs, management costs, and more.

In addition to this, CPU speeds are adhering to Moore's law (the doubling of processor speeds every 18 months), but disk controller arms are not. This means that for every 100% increase in a computer's CPU speed, the data pipe to and from the disk is a fraction (perhaps increasing at a rate of 10%) of the CPU advancements. Clearly, there has to be a better way to feed the pipe and leverage faster CPUs.

DB2 UDB v8 introduces a fresh, unique, innovative approach to the concept of data access and storage with support for MDC tables. In fact, this approach is so revolutionary that IBM has multiple patent applications surrounding this technique—further demonstrating why DB2 UDB leads all other relational vendors combined in database patents.

MDC provides an innovative method to provide flexible, continuous, and automatic clustering of data along *multiple* dimensions. This new feature can result in significant improvement in the performance of queries, as well as a significant reduction in the overhead of data management operations such as reorganization and index maintenance after INSERT, UPDATE, and DELETE (I/U/D) operations. In this chapter you will learn how MDC provides users with the following benefits:

- Faster query speed via access to only those data pages that contain the requested data, without erroneous searching and fewer disk accesses. This reduces CPU and disk I/O and sustains these resources for other applications.
- An environment well suited for OLAP-style hierarchical analysis like executive reports and summaries.
- Reduced index size, which leads to disk savings and faster queries
- Virtual elimination of some maintenance operations like table reorganizations for re-clustering
- Faster deletes
- Faster inserts

Basically, MDC enables a table to be physically ordered on more than one dimension simultaneously (similar to having multiple clustered indexes on a single table, if it were possible to do so). In particular, an MDC table ensures that rows are organized on disk in blocks (in MDC terminology, a block is synonymous to an extent) that contain contiguous pages, such that all rows within any block have the same predefined dimensional values. All blocks contain the same number of pages and multiple blocks can have the same dimension values when there are enough records having those dimension values to warrant it.

Dimensions for an MDC table are specified when the table is created. Special lightweight indexes are then automatically created for each dimension, and in many cases, a composite index for the entire set of dimensions.

MDC tables are for the most part treated like any other table; that is, triggers, referential integrity, views, and materialized query tables (referred to as automated summary tables [ASTs] in DB2 UDB 7.x) can all be defined on them.

Some of the terminology used to describe MDC tables (slices, dimensions, etc.) are familiar to OLAP users. It is important to clarify that MDC tables are not solely for OLAP, though they can be beneficial to those operations. MDC tables should be thought of from the perspective of how the data is hardened to disk—a colocation of data if you will.

This chapter gives you an overview of MDC tables, how to use them, when to use them, why they can be better than traditional tables or alternative partitioning schemes, and a whole lot more! Throughout this chapter we present illustrations to conceptualize what is going on "underneath the covers." When it is easier to illustrate concepts in two dimensions, we do so; likewise with more. For more information, you can also refer to the Information Center or the *DB2 UDB Version 8 Administration Guide*.

MDC 101: A SIMPLE CONTRAST BETWEEN TRADITIONAL AND MULTIDIMENSIONAL CLUSTERING TABLES

To best understand the advantages of MDC tables and what they can offer your environment, a contrast and comparison with traditional tables is beneficial. Let's look at a business that is most interested in three specific dimensions of data: an associated stock keeping unit (SKU) that represents a sold product, the store location where the product was sold, and the date the sale took place.

Figure 2.1 illustrates a sample of data stored in a traditional table.

Assuming you want to organize your data across these multiple dimensions using a traditional table, you would run into some limitations. To help maintain data order for more efficient retrieval, your best choice is to create a clustering index to provide ordered data access across a single dimension (e.g., a clustering index on NATION as shown in Figure 2.1). This index would physically cluster data on I/U/D operations according to its order. This order would yield performance advantages via DB2 UDB's prefetchers because like data is being stored sequentially and DB2 UDB can leverage "big block" I/O (more bang for the buck). In fact, with good clustering, only a portion of the table ever needs to be accessed with queries that are focused on the NATION attribute.

A clustering index will deliver better performance for range queries involving the qualifying dimension (in this case, NATION). So what's wrong with a clustering index?

The first limitation of traditional tables is that you can only create one clustering index on a table, all the other indexes must be nonclustered indexes. The problem with this comes into play when you're interested in fast access to NATION and YEAR, not just the NATION dimension.

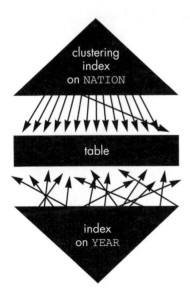

Figure 2.1
A traditional table.

Another issue to consider with traditional tables is what happens over time to your ordered data. Chances are you are inserting, updating, and deleting the data values in your table. Perhaps each tuple contains a new or duplicate NATION (depending on what product was ordered). Each time you insert a row with a NATION attribute, the INSERT algorithm attempts to find a data page where common dimension values are being stored. A traditional table with a clustering index is usually set up initially with a percentage of free space left at the end of each data page for future insertions to allow for new data. This is where the INSERT algorithm will first find space for the new record.

Over time, however, this preallocated free space fills up. If space on the target page cannot be found, the INSERT algorithm will search in a spiral fashion through the current target free space control record (FSCR) for suitable data placement. If it can't find any space in the FSCR, the INSERT algorithm will search through other FSCRs with a "best-it-can-do" search as used for INSERTs on regular tables. The number of FSCRs searched can be limited by the MAXFSCR registry variable. If no free space is available, the INSERT algorithm will ultimately insert the data at the end of the table.

With this in mind, you can see how the table data stored can become fragmented over time. Data in the page gets placed out of order as the free space fills up—this is why tables need to be maintained and reorganized (this is shown by the stray arrows for NATION in Figure 2.1). This leads to a management and availability cost to reorganize the table along the clustering index to better maintain order and yield better performance. (Incidentally, DB2 UDB v8 introduces online table and index reorganization. For more information, see Chapter 15. This is beneficial, without question, but MDC tables help to solve this issue entirely.)

Access to the data across the NATION dimension in our example is through a clustering index. A clustering index is a record ID (RID)-based index that points to specific ordered entries in a table. An index could be created for other dimensions on a regular table (like YEAR), but the data could not be ordered in the table (hence the chaotic arrows in Figure 2.1 for YEAR). This introduces another limitation of the traditional method for tables. RID-based access, in comparison with MDC which performs block ID (BID)-based access (you will learn more about this later), comes with a performance penalty as each data record needs to be pointed to. In addition to this, if the table is very large, the RID index is likely to be very large (because it has an entry for each and every row in the associated base table). Large indexes not only have to be maintained, but stored as well. Depending on the size of a table, they can take up a significant amount of space.

In summary, traditional tables and indexes add performance and management costs to relationally leveraging interesting dimensions of data because they can only be clustered along a single dimension (all other supporting indexes are nonclustered), the clustering degrades over time and requires maintenance, indexes are record-based, and they are correlated in size to their associated tables.

MDC tables solve these problems by allowing data to be physically clustered along extent boundaries according to multiple (*n*) dimensions (shown in Figure 2.2). In essence, MDC tables provide the abil-

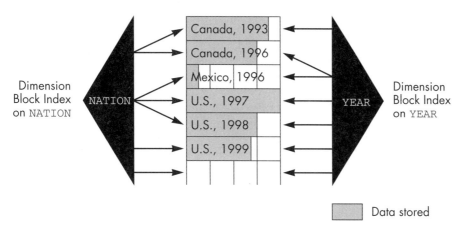

Figure 2.2
Extents (referred to as BLOCKS with MDC tables) making up an MDC table with dimensions NATION and YEAR.

ity to have multiple clustering indexes on a table. This can obviously lead to improved performance (for clarification, the squares in Figure 2.2 represent data pages).

MDC tables also support a new and efficient block index that is very compact and allows for fast access to data, not by record, but by block. These indexes point to the blocks of data allocated to specific dimension values. Because block-based indexes are not pointing to each and every record in the table (just the block that is housing the colocated data), they are much smaller than RID indexes and have much less overhead for logging and maintenance.

The new MDC feature provides a mechanism by which clustering is automatically and dynamically maintained over time. Table reorganizations for MDC tables are only really needed to compact fragmented space caused by sparse deletes or to clean up pointer/overflow pairs: they are not necessary for reclustering.

Finally, the syntax to create MDC tables is simple and flexible: CREATE TABLE...ORGANIZE BY DIMENSIONS(X,Y,...).

The end result is a mechanism that provides a powerful method of improving performance for many different queries and I/U/D operations, and some roll-in/roll-out features for range partitioning, all with a decreased imposition on DBAs, less resource requirements to store the data, and faster performance.

Going back to our example, let's look at our business problem (wanting to relationally look at your business across multiple dimensions, in an organized, compact, and efficient fashion). MDC allows you to create multiple dimensions and store the table data across these dimensions. To keep things simple, let's look at just two dimensions. Figure 2.2 illustrates an MDC table organized across two dimensions: NATION and YEAR.

In Figure 2.2 you can see that the table has been organized across two dimensions. In the declaration of the MDC table, the DBA would have specified that the table be organized across the dimensions NATION and YEAR. In Figure 2.2, you can see that each unique combination of the declared interest data is allocated to its own block (a block is an extent of data pages that houses records having the same dimension values).

Without MDC, you would have to keep an index on both columns of interest, and only one of these could be clustered (as in Figure 2.1). When a request would come in for analysis of NATION='CANADA', DB2 UDB may have to access many extents to find all the occurrences of NATION='CANADA'. With an MDC table, DB2 UDB stores the rows having different dimension values in separate data pages or blocks. Only rows with the same value in all dimensions are stored together in a block. When a SELECT comes to the database manager that is interested in NATION='CANADA', DB2 UDB only has to retrieve the blocks containing rows having those dimension values. All this is maintained for the DBA automatically by DB2 UDB every time a row is inserted, updated, or deleted.

TERMINOLOGY REQUIRED TO UNDERSTAND MDC TABLES

Before looking at how to use this technology and the details about what it is, it is important to understand the terminology used when discussing MDC tables. This section details the key terms that you will encounter throughout this chapter and briefly describes them. Details on each and their use follows in this chapter.

MDC Table

An MDC table is a table with data that is physically clustered on more than one table column (or dimension) simultaneously. It is created using the standard CREATE TABLE statement, using the ORGANIZE BY DIMENSIONS clause.

Dimension

A particular defined area of interest, specified at table creation time. An MDC dimension is a clustering key for a table. Data having particular dimension values can be found via that dimension's axis in the cube figures that follow (a cube is a simple way of conceptualizing how data is organized in an MDC table having three dimensions; see Figure 2.3). Remember, although MDC tables can be used to aid OLAP-type operations, the term dimension in this context does not relate to a multidimensional database. Rather, it refers to like data that is stored together on disk.

Slice

A slice is the set of blocks that contain pages with data having the same value of one of the clustering dimensions specified when the MDC table is created. For example, if a specified dimension at table creation time was NATION, and one of the values that the distribution of the data took was 'CANADA', a slice of the MDC table could look like Figure 2.4. (Note in Figure 2.4

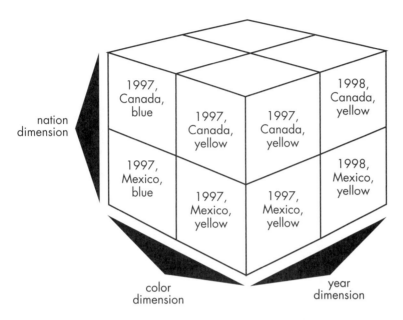

Figure 2.3
A table organized along the NATION, COLOR, and YEAR dimensions.

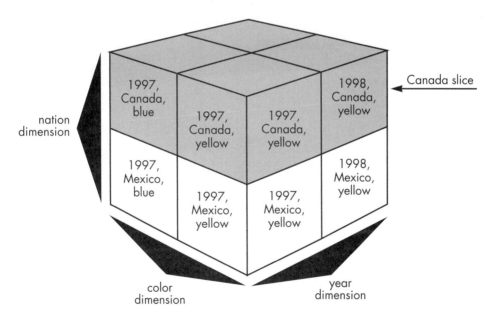

Figure 2.4
A table organized along the NATION, COLOR, and YEAR dimensions, with the value 'CANADA' comprising a slice.

there is another slice that is part of the NATION dimension because the range of values includes 'MEXICO'.)

Any value of a particular dimension will define a slice of the table and that slice will contain *all* of the data in the table having a value of that particular dimension, and *only* that data.

There are as many slices of the data as there are dimension values. For example, Figure 2.5 shows the COLOR slice for the value 'YELLOW'. Note that this slice overlaps the slice depicted by Figure 2.4 in part. This indicates that some records have both NATION of 'CANADA' and COLOR of 'YELLOW', and others don't.

Cell

Every unique combination of the dimension values comprises a logical cell. Physically, a cell is comprised of one or more blocks of pages with records that all share the exact same values for each clustering column (to keep things simple, we are assuming that all the data for a particular cell can fit into one block of data pages). A cell is a portion of the table containing data values having a unique set of dimension values—the intersection formed by taking a slice from each dimension. For example, the combination of the dimensional values NATION='CANADA', COLOR='YELLOW', and YEAR='1997' is depicted in Figure 2.6. The depicted cell only houses the data specified by these specific attributes of the defined dimensions.

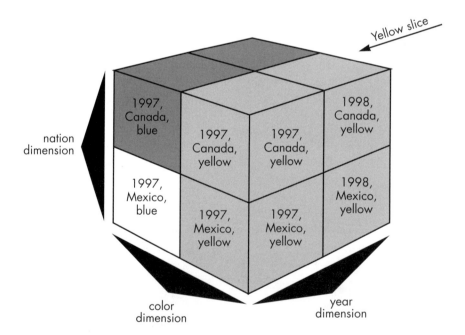

Figure 2.5
A table organized along the NATION, COLOR, and YEAR dimensions, with the value 'YELLOW' comprising a slice.

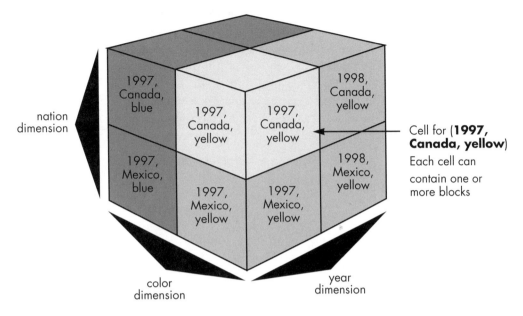

nation dimension

1997, Canada, blue

1997, Canada, yellow

1997, Canada, yellow

1998, Canada, yellow

1997, Mexico, blue

1997, Mexico, yellow

1997, Mexico, yellow

1998, Mexico, yellow

Cell for (**1997, Canada, yellow**)

Each cell can contain one or more blocks

color dimension

year dimension

Figure 2.6
A cell (which on disk comprises one or more blocks of data pages) that only contains data with the values 'CANADA', 'YELLOW', and '1997'.

Block

A block is a set of consecutive pages of disk. The term *EXTENT* is a synonym for a block when discussing MDC tables. Multidimensional tables allocate and fill blocks for each unique combination of values for the specified dimensions. If more than one block is needed for a specified combination of dimensions, then multiple blocks will be assigned to house the like data. Note that if there are no records having a particular cell value, there is no need to allocate a block for it. For the most part, blocks are only allocated for cells containing records.

Block Size or Blocking Factor

The block size or blocking factor specifies the number of pages in a block. It is equal to the extent size of the tablespace. This factor serves as a critical piece to an MDC solution in terms of how the data is laid on a disk. The larger the blocking factor, the more space will be allocated each time a new block is added to the table to house records having a specific dimension. It would not be a good idea to have a large blocking factor for data that had very high cardinality.

Block Index

A block index is a new index structured in the same manner as a traditional RID index, except that at the leaf level, keys point to BIDs instead of RIDs. This means that the size of block indexes are very small in comparison to RID-based indexes because they point to block numbers (many records that have the same dimension values exist in a block) in contrast to traditional indexes, which have entries that point to each data record. An example of a dimension block index is shown in Figure 2.7, which indicates that the dimension `CANADA` has data that is stored in 12 different blocks.

Notice how the block index is pointing to specific block numbers. These are the blocks where data containing the value `CANADA` in our example are stored. A block index on a specific dimension is called a *dimension block index*. The blocks listed in this index logically correspond to the `CANADA` slice in Figure 2.4. In our example, there is another dimension value for NATION = `MEXICO`. `MEXICO` would have its own dimension BID list, similar to Figure 2.7 (but it would obviously have pointers to the blocks that contain NATION = `MEXICO` instead of `CANADA`).

Block-based indexes are considered by the DB2 UDB optimizer when determining possible access plans for queries just as RID indexes are. They are also treated just like RID indexes during processing. They can be ANDed or ORed (these concepts are discussed later in this chapter) with each other and with other RID indexes; reverse scans can be done on them; and so on.

A dimension block index is automatically created for each dimension when an MDC table is created. These indexes cannot be dropped; however, they can be renamed (as a system-generated name is assigned to each for you). The ability to rename indexes is a new feature in DB2 UDB v8.1.

Block ID

A BID is stored along with a key value in the leaf node of a block index and references a particular block in the MDC table. BIDs are shown in Figure 2.7, to the right of the NATION key `CANADA`. The set of BIDs for a referenced dimension can be referred to as a BID list.

Generated Column

A generated column is a column that is derived from an expression that involves one or more columns in a table. Generated columns have been supported in DB2 UDB since DB2 v7. They can be used to control the granularity of a dimension or rollup dimension values into coarser representations for more efficient blocking. For example, if you wanted to implement ranges for customer numbers, you could represent values 1 through 100 in the dimension CUSTGROUPID=`1` and values 101 through

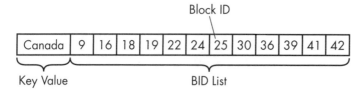

Figure 2.7
An example of a block index on the dimension NATION.

200 in dimension CUSTGROUPID='2', and so on. This would be a better approach than to have one block allocated for each customer ID (if customer was a unique column for example).

Monotonicity

Princeton University (WordNet v1.6 ©1997) defines *monotonicity* as "(in mathematics) a sequence or function; consistently increasing and never decreasing or consistently decreasing and never increasing in value."

For example, the function $B = A/100$ is a monotonic expression. Plugging in the set of values where $A = 1$, 10, 250, and 378 into this function, yield results where B's approximation is equal to 0, 1, 2, and 3, respectively. We can determine that the expression $B = A/100$ is monotonic because as A increases in value, B never decreases in value.

An example of a nonmonotonic expression would be the function $B = month(date)$. If inputs into this function were the set (1999/03/03, 1999/05/17, 2000/02/01, and 2001/05/04), result values would be (03, 05, 02, and 05), respectively. As you can see, the dates are going up, but the *month(date)* values go up and then cycle through to a lower value where each value represents a month of the year.

Monotonicity is important in MDC when it comes to range scans. You will learn more about this later. Just understand what the term is for now.

HOW MDC TABLES WORK

MDC enables a table to be physically clustered on more than one dimension simultaneously. Without MDC tables, DB2 UDB would only be able to relationally support single dimensional clustering of data via a clustered index. With MDC, these benefits are extended to more than one dimension or clustering key.

In the case of query performance, queries involving any, or combination thereof, specified dimensions of the table will benefit from clustering. Not only will these queries access only those data pages having records with the correct dimension values; these qualifying pages will be colocated as well. Furthermore, although a table with a clustering index can become unclustered over time as space fills up in the table, an MDC table is able to maintain its clustering over all dimensions automatically and continuously, eliminating the need to reorganize the table to restore the physical order of the data.

When creating a table, a DBA can specify one or more keys as dimensions along which to cluster the table's data. Each of these dimensions can consist of one or more columns, as index keys do. In fact, a dimension block index will be created automatically for each of the dimensions specified, and will be used to quickly and efficiently access data along each dimension. A composite block index may also be created automatically (a composite block index will not be created if you have a dimension that already includes all the columns in a specified dimension).

This index contains all dimension key columns, and will be used to maintain the clustering of data over INSERT and UPDATE activity.

Every unique combination of dimension values forms a logical cell, which is physically comprised of one or more blocks of pages, where a block is a set of consecutive pages on disk. The set of blocks that contain pages with data having a certain key value of one of the dimension block indexes is called a *slice*. Every page of the table is part of exactly one block, and all blocks of the table consist of the same number of pages: the blocking factor. The blocking factor is equal to extent size, so that block boundaries line up with extent boundaries.

To keep things simple, let's look at blocks within MDC tables that have two dimensions. Figure 2.8 logically illustrates an MDC table that is clustered across two dimensions: YEAR and NATION. Records in the table are stored in blocks, which contain an extent's worth of contiguous pages on disk. In Figure 2.8, a block is represented by an oval, and is numbered according to the logical order of allocated extents in the table. For example, Blocks 1, 6, and 12 contain only those rows having the year '2001', and the nation 'CANADA'.

The grid in Figure 2.8 represents the logical partitioning of these blocks, and each square represents a logical cell. A column or row in the grid represents a slice for a particular dimension. For example, all records containing the value 'CANADA' in the NATION dimension are found in the

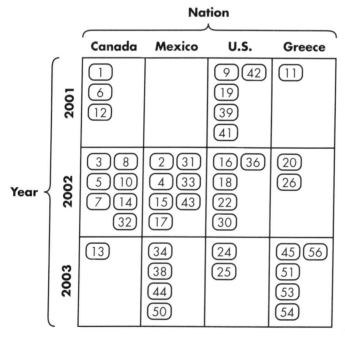

Figure 2.8
A two-dimensional MDC table.

blocks contained in the slice defined by the 'CANADA' column in the grid (blocks 1, 3, 5, 6, 7, 8, 10, 12, 13, 14, and 32). In fact, each block in this slice only contains records having 'CANADA' in the NATION field. Thus, a block is contained in this slice or column of the grid if and only if it contains records having 'CANADA' for the NATION field.

Creating an MDC Table

Creating MDC tables is easy and flexible. The syntax is a simple extension of DB2 UDB's CRE-ATE TABLE data definition language (DDL). Specific details of the DDL used to create MDC tables are covered in Chapter 7 "SQL Enhancements."

The DDL to create a traditional table that encompasses the information YEAR, NATION, and COLOR (as our examples do in the earlier definitions section) could look like this:

```
CREATE TABLE NOTMDC (YEAR INT NOT NULL, NATION VARCHAR(25) NOT NULL,
     COLOR VARCHAR(25) NOT NULL)
```

To create an MDC table, simply add the ORGANIZE BY DIMENSIONS clause to define the dimensions that you want to organize the table by. Pay careful attention to the dimensions you choose to organize your table by at creation time (see the section "Picking a Dimension for an MDC Table" later in this chapter for more information). Once you define the dimensions in an MDC table, you cannot change them without dropping and re-creating the table. Enter the following commands to create the table in the previous example as an MDC table:

```
CREATE TABLE MDC (YEAR INT NOT NULL, NATION VARCHAR(25) NOT NULL,
     COLOR VARCHAR(25) NOT NULL)
          ORGANIZE BY DIMENSIONS (YEAR, NATION, COLOR)
RUNSTATS ON TABLE MDC ON ALL COLUMNS
```

You can have a maximum of 16 distinct columns included in the set of dimensions for an MDC table.

> **TIP**
> Dimensions, being index key definitions, can actually have composite keys. For example, if two dimensions of interest were YEAR and NATION, you could combine the dimensions as: CREATE TABLE . . . ORGANIZE BY DIMENSIONS ((YEARandMONTH)).

Unlike other partitioning schemes (e.g., the List or Range partitioning schemes implemented by other database vendors), there is never a need to define an explicit range or a list of values for a dimension, or to add new range boundary values to existing dimensions as the data range changes. This is an administrator's dream when it comes to ease of implementation. Think about it for a moment. Many DBAs like the idea of Range partitioning because it allows them to easily rollin and rollout partitions (or ranges) of data. For example, sales for Quarter 1 Year 1999 (Q1Y99) might be relevant for two years, at which time it should be rolled out; each rollout comes with an associated new rollin for a new quarter and year combination. There are many advantages to this technique, but notable disadvantages as well. Both issues are solved by MDC tables.

The first issue is that Range partitioning can produce hot spots in the disk subsystem. For example, typically a DBA would spread his or her QY data across each partition. Q1Y99 would be on Partition 1, Q2Y99 would be on Partition 2, and so on. Well, it is likely that when the latest quarter data is available, everyone is going to want to look at that data, so all the users are going to do searches that involve a range or equality predicate on the newest QY. All of these queries will be directed (and consequently must be handled) by that one node, while the other nodes sit idle, responding to requests for the data that they own. Therefore, there are often performance issues with Range partitioning. In a Hash partitioning scheme, as implemented by DB2 UDB, these issues do not arise because each database partition owns a piece of the data set described by the partitioning key. Using MDC and DB2 UDB Enterprise Server Edition's Database Partitioning Feature, you could create Range partitions that are hashed over many tables or that are segregated to reflect the preceding example.

The second issue is that although Range partitioning offers operational ease of use (rollin, rollout), it does have management and aggregation trade-off costs as well. The following Data Definition Language (DDL) shows how a DBA would create a Range partition using a different vendor's database:

```
CREATE TABLE PART1 (Date DATE, Province CHAR(2), Color VARCHAR(10), ... )
  PARTITION BY RANGE ( Date)
    (PARTITION cell1 VALUES LESS THAN (1999/02/01) TABLESPACE TB1,
     PARTITION cell2 VALUES LESS THAN (1999/03/01) TABLESPACE TB2,
     PARTITION cell3 VALUES LESS THAN (1999/04/01) TABLESPACE TB3,
     PARTITION cell4 VALUES LESS THAN (1999/05/01) TABLESPACE TB4,
       ...)
```

Note that this syntax can get quite cumbersome and lengthy. As well, it isn't very extensible either. Efforts have to be made to handle all current and future data values ahead of time. For example, if you want to create a new range, you must do this at the DDL level, which could involve creating and dropping the table (imagine having a new color; you would need to manually add a new range partition for it). With an MDC table, the new dimension block is allocated dynamically when a data row containing a dimension value is inserted into the table (if it exists, it goes into a preallocated block, and if it doesn't, one is automatically created). Another example would be environments where DBAs have to create a "catch-all" range at the high end, and over time need to split it out into new ranges from it.

What if your company wants to derive better insight into their data? A telecommunications company (telco) might be interested in scanning phone calls on a monthly basis to devise new consumer vulnerability models. This is easy: 12 ranges. What if they want to move to more of an operational data store (ODS) and work with their information on a daily basis (now you have to manage 365 ranges), and from there on an hourly basis (8,760 ranges). Well, you get the point.

Indexes and MDC Tables

There are two types of indexes that can be automatically created with MDC tables: dimension block indexes and composite block indexes. If an MDC table is created with only one defined dimension or you specify a composite dimension in an MDC table that is only organized along it, then a composite block index is not created. Otherwise, you will have a dimension block index for each dimension specified, as well as an additional composite block index.

Both of these index types are block-based indexes, as opposed to RID-based indexes. Block indexes are structurally the same as regular record indexes, but they point to blocks instead of records. This results in block indexes being much smaller than RID indexes. For example, there is one pointer for every record in a traditional table in a RID index, but there is only one pointer for every block in an MDC table. These slimmer indexes result in faster performance and lower maintenance costs (MDC tables are especially well suited for rollin and rollout). The size of a block is equal to the number of pages in an extent. This value can be between 2 and 256 pages and its default is defined at database creation time, while an overriding value can be defined when the tablespace is created.

Dimension Block Indexes

Dimension block indexes facilitate the determination of which blocks comprise a slice of an MDC table. A dimension block index is automatically created for each dimension when the table is created and is required by the system for that MDC table.

In Figure 2.8, blocks 1, 6, and 12 are pointed to by the 'CANADA' key in the NATION dimension block index.

Consider the table *MDC* for which we presented the DDL as a sample in the previous section. If you created this table, run the following DML statement:

```
INSERT INTO MDC VALUES (1997, 'CANADA', 'YELLOW'), (1997, 'MEXICO',
'YELLOW')
```

Now issue the following DML statement:

```
SELECT * FROM MDC WHERE NATION = 'CANADA'
```

This DML yields a single result set showing a row for YEAR = 1997, NATION = 'CANADA', and COLOR = 'YELLOW'. More interesting is to see how this information was accessed by the DB2 UDB engine. Try running a visual explain on the previous SELECT statement by starting the Control Center, right-clicking the database in which the MDC table you created resides, and selecting Explain SQL. Enter the SQL statement in the SQL text box, and select OK. You may see output that is similar to Figure 2.9 (environments may vary).

Take note of the index that was used to solve the query in Figure 2.9 (it's boxed in Figure 2.9). Now issue the following SQL statement to see what type of index it is:

```
SELECT INDEXTYPE, INDNAME FROM SYSCAT.INDEXES
```

The output you receive will be similar to Figure 2.10.

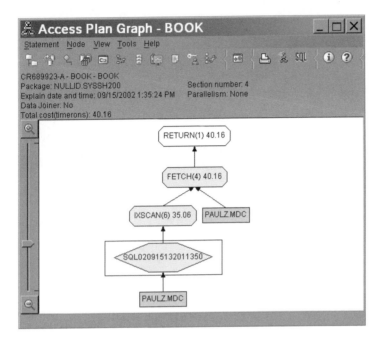

Figure 2.9
A Visual Explain of a SELECT from an MDC table along a single dimension.

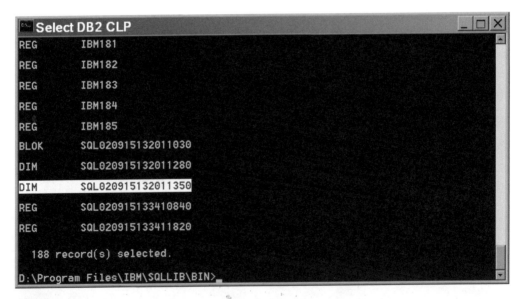

Figure 2.10
Access to data in an MDC table through a dimension block index.

Take note of the DIM keyword in Figure 2.10. This keyword indicates that the information requested was accessed through a dimensional block index (remember those block id-based indexes that just point to the block where the data is located). The key benefit here is that MDC can circumvent a significant amount of random and/or sequential I/O that would typically pull in pages that can contain a mix of qualifying and unqualifying rows. In essence, MDC is like guaranteed big-block reads of interested data.

To complete this example, try running the exact same INSERT DML statement on the NOTMDC table for which we gave you the DDL in the previous section as well. Perform the exact same steps as you did with the MDC example, only run the following command to create an index on the NOTMDC table before issuing the SELECT statement:

```
CREATE INDEX IDXNATION ON NOTMDC(NATION)
```

If you were to run a visual explain on the same SELECT statement for the NOTMDC table, you would see that a REG (regular) index was used to access the table. (Instead of a system name for the index, you will see the name specified in the CREATE INDEX statement. You can rename MDC indexes in DB2 UDB v8.1 if you want.)

Block indexes are much smaller then RID indexes because they only have to point to blocks and not to individual records. Imagine if 1,000 records could be stored in each block. In the MDC case, that would require one index entry to the block. In the RID example, it would require 1,000 entries, one to each record. In fact, the dimension block index is smaller by this factor:

```
block size * avg. # of records in page
```

where block size = the number of pages in an extent (2–256).

Because the indexes are much smaller, access to the data is much faster than would have been with a clustering index, as there is one pointer per qualifying block of pages versus one pointer per qualifying row. Given a BID from a block index, DB2 UDB can do a very efficient scan of the corresponding block in the table.

Again, a dimension block index is created for each dimension specified for an MDC table. So, for our MDC table example, a dimension block index is created on each of the YEAR, NATION, and COLOR dimensions automatically. These indexes are illustrated in Figure 2.6 if you consider each triangle to be a dimension block index.

Since each dimension block index is structured in the same manner as a traditional RID index, except that at the leaf level the keys point to BIDs instead of RIDs. This allows for block-based and record-based indexes to coexist and interoperate together on MDC tables (more on that in a bit). Because each block contains potentially many pages of records, these block indexes are much smaller than record indexes and need only be updated as new blocks are needed and so added to a cell, or existing blocks are emptied and so removed from a cell.

A slice, or the set of blocks containing pages with all records having a particular key value in a dimension, is represented in the associated dimension block index by a BID list for that key value.

So, in our example, we wanted to find the slice of blocks containing all records with 'CANADA' for the NATION dimension. To facilitate this, DB2 UDB looks up this key value in the NATION dimension block index, and finds the appropriate keys, such as those shown in Figure 2.11.

The key in Figure 2.11 is comprised of the key value, namely 'CANADA', and a list of BIDs. Each BID contains a block location. We see that, in this example, the block numbers listed are the same ones found in the 'CANADA' slice in the grid for the MDC table represented in Figure 2.8.

Remember that a dimension block index is automatically generated (and maintained) for each specified dimension. So, similarly, to find the list of blocks containing all records having '1997' for the YEAR dimension, DB2 UDB would look up this value in the YEAR dimension block index.

Dimension block indexes *cannot* be used in conjunction with a RID-based *clustering* index (remember, they can be used in conjunction with regular indexes). However, you wouldn't have a need for a clustering index with MDC tables because they guarantee clustering. Block indexes can be used alongside RID indexes and when generating an access plan for a query, the DB2 UDB optimizer will look at their use individually and in conjunction with each other via index ANDing and ORing (see the appropriate section later in this chapter for more information).

Composite Block Indexes

A composite block index comprises pointers to blocks that form a combination of all defined dimensions on the MDC table. Therefore, this block index is an index on all the dimension columns of the table, so that each key value corresponds to a particular cell in the table, and its BID list corresponds to the list of blocks comprising that cell.

The composite block index maps cell values to the list of blocks for each cell. Its key is made up of all columns involved in the dimensions. Therefore, in our example of an MDC table with three dimensions, four indexes will be created: one dimension block index for each dimension

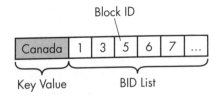

Figure 2.11
A key from the dimension block index on NATION.

(YEAR, NATION, and COLOR), and one composite block index on NATION, YEAR, and COLOR. This index can be used by DB2 UDB to very quickly determine whether a particular cell exists, and if so, exactly which blocks contain those cell values.

Composite block indexes are mainly used for INSERT operations because they allow DB2 UDB to quickly determine if a cell exists for its dimension values. They are also used for queries with predicates that include all of the dimensions in the MDC table, as well as for other queries (especially if they involve any sequential subset of the first keyparts).

Try running a visual explain on the following query to see how DB2 UDB chooses to use the composite block index when retrieving the requested result set:

```
SELECT * FROM MDC WHERE NATION = 'CANADA' AND COLOR = 'YELLOW' AND
YEAR = 1997
```

If you follow the same steps that you did to investigate the use of a dimension block index, you will see the index usage output may match the visual explain and show the use of a composite block index instead (denoted as BLOK in Figure 2.12). In Figure 2.12 you can also see the IDX-NATION index that we asked you to create for the NOMDC table.

In a composite block index, a key is only found for each cell of the table containing records. This block index assists in quickly and efficiently finding those blocks with records having a particu-

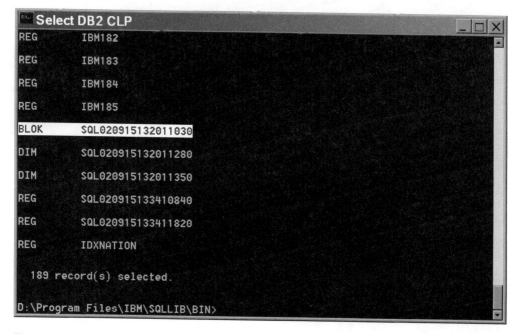

Figure 2.12
A query across all dimensions uses a composite block index.

lar set of values for their dimensions. It also is used to dynamically manage and maintain the physical clustering of data along the dimensions of the table over the course of INSERT activity.

For example, if we wish to find all records in the table having NATION of 'CANADA', COLOR of 'YELLOW' and YEAR of '1999', DB2 UDB would look up the key value for each dimension 'CANADA', 'YELLOW', '1999' in the composite block index, and find the block(s) for each one that would match. These operations are shown in Figure 2.13.

Again, the key is comprised of each dimension's key values, namely 'CANADA, YELLOW, 1999', and a list of BIDs that identify the blocks (extents of data pages) that house this data. We see that the only BIDs listed are 52 and 292 (for the predicate NATION='CANADA', COLOR='YELLOW', and YEAR='1999'), and this would indicate that there are only two blocks in the MDC table containing records having these two particular values.

Index Operations

Block indexes can be combined (ANDed, ORed) with each other and with RID-based indexes. These operations can be performed to quickly identify blocks that contain interested data for quick scanning, while providing clustered data access. Examples of these operations are covered in this section.

Index ANDing

Block ANDing utilizes dimension block indexes to combine slices of data to quickly and efficiently arrive at a result set that includes interested data. Consider the following query:

```
SELECT * FROM MDC WHERE COLOR='YELLOW' AND NATION='CANADA'
```

The DB2 UDB optimizer would use ANDing to quickly and efficiently arrive at the result blocks of data that contain the values 'YELLOW' and 'CANADA'. Because these are defined dimensions

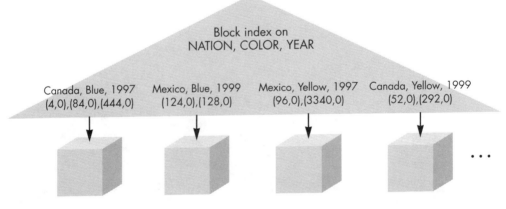

Figure 2.13
A composite dimension block index.

on our example MDC table, DB2 UDB knows that block indexes exist for these dimensions and would choose to use them to arrive at the result set. In the previous query, DB2 UDB did an index lookup on the dimension block indexes, block ANDed the two indexes, and performed a minirelational scan of the resulting blocks, yielding great performance benefits. This is illustrated in Figure 2.14.

Suppose you have created an index on a business value that was not defined as a dimension when the MDC table was created. For example, unless you generated a materialized aggregation or transformation of a stock keeping unit (SKU), it would not be a good choice as a dimension. (Imagine having 100,000 SKU numbers and SKU being a dimension, resulting in 100,000 blocks!)

As previously stated, DB2 UDB can leverage block-based and RID-based indexes together. Consider the following query that ANDs a block-based and RID-based index:

```
SELECT * FROM MDCTABLE WHERE COLOR='YELLOW' AND SKU-# >= 1000
```

DB2 UDB would process this query as shown in Figure 2.15.

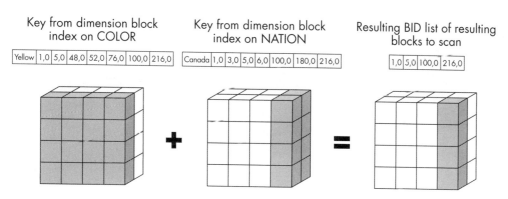

Figure 2.14
Dimension block ANDing for quick results with MDC.

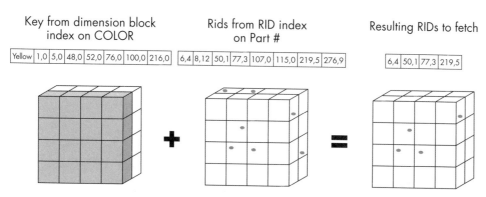

Figure 2.15
Dimension block and RID index ANDing for quick results with MDC.

The result set is only those RIDs belonging to the qualifying blocks.

Index ORing

DB2 UDB can use index ORing to arrive at a result set just as it can use ANDing techniques. Obviously the query has to have an OR predicate for the DB2 UDB optimizer to decide to use this type of operation, so consider the following query:

```
SELECT * FROM MDCTABLE WHERE COLOR='YELLOW' OR SKU-# >= 1000
```

This query would be processed as shown in Figure 2.16.

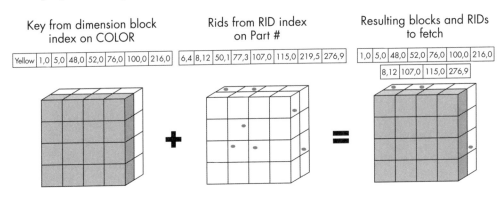

Figure 2.16
Dimension block and RID index ORing for quick results with MDC.

The result set includes all records in the qualifying blocks, plus additional RIDs outside of those blocks because of the OR condition. Of course, DB2 UDB could also OR two dimension block indexes, just like it did in the AND example—depending on the query.

So, one of the index benefits of MDC tables are that DB2 UDB can take advantage of block and RID-based indexes to quickly and easily narrow down a portion of the table having particular dimension values or ranges of values (block elimination). It can do this while performing very fast index lookups, as block indexes are small and relational scans of blocks are faster than RID-based retrieval. MDC tables have a new performance enhancing method for prefetching called *block lookahead prefetching*. This involves scanning ahead in the block index, and bringing entire blocks of data into memory without sequential detection. Because data is guaranteed to be clustered on dimensions, data retrieval is much faster, as the existence of block indexes provide additional access plans for the DB2 UDB optimizer to choose from, with no prevention of the use of traditional access plans (RID scans, joins, table scans, etc.).

MDC and Query SELECT, INSERT, UPDATE, and DELETE Operations

This section looks at the different processing operations that are performed on relational tables and how they are handled by MDC tables.

SELECT Operations

MDC tables provide alternative efficient access plans that can be evaluated by the optimizer for a wide variety of queries. Queries affected include those having star joins, as well as those with range, equality, and IN predicates.

In a star join scenario, consider an MDC fact table such that its clustering dimensions are one or more foreign keys of the dimension tables. In this case, the optimizer can use the dimension block indexes, which are small, to quickly find the list of qualifying blocks that contain records to be joined with the dimension tables. Block index ANDing can be used if necessary, and a mini-relational scan of the rows in these blocks can be done, which might be much more efficient retrieving these rows than RID-based fetching would be (especially when you take into account the new block lookahead prefetching). In addition to this, the bufferpools in DB2 UDB v8.1 have a blocked based option which allows prefetching to be done in blocks that correspond to the same size as the blocking factor.

In a nonstar join scenario, when one or more range or equality predicate terms match an MDC dimension, the optimizer can choose to perform block processing instead of RID processing (with block ANDing if necessary) to quickly narrow down a small set of large blocks of qualifying records to scan.

As you have seen, DB2 UDB can be very efficient using block indexes to access data, leading to the potential to achieve incredible SELECT performance. DB2 UDB can be so efficient with block indexes because once it has a BID from a block index, it has the first pool page of that block, so it can go directly to it and scan the entire block of pages. DB2 UDB guarantees that every record found in these pages will have the dimension value of the block index key found. Scans on any dimension index provide clustered data access because each BID corresponds to a set of sequential pages in the table guaranteed to contain data having that dimension value. Clustered access is possible for any plan that involves a block of data (range or equality, IN, etc.).

Let's look at DB2 UDB processing with SELECTs on an MDC table. (Most of this processing should have become apparent in the "Indexes and MDC Tables" section, so we cover it briefly here. If you are still unclear, reread that section.) Let's assume that a user has a SELECT statement that he or she wants to issue (the same one we used in the first index ANDing example):

```
SELECT * FROM MDC WHERE COLOR='YELLOW' AND NATION='CANADA'
```

To process this query, DB2 UDB would first determine the slice containing all blocks with COLOR equal to 'YELLOW' by looking up the YELLOW key in the COLOR dimension block index, finding the appropriate key that corresponds to a slice of data, as shown in Figure 2.17.

DB2 UDB would then determine the blocks containing all the records having NATION equal to 'CANADA' by looking up the CANADA key in the NATION dimension block index, and finding the appropriate key that corresponds to a slice of data as shown in Figure 2.18.

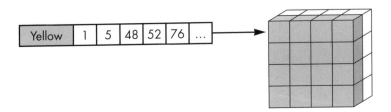

Figure 2.17
Identifying the first block of qualifying data on an MDC table.

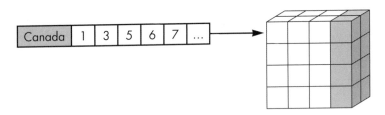

Figure 2.18
Identifying the second block of qualifying data on an MDC table.

To find the set of blocks containing all records having both values, DB2 UDB has to find the intersection of these two slices. This is done by index ANDing the two BID lists. (Of course if we chose to illustrate a different SELECT processing example, the blocks might have been ORed or perhaps combined with a RID-based index as discussed in the "Indexes and MDC Tables" section.)

The common BID values are 1, 5, 100, and 216 and this corresponds to the result set in Figure 2.14. Once DB2 UDB has a list of blocks to scan, it can do a mini-relational scan of each block. This will involve just one I/O per block as a block is stored as an extent on disk and can be read into the buffer pool in the same manner. If the isolation level is Cursor Stability or Read Stability, and predicates for the query are only on dimension values, DB2 UDB needs to reapply the predicates on records in the block, as all records in the block are guaranteed to have the same dimension key values. If other predicates are present, DB2 UDB only needs to check these on the remaining records in the block, but does not need to reapply the dimension predicates on any but the first record. (For Repeatable Read, locks are obtained up front so predicates need not be reapplied at all.)

INSERT Operations

MDC tables can help with INSERT operations as well. Consider the following INSERT statement:

```
INSERT INTO MDC VALUES (1999, 'CANADA')
```

When DB2 UDB inserts a new record into this table, how does it most efficiently determine where to store it? To maintain clustering of the MDC table, DB2 UDB needs to find the unique cell for the dimension values NATION='CANADA' and YEAR='1999'. (Incidentally, in this example, we purposely left out the third dimension COLOR. DB2 UDB would assume that COLOR='NULL' in this example and proceed with INSERT operations, unless the COLOR column was defined with the NOT NULL option, in which case it would fail the INSERT.)

If you recall, when an MDC table is created, a dimension block index for each dimension is automatically generated and maintained. Therefore, DB2 UDB has the option to find each dimension's slice and determine the cell from the intersection of these slices. This is the scenario that was shown in Figure 2.14.

In other words, DB2 UDB can search each dimension's index for a list of blocks corresponding to their respective key value and do an ANDing of the BID lists to find the set of blocks in the table for this cell. The resulting blocks contain the entire set of records with the specified dimension key values. DB2 UDB therefore inserts the new record in one of these blocks if there is space on any of their pages. If there's no space on any pages in these blocks, DB2 UDB uses a previously emptied block in the table or allocates a new block for the table.

However, remember the composite block index? A composite block index has keys that consists of all the columns defined as dimensions and maps cell values to the list of blocks for each cell. In our example, the composite block index of (NATION, COLOR, YEAR) would be used for INSERT processing. DB2 UDB chooses to use this index, instead of ANDing the dimension block indexes, to quickly determine whether a particular cell exists (if it doesn't, it will need to be created), and if so, exactly which blocks contain those cell values.

So, on INSERT operations, DB2 UDB probes the composite block index (if it exists) for the cell corresponding to the dimension values of the record to be inserted. If it finds the cell's key in the index, its list of BIDs gives DB2 UDB the complete list of blocks in the table having that cell's dimension values. Therefore, using a composite block index, DB2 UDB is able to limit the number of blocks of the table it has to search for space to complete the insert. If the cell's key is not found in the index, or if the extents containing these values are full, DB2 UDB needs to assign a new block to the cell. If possible, it reuses an empty block in the table first before extending the table by another new extent of pages.

Whether or not a cell exists for the new data can impact the processing DB2 UDB must follow to complete an INSERT. An INSERT probes the composite block index for matching cell values. If they exist, it scans the list of BIDs. For each BID, DB2 UDB scans the block for space using the block's free space control record (FSCR). If space is found on a page in the block, DB2 UDB logs the operation and inserts the data record.

If RID indexes exist on the MDC table, DB2 UDB has to log the appropriate key and RID values. If, on the probe of the composite block index, the cell values do not exist for a new record, or the cells exist but no space is found in any of its blocks, DB2 UDB scans a block map for a block that has been previously emptied and freed from any cell, in order to reuse the block for this cell. The block map is an internal structure MDC uses to identify free blocks. If a free block is found, DB2 UDB logs and changes the block status to in use. If a free block does not exist, it allocates one and finishes the insert as in the previous case.

UPDATE Operations

How DB2 UDB handles UPDATE operations on an MDC table depends on the value that is being updated. If the UPDATE statement is for non-dimension values, then they occur in place, just like regular updates.

If the UPDATE is for a varying length data type and can no longer fit on the data page as a result of the updated value, DB2 UDB will have to search for another page to place the record. DB2 UDB tries to first find this extra space within the same block. If no space is found in the current block where the data record resides, the INSERT algorithm is used to search the other blocks in the cell or allocate a new one in the cell as needed. DB2 UDB does not need to update the block index (unless the insert of an overflow record requires a new block to be added to the cell).

If an UPDATE is performed for a dimension value, DB2 UDB needs to move that record to a different cell. DB2 handles updates to dimension values by first converting the operation into a DELETE operation, and then handling the changed data as an INSERT operation into the appropriate cell.

DELETE Operations

DELETE operations differ in their operation depending on whether the delete empties the block or not.

In the simplest case, DB2 UDB is just removing a record from a block, but other records still exist in it. Take, for example, removing an order for a customer in NATION='CANADA'. In this case, DB2 UDB logs and deletes the record from the table. (Remember, in this case, the block is not emptied.) If a RID index exists, DB2 UDB must also log and delete RID from each index too.

DB2 UDB has more work to do if the DELETE operation involves the last record in the block. When a block is emptied, DB2 UDB must disassociate it with its current cell values so that it can be reused by another cell when needed. This is more efficient than always allocating a new block to the MDC table when a new block is needed. In this scenario, DB2 UDB still logs and deletes the record from the table, but this time, the block is now empty. This must be reflected in the block map because the block is now available for reuse. To accomplish this, DB2 UDB finds the corresponding block entry in the block map, logs and changes the block status to *free*, logs and removes the BID from each block index (dimension and composite), and handles any existing RID entries as well.

In the end, block indexes only need to be updated when an insert of a first record for a block occurs, or a delete for the last record from a block happens. This enormously reduces index overhead by a factor of cell cardinality for maintenance and logging for every block index that would have otherwise been a RID index.

PICKING A DIMENSION FOR AN MDC TABLE

MDC tables can deliver incredible performance advantages over regular tables. However, when defining MDC tables, you must give careful consideration to dimension selection. Having too granular of a dimension (e.g., customer number) could cause too few individual records to have their own blocks of like information—the worst case would be if that information is unique. Clearly this would not benefit from any performance benefits of an MDC table, and would have excessive space requirements.

When choosing dimensions for a table, consider the fact that you are enabling fast query access, so the best place to start is by looking at your expected queries. Columns in equality or range queries, as well as those with coarse granularity, will benefit the most from block-level clustering. Remember, you can use a generated column to add coarseness to a proposed dimension.

Before creating an MDC table, you should first identify candidates for dimensions. The best starting point is to examine the query workload that you plan to run against your MDC tables. For the most part, you should pay attention to the following query characteristics:

- Range, equality, or IN-list types of predicates on attributes; for example:

```
shipdate > 1999-01-01 or shipdate = 1999-01-04
```

- Rollin or rollout of data; for example, loading data for the quarter 2002–01 and deleting data for the quarter 2001–01
- Group By clause attributes; for example, group by ship date
- Join clauses, especially in a star schema; for example:

```
Lineitem.partkey = Part.partkey and Part.partkey < 1000
```

- Any combinations of these

It is quite possible that a workload can have several candidate attributes that satisfy these criteria. If this is the case, it is important to rank these attributes based on the workload characteristics so you can choose the appropriate subset of the candidates. Choosing an MDC dimension is not an exact science. It might require iterations and variations with the set of dimension candidates before converging to an appropriate selection.

Order matters with the selection of MDC dimensions. The dimension with the lowest cardinality is a good choice. Take, for example, clustering a table on three dimensions: DAY, NATION, and COLOR. If the number of years spanned is 20 and there are 100 different nations and 5 different colors, the potential number of cells is $20 \times 100 \times 5 \times 365 = 3,650,000$. If the skew of the data is such that some cells will be sparsely populated whereas others will be densely populated, and space consumption is a concern, you might wish to have a smaller block size so that the sparse cells will not take up as much wasted space. On the other hand, if you were to cluster on a coarser measurement like YEAR instead of DAY, this would increase the density of cells, and the potential number of cells becomes $20 \times 100 \times 5 = 10{,}000$.

MDC Utilities

With regard to utilities, loading an MDC table by default organizes the input data along the dimension values. Note that the load design need not distinguish between ordered and non-ordered input data. In the ordered case, the LOAD utility manages the input optimally by writing directly to the target table without significant overhead.

In the unordered case, the LOAD utility will order data internally, using a cache and a system temporary table. Load examines the incoming data stream, clustering a portion of data at a time in a memory buffer. Data in the buffer is separated into blocks according to cell values, and as blocks are filled, they are written directly to disk. Partially filled blocks are stored in a dynamic cache, to be further filled as data for the same cell is found later in the data stream. If the cache fills up, it spills directly to the database container, where it eventually belongs. The temporary table stores cell values found in the data stream, and maps each cell value to the block in the dynamic cache being filled with data for that cell.

Note that MDC support will affect duplicate record processing and deletion for LOAD too. In the non-MDC case, when a duplicate record is detected, the LOAD utility is able to discern (and keep) the oldest record of a unique key. However, when an attempt is made to insert a duplicate record into an MDC table, there are two possible outcomes:

- If the unique key was present in the table before LOAD started: the original record prevails and only the new, duplicate, or loaded records are deleted.
- If the unique key did not previously exist in the table, then only one of the loaded records will prevail (the one with the lowest object relative page number). Furthermore, there is no guarantee (nor an easy way to calculate) which of the candidate records this will be.

Reorganization of an MDC table is required less often than for a table with a clustering index. Because clustering is automatically and continuously maintained, reorganizations are no longer required to recluster data. They can still be used, however, to reclaim space in the table (specifically, to reclaim space within cells), to clean up overflow records, and so on. Online reorganization is not yet available for MDC tables. All other DB2 UDB utilities are supported. Finally, MDC tables can coexist with and complement data partitioning. Each partition will contain an MDC table with those slices of the logical cube corresponding to the partition's key. The partitioning key can also be a dimension, or not.

SUMMARY

As you can see, MDC tables provide a unique and powerful solution for large database performance and high availability. MDC benefits include the following:

- Extending the performance advantages of clustering to multiple dimensions.
- Automatic and dynamic maintenance of clustering over time.
- The need for reorganizations are reduced to space reclamation only.
- Data organization provides benefits of partition elimination.
- Block-based indexes provide additional high-performance access plans and block elimination in queries.
- Block index size results in faster scans and reduced overhead for logging and maintenance.
- A simple, flexible syntax makes it easy to set up and maintain.

Declared Global Temporary Tables

A *declared global temporary table* (DGTT) is created using the DECLARE GLOBAL TEMPO-RARY TABLE statement and is used to hold temporary data on behalf of a single application. The DECLARE statement is very similar to the CREATE statement used to create persistent tables.

A DGTT is dropped implicitly when its owning application disconnects from the database. DGTTs are often used by application developers when they need a temporary location to store data that will be used for further processing. Without these types of tables, the database engine would go through overhead activities (e.g., logging, locking, etc.) to persist and manage a table that wasn't needed in the long run. The application developer would also be charged with the responsibility of dropping the table when the application was finished with it (which would spawn more activity for the database).

DGTTs behave very much like other tables (you can DROP and ALTER them), but they are limited in their support of database objects (e.g., they do not support triggers).

DGTTs must be placed in a user temporary table space. User temporary table spaces are not created by default at database creation time (you must create them before creating a DGTT). At least one user temporary table space should be created with appropriate USE privileges to allow the definition of declared temporary tables.

DB2 UDB v7 supported DGTTs, however, they did not have any optimization support or indexes available to them. Although DGTTs were still efficient and useful to developers in DB2 UDB v7, they came with an inherent performance hit whenever an application had to query a temporary table. Because indexes could not be created and there were no statistics available to the optimizer for these tables, whenever an application had to read data from these tables, the database manager had to perform a relational table scan of all the rows in the table.

Consider an application that inserts 500,000 rows into a temporary table for further processing. In DB2 UDB v7, when the application went back to reference or search through this table, the optimizer would have to perform a relational scan, row by row, through the table.

DB2 UDB v8 solves the performance issues once associated with DGTTs with new features that include the following:

- Index support: The ability to create indexes using the CREATE INDEX statement.
- Minimal undo logging: You now have the option to log DGTTs, giving developers access to the atomicity and save points for these tables.
- Statistics support: Performance of relational operations on DGTTs is improved as a result of support for the RUNSTATS utility that can be used to update statistics about the physical characteristics of a DGTT and its associated indexes.

INDEX SUPPORT FOR DGTTs

DB2 UDB v8 gives DBAs the ability to create multiple indexes on DGTTs. Each index that is created will be created in the same table space in which the temporary table resides. (Remember, you have to define a user temporary table space before you can create these types of tables.)

Indexes on DGTTs can be created using the CREATE INDEX statement and dropped using the DROP INDEX statement. Due to the nature of temporary tables, they are implicitly dropped when the session is closed and do not have any persistence in the catalog (they only exist within the duration of a database connection.)

If you create an index on a temporary table, the PUBLIC group is given the INDEX privilege on the table. The qualifier for a DGTT (or an index on a DGTT) will always be SESSION.

Index Restrictions on a DGTT

Some features of the CREATE INDEX statement are not supported for DGTTs because they are either not applicable or common to them.

DB2 UDB v8 adds the ability to rename an index using the RENAME INDEX statement. However, this feature is not supported for indexes defined for declared global temporary tables.

Indexes on DGTTs cannot be reorganized either. However, due to their inherent temporary nature, there isn't really the opportunity for them to become defragmented. An attempt to perform either of these actions would result in the following error:

```
SQLSTATE 42995: The requested function does not apply to global temporary
tables.
```

The following list details the supported clauses for indexes on DGTTs:

- UNIQUE
- INDEX *index-name*

- ON `table-name`
- `column-name` ASC/DESC
- DISALLOW REVERSE SCANS
- ALLOW REVERSE SCANS
- INCLUDE
- PCTFREE
- MINPCTUSED

The following clauses are not supported with the CREATE INDEX statement on DGTTs:

- SPECIFICATION ONLY
- EXTEND USING
- CLUSTER
- SHRLEVEL

The SPECIFICATION ONLY and EXTEND USING options do not really apply to DGTTs and consequently they are not supported.

The CLUSTER option would typically not be used with DGTTs, but could be considered as an added option at a later time.

> **NOTE**
> If you specify the SHRLEVEL option, it will be ignored as opposed to blocked like the previous options.

Creating an Index on a DGTT

You create an index on a DGTT the same way that you would create an index for any regular table: There is no change to the CREATE INDEX statement. (The samples in this section assume that you have created the SAMPLE database. If you have not done this, you can do so now by entering the DB2SAMPL command from a command prompt.)

To create a temporary table space, you first must create a temporary user table space. For example, issue the following command:

```
create user temporary tablespace WHATSNEWTEMPSPACE pagesize 4k managed
by system using
            ('D:\Tablespaces\DGTTsWhatsNewContainer')
```

After creating a temporary table space, create and populate the DGTT by issuing the following commands:

> **TIP**
> Don't forget to substitute the appropriate schema name for `paulz`.

```
declare global temporary table indextemptable like
        paulz.staff on commit preserve rows not logged

insert into session.indextemptable
        select * from paulz.staff
```

The first command creates a declared global temporary table called INDEXTEMPTABLE that is a copy of the STAFF table in the SAMPLE database. The second command inserts all of the values in the SAMPLE database's STAFF table into the temporary table: INDEXTEMPTABLE.

You can verify that you have populated the INDEXTEMPTABLE table by entering the following command:

```
select * from session.indextemptable
```

Suppose you needed to find specific employees in your temporary data set based on the department they work for. This need would benefit from the ability to create an index for quicker access to the table. You can use the new index support in DB2 UDB v8 for DGTTs to create an index. For example:

```
create index session.tempdeptindex on session.indextemptable(dept)
```

Now queries that need to access the temporary table along the *dept* key can use the index you created. Each index created on a DGTT implicitly has PUBLIC authority granted to it and its qualifier is always SESSION.

When an application disconnects from the database, all temporary objects created cease to exist. Enter the CONNECT RESET command, reconnect to the database, and try to issue that same query again. You will receive an SQL0204N error because the table (and the index for that matter) no longer exists.

MINIMAL UNDO LOGGING TO SUPPORT THE ROLLBACK OF DATA CHANGES TO DGTTS

In DB2 UDB v7, the NOT LOGGED clause was mandatory when creating a DGTT (notice that we used this option in the preceding example). In DB2 UDB v8, this clause is optional and DGTTs are logged by default to support the rollback of a unit of work or a rollback to an application save point. (For the rest of this section, we refer to rollback as either the rollback of a unit of work or the rollback to an application save point.)

The NOT LOGGED option reduces the amount of overhead that a database manager needs to perform to manage a DGTT, but it has its drawbacks. For example, applications leveraging data in temporary tables might require atomicity or the ability to leverage save points within a transaction. For these types of applications, logging would be beneficial in that it could support the roll-back of transactions.

When a DGTT is created with the NOT LOGGED option in DB2 UDB v8, changes to the table (including its creation) are not logged. However, if a transaction needs to roll back, the rows in the DGTT are either deleted or preserved, depending on how the DGTT is specified in the DECLARE statement. In DB2 UDB v7, there were no rollback options and the behavior was fixed (you lost all the data in your DGTT).

DB2 UDB v8 supports two new options that you can use with the DECLARE statement:

- **ON ROLLBACK DELETE ROWS**—Specifies that a DELETE should occur on the DGTT when a rollback operation is performed. If the table data has been changed, all the rows are deleted. This is the default behavior in DB2 UDB v8.
- **ON ROLLBACK PRESERVE ROWS**—The rows are deleted or preserved depending on whether the table data has changed or not. If this option is specified, all the rows are preserved at statement rollback. This means that if a statement changed the rows in a DGTT and then failed in the middle of its work, the rows that have been already changed are preserved.

STATISTICS SUPPORT ON DGTTS

In DB2 UDB v7 there were no statistics collected on DGTTs. To improve their performance, DB2 UDB v8 adds support for the RUNSTATS utility over DGTTs. Application programmers can now invoke the RUNSTATS utility to update statistics about the physical characteristics of a DGTT and its associated indexes. There is no change required for the syntax of the RUNSTATS command. Just ensure that you identify the DGTT with the SESSION schema as with all other operations on these tables.

For example, to collect statistics on the table we created earlier in this chapter, you could enter a command similar to the following:

```
runstats on table session.indextemptable on columns (id)
```

DB2 UDB v8 does not support the viewing of statistics on DGTTs or their associated indexes. Because DGTTs exist only within the scope of an application, and you cannot reorganize them, there isn't really a need to see this data.

For more information on DGTTs, refer to the Information Center or the *DB2 UDB v8 SQL Reference* manual.

System Default Value and NULL Compression

I n DB2 UDB v7.2, the record format used to store a table's data consumed a fixed amount of space for all columns, regardless of the data value for the column. There is a growing demand for all databases to consume less space. One of the ways that a database could save space is to not set aside a fixed amount of space if the column value is NULL, or by simply not hardening the column's value to disk if it can be easily known (e.g., system default values are always easily known and available to the DB2 UDB engine during record formatting and column extraction).

DB2 UDB v8.1 provides a new ability to compress NULLs and system default values, thereby storing this data more efficiently and reducing space requirements. This new feature is particularly useful for data warehousing environments. The benefits that accrue from the ability for a database engine to provide data compression techniques are twofold:

- Significant disk savings can be attained, resulting in lower costs attributed to decreased DASD requirements and the time it takes for maintenance operations.
- Improved query performance can be achieved by effectively packing more data per page and unit I/O—a bigger bang for the buck.

How Data Compression Works in DB2 UDB

Compression in DB2 UDB v8.1 can take place at the table level, as well as at the column level, depending on the data you want to compress. There are two ways in which DB2 UDB tables can occupy less space when stored on disk:

- If the column value is NULL or a zero-length varying character, the database manager can use a mechanism at the table level by which the defined fixed amount of space reserved for the data is not allocated and no data is stored on disk.

- If the column value can be easily known or determined (like system default values) and if the value is available to the database manager during record formatting and column extraction, the database manager can replace this value at run time and not store it on disk. This type of compression happens at the column level, but compression must be enabled for the table (enabling NULL compression) for this to happen.

Compression in DB2 UDB v8.1 is implemented via a new optional record format, which you will learn about later in this chapter.

Use the CREATE TABLE or ALTER TABLE commands with the ACTIVATE COMPRESSION or DEACTIVATE COMPRESSION option statements to disable or enable compression on a DB2 UDB table. When compression is enabled, DB2 UDB uses the new row format to store the table's data. A table created in DB2 UDB v8 can have mixed record row formats. For example, if you add new rows to a table after compression has been enabled, they will use the new format. All of the rows that existed before compression was activated would use the old record format and can be converted to the new record format using a table reorganization.

The new VALUE COMPRESSION clause is used to direct a table to use the new row format and therefore enable compression. When the VALUE COMPRESSION clause is activated for a table, NULLs and zero-length varying-length data (VARCHARs, LONG VARCHARs, VARGRAPHICs, LONG VARGRAPHICs, BLOBs, CLOBs, and DBCLOBs) are not stored on disk. The only disk space allocated on INSERT and UPDATE operations for this data is that which is required overhead to support this feature. The VALUE COMPRESSION clause is specified at the table level.

If VALUE COMPRESSION is activated, another option, COMPRESS SYSTEM DEFAULT, provides another layer of compression that can compress the column's system default value. This feature is enabled at the table level. In this case, as with the NULL values, the data is not stored on disk.

> **T I P**
> It would be redundant (although it would not return an error) to specify the COMPRESS SYSTEM DEFAULT option for all varying-length data type columns.

If the COMPRESS SYSTEM DEFAULT option is specified for a column when VALUE COMPRESSION has been deactivated for the table, an SQLSTATE 01648 warning is returned and DB2 UDB does not compress any data.

If you ALTER a table using the DEACTIVATE VALUE COMPRESSION option, it disables the COMPRESS SYSTEM DEFAULT option for each column implicitly, even though each individual column retains the COMPRESS SYSTEM DEFAULT attribute. In this case, an SQLSTATE 01648 warning is also returned.

For a typed table, altering the record row format is only supported on the parent table of the table's hierarchy. If a column in a typed table is altered to compress the system-generated defaults at the column level, that column must not be inherited from a super table.

When you create a table with the VALUE COMPRESSION option, 2 bytes for the row and an additional 2 bytes for every column (regardless of their eligibility for compression, with an exception for large objects [LOBs] and double-byte character set [DBCS], etc.) are added for overhead and feature support. If you enable compression and your data does not contain NULLs and system-generated defaults, your table could actually grow in size.

For complete details on these options, refer to the DB2 UDB Information Center or the *DB2 UDB SQL Reference* manual.

The New Row Record Format

Without getting into too much detail, DB2 UDB v7.2 used two record headers (an inner and an outer), each consisting of 4 bytes.

This old record format has a known fixed offset following the record headers for each column in the table. This offset is determined by all preceding column types, lengths, and the nullability of the column. The offset for Column 0 is 0, and from there, the other rows fall into place, depending on the size of the preceding columns.

With the old record format, all columns have a fixed-length portion that is kept at the column's offset in the fixed portion of the record. This fixed portion consumes 4 bytes and consists of two unsigned short elements for variable column types. The unsigned elements consist of the length of the variable data and the offset where the variable data can be found (offset from the beginning of Column 0).

Each column that is nullable has an additional null byte indicator that is part of the fixed-length portion for the column. The null byte indicator follows the space for the column data.

For example, consider the following table, T1:

```
CREATE TABLE T1 (C1 INT NOT NULL WITH DEFAULT, C2 CHAR(30),
C3 VARCHAR(10), C4 VARCHAR(56))
```

This table would have the storage requirements shown in Table 4.1.

The minimum row size for the fixed-length portion of table T1 in this example is 44 because it could have a zero-length VARCHAR for Column C3, and a NULL value for Column C2 and C4. The maximum size of a row in T1 is 110 bytes: 44 + 10 + 56.

Table 4.1   Storage Requirements for Table T1

Column	Size of Fixed Length Portion	Column Offset
C1	4 (size of integer)	0
C2	31 (column length + null byte indicator)	4
C3	4 (fixed-length portion of variable column)	35
C4	5 (fixed-length portion of variable column + null byte indicator)	39

Exclusive whether or not the values of Columns C2 and C4 are NULL, DB2 UDB v7.2 would set aside 36 bytes in the fixed-length portion of the record for these two columns. If both Columns C2 and C4 are NULL, then 34 out of the 44 bytes are not used, but still allocated to disk.

If 70% of T1's column values are NULLs, 22% to 54% of the disk space will not be used with the old record row format. If Column C1 was defined with the system default value 0, the 4-byte fixed-length storage for the value 0 would also still be allocated.

The new record format in DB2 UDB v8.1 frees DB2 UDB from consuming a fixed amount of space for all columns (for the most part), regardless of the value for the column. The new record row format no longer reserves the corresponding fixed-length column portions that it did in the previous release.

There are some overheads and maximum data sizes that must be taken into consideration with the new record row format. It is possible that rows could therefore be larger or smaller than the old record format (it depends on the number of compression-eligible data values that populate the table). Generally speaking, sparsely populated tables benefit from using the new row format.

When a table is altered such that it will use the new record format, if the sum of the bytes required by the columns in the destination row format becomes greater than the row size limit that is based on the page size of the table, an SQL0670N error is returned.

During processing, DB2 UDB might make use of system temporary tables to store intermediate results while processing complex queries. Many application developers also choose to leverage declared global temporary tables for transient data. The new record row format (and therefore the compression feature) is not supported for temporary system or declared global temporary tables.

COMPRESSION EXAMPLE

To get a feel for how compression works, you can work through the example in this section.

First create a table using the following DDL:

```
create table compression (groupid int not null, greeting varchar(200)
not null, message varchar(200) compress system default, txid int
not null) value compression
```

Now create a table that is the same as the COMPRESSION table you just created, but without the compression feature turned on by entering the following command:

```
create table nocompression like compression
```

> **TIP**
> When creating a table using the LIKE function, the new table does not inherit the compression attributes of the original table.

If you want to ensure compression is on for the COMPRESSION table and not on for the NOCOM-PRESSION table, see the section "How Do I Know if Compression Is Turned On?" later in this chapter.

You should now have two tables: one with the compression feature turned on (called COMPRES-SION) and one without (called NOCOMPRESSION). To complete the example, we need to populate these tables with data and see the impact that the compression feature can have on a table's disk requirements.

You can easily create a sample input file using any scripting lanuage to run this example in your own environment. In this example, our sample input file had 13,000 records and was called compressionsample.txt.

A sample file, called SAMPLECOMPRESSION is provided on the Web at: *http://authors.phptr.com/zikopoulos/*. You can copy and paste the two commands in this file into the Command Cetner to setup your own compression table example.

To import all of the sample records into your sample tables, enter the following commands.

You might need to adjust your database's logging properties to accommodate the INSERT activity generated by the preceding IMPORT commands.

```
import from
c:\writing\books\WhatsNewV8\PaulZChapters\COMPRESSIONSAMPLE.txt
of del messages c:\temp\intocompressiontable.txt insert into
paulz.compression

import from
c:\writing\books\WhatsNewV8\PaulZChapters\COMPRESSIONSAMPLE.txt
of del messages c:\temp\intonocompressiontable.txt insert into
paulz.nocompression
```

> **TIP**
> To avoid any logging issues with this IMPORT operation, you can use
> the NOT LOGGED INITIALLY TABLE option with the CREATE TABLE
> statement. Don't forget to commit once the IMPORT is finished.

After you have run these commands successfully, both tables are populated with the same data. At this point, you can use the Control Center's ESTIMATE SIZE function to approximate the size of these two tables and see the space savings that the new compression feature can give.

After starting the Control Center, select the COMPRESSION table, right-click on this object, and select the Estimate Size option. This utility is shown in Figure 4.1.

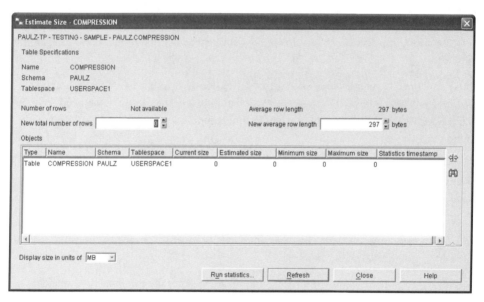

Figure 4.1
The Estimate Size function in the Control Center.

Before you can estimate the size of your tables, you must ensure that all the database statistics are current.

If you just created these tables, the statistics are likely not current and therefore DB2 UDB cannot perform a size estimation. To update the statistics, click Run statistics. (For this example, because the tables are relatively small, just select the Collect basic statistics on all columns radio button and run it now.)

After the statistics have been updated or created for a table, you can estimate the size of that table. The estimated size of the COMPRESSION and the NOCOMPRESSION tables is shown in Figures 4.2 and 4.3, respectively.

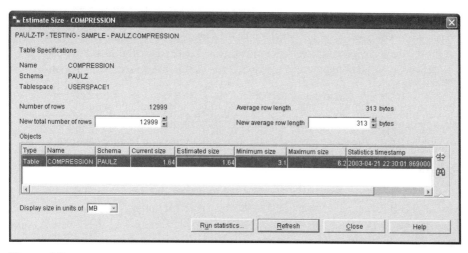

Figure 4.2
The estimated size of the COMPRESSION table.

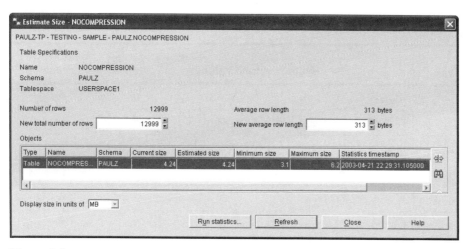

Figure 4.3
The estimated size of the NOCOMPRESSION table.

As you can see in this simple example, the compression feature available in DB2 UDB v8.1 can have a considerable impact in terms of disk savings. Notice in the figures the minimum size of both tables is the same, 3.1 MB. This is the minimum size of the table without compression.

SUPPORTED DATA TYPES FOR COMPRESSION

For DB2 UDB v8.1 to compress data and not store the data on disk, the column's value must be easily known to the database engine during record formatting and data extraction. There are data values and situations when data is not eligible for compression and is therefore always stored on disk.

As of DB2 UDB 8.1.2, only system-generated default values are eligible for compression. User-defined data defaults for columns are not eligible for compression and are stored on disk. However, the new row format does provide the underlying architecture so that this might become an option in a future release of DB2 UDB.

All of DB2 UDB's data types are eligible for compression, except for the TIME, DATE, and TIMESTAMP data types. Time sensitive data is dynamic in nature and their system default values always equate to the time that the INSERT or UPDATE occurred for that column. Because it is not possible for DB2 UDB to know these values during SELECT processing, these values must always be hardened to disk.

Table 4.2 lists all the system default values for each data type. For complete details, refer to the Information Center or the *DB2 UDB SQL Reference* manual.

Table 4.2 System Default Values for Each Data Type.

Data Type	System Default Value	Eligible for Compression?
ANY NUMERIC	0	Yes
CHAR	Blanks	Yes
VARCHAR	A string length of 0	Yes
GRAPHIC	Double-byte blanks	Yes
VARGRAPHIC	A string length of 0	Yes
DATE	For existing rows, a date corresponding to January 1, 0001. For added rows, the current date.	No
TIME	For existing rows, a time corresponding to 0 hours, 0 minutes, and 0 seconds. For added rows, the current time.	No
TIMESTAMP	For existing rows, a date corresponding to January 1, 0001, and a time corresponding to 0 hours, 0 minutes, 0 seconds, and 0 microseconds. For added rows, the current timestamp.	No
Large Object	A string length of 0	Yes

HOW DO I KNOW IF COMPRESSION IS TURNED ON?

You can use the information stored in the DB2 UDB v8.1 system catalogs to determine if compression has been activated on a table or not.

A new column called COMPRESSION, defined as CHAR(1), has been added to the SYSIBM .SYSCOLUMNS catalog table in DB2 UDB v8.1. This column can be used to indicate if VALUE COMPRESSION has been activated on a table or not. If the value in this column is V, this indicates that value compression has been turned on. If it is N, then value compression has not been enabled.

Figure 4.4 shows a query with a result set that includes a table that was created and enabled for value compression.

Another column called COMPRESS, defined as CHAR(1), has also been added to the SYSIBM.SYSTABLES table to indicate whether system-generated default value compression is in use. If the COMPRESS column has an S, then system-generated default compression is turned on, and if it has an O, it is turned off.

DB2 UDB v7.2 tables that are migrated to the DB2 UDB v8.1 format have a migrated value of N for the COMPRESSION column in the SYSIBM.SYSTABLES table and an O for the COMPRESS column in the SYSIBM.SYSCOLUMNS table.

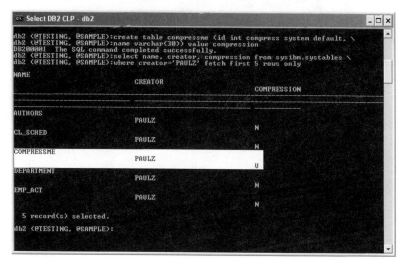

Figure 4.4
Using the catalog tables to identify tables using value compression.

ESTIMATING COMPRESSION SAVINGS

It can be advantageous to estimate the savings that could be gained by using the compression techniques available in DB2 UDB v8.1 without creating, altering, or loading a table.

We have provided you with a query that you can download from the Web that makes a rough estimate of the cost benefit of activating value compression (npage_ohead_est in the result set of the query) and system default compression (new_npage_est in the result set of the query) on columns where most or all values are defaults. This query is available at: *http://authors.phptr .com/zikopoulos/*

This query is completely dependent on the accuracy of the distribution statistics—the more up to date that information is, the better chance this query has of being accurate. This query can be used to get an idea of whether compression might be of value for a particular table, but it is in no way 100% accurate or an IBM-supported decision criteria.

Informational Constraints

DB2 UDB v8.1 introduces a new type of constraint called *informational constraints*. Informational constraints are additional data model information that can be used in query rewrite to improve performance, but you have the option to have the database manager enforce them. This feature leverages the performance gains that can come from constraint checking in the database, but avoids the overhead with revalidation checking in the engine during INSERT, UPDATE, DELETE, and LOAD operations.

WHY INFORMATIONAL CONSTRAINTS?

DB2 UDB introduced support for constraint checking in the DB2 Common Server version 2 release. Both check constraints and referential integrity constraints were included and used to enforce business logic and schema rules in the database.

Constraints are really used for two purposes:

- Ensuring the integrity of the database and its data.
- Enhancing the performance for query workloads.

Query performance improvements as a result of defining constraints in the database were introduced in DB2 UDB version 6. The ability to use constraints as a performance enhancer comes from the integration of check and referential integrity constraints into the query graph model (QGM). This integration gives the DB2 UDB optimizer more information and the ability to rewrite the query into an even more efficient form.

For example, consider a UNION query over a set of tables partitioned by quarters of a year. When a query against only one month of the year is issued, all but one branch of the UNION can be dropped.

Each release of DB2 UDB builds on its predecessor with respect to the amount of query performance improvements that can be leveraged from constraints. With the increased usage of constraints for performance enhancements, DBAs are adding more and more constraints to the database than are truly needed for database integrity. Examples include applications that already ensure data integrity through some other median, but want to benefit from performance enhancements in the engine. The transitive closure of constraints on a table might give the optimizer choices it might not discover on its own.

Although constraints can be used for business rule enforcement and performance advantages, they do result in overhead, as the defined constraints need to be reverified during INSERT, UPDATE, DELETE, and LOAD operations. On one hand you can leverage benefits with query type workloads, but you also pay a cost for some data change operations.

Data warehouses typically use star schemas. An example of a Star Schema is shown in Figure 5.1.

A star schema is used to model the business view in a highly normalized database. At the heart of a star schema is the FACT table. Surrounding the facts of the business are attributes, which are stored in what are called DIMENSION tables.

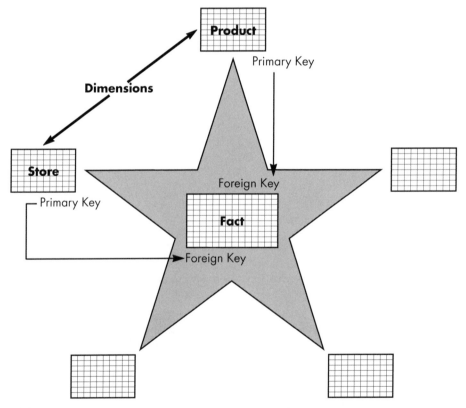

Figure 5.1
A Star Schema.

A company's sales data and its attributes typically leverage a star schema (or its more advanced representation, a snowflake schema) in a data warehousing environment. Setting up referential integrity between the FACT and DIMENSION tables is beneficial for query processing, but presents overhead for other operations. Think about the potential performance penalty for large operations that refresh, update, or insert data into a large data warehouse; there is the potential for a lot of overhead!

Take for example telecommunication companies (telcos). Telcos often persist data in operational data stores (ODSs) that are populated and analyzed with call data to detect fraudulent usage. In this environment, having heavy referential integrity checking could slow down load times and hence the critical fraud detection mining algorithms.

Another example where constraints can be redundant is with a front-end tool (FET). Quite often, a FET has been coded such that the business rules are enforced through the application logic, as shown in Figure 5.2.

In Figure 5.2 you can see that both the application and the database engine ensure that the Sex field can only take one of two discrete values: Male or Female. This is typical of DB2 UDB implementations in which the application programmatically verifies and protects the constraint itself, but DBAs want the leverage constraints in the database to improve query performance.

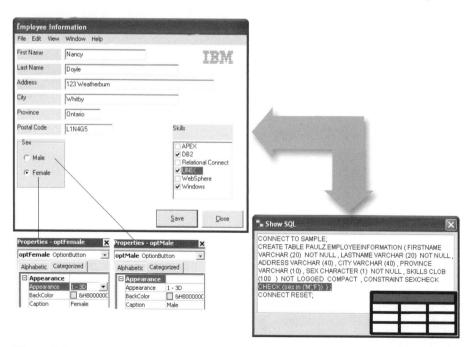

Figure 5.2
Redundant checking at the application layer and in the database.

Informational constraints are well suited for complex queries, especially those that run against a star or snowflake schema. Typically, informational constraints are set up between a FACT table and its associated DIMENSION tables. This new constraint allows applications to circumvent the referential integrity and constraint checking during LOAD (to round out our previous example), but still get good performance at run time. In essence, the database manager is aware of the relationships (so it can optimize around them), but does not spend cycles enforcing them.

It is important to note that informational constraints do not tell the optimizer how to get to the data. Some databases rely heavily on rules-based optimizers, which require hints that tell the database engine how to get to the data in the most efficient manner. Think of informational constraints as tips: the optizmizer is free to do with them as it will when trying to determine the most efficient access plan to the data. Information Constraints simply provide more data for the optimizer to consider when making a decision for efficient data access.

USING INFORMATIONAL CONSTRAINTS

You can define informational constraints using the CREATE TABLE or ALTER TABLE statements. Within these statements, you add referential integrity or check constraints. You then associate constraint attributes to them, specifying whether you want the database manager to enforce the constraint or not and whether you want the constraint to be used for query optimization or not.

This section takes you through an example using informational constraints. Complete details on how to use them are available in the Information Center or the *DB2 UDB SQL Reference* manual.

Informational Constraints Example

To illustrate the use of informational constraints, first create a table called EMPLOYEEINFORMATION using the following DDL:

```
CREATE TABLE EMPLOYEEINFORMATION
(FIRSTNAME VARCHAR(20) NOT NULL,
  LASTNAME VARCHAR(20) NOT NULL,
  SEX CHARACTER(1) NOT NULL,
    CONSTRAINT SEXCHECK CHECK (sex in ('M','F'))
    NOT ENFORCED
    ENABLE QUERY OPTIMIZATION)
```

The EMPLOYEEINFORMATION table that this DDL creates has a constraint called SEXCHECK. This constraint enables the DB2 UDB engine to optimize queries with the information that the only values in the SEX column are M (for male) or F (for female); however, DB2 UDB will enforce this rule in the database since we used the NOT ENFORCED clause in the DDL.

There are two new parameters on the CREATE and ALTER table statements that are of particular interest when using informational constraints:

- NOT ENFORCED | ENFORCED: The constraint is, or is not, enforced by the database manager during normal operations such as INSERT, UPDATE, and so on.
- DISABLE QUERY OPTIMIZATION | ENABLE QUERY OPTIMIZATION: The constraint is, or is not, used for query optimization by the DB2 UDB engine.

Now run the following INSERT statement:

```
db2 insert into paulz.employeeinformation values
        ('Kelly','Doyle','F'),
        ('Erin','Sweeny','F'),
        ('John','Knotek','M'),
        ('Jeff','Jacobs','M'),
        ('Michael','Craig','C')
```

Because this table was created with the NOT ENFORCED option, the row (Michael,Craig,C) was allowed to be inserted into the EMPLOYEEINFORMATION table. (If you had created this table without the NOT ENFORCED option, this INSERT statement would have been rejected; try it with the same DDL using a different table name.)

Figure 5.3 shows two queries that are run against the EMPLOYEEINFORMATION table.

Do you notice anything peculiar about the second result set? The first query returned a result set that contained all of the data in the table because the SELECT statement used the * operator. The second query restricted the result set to only include those employees where SEX='Q'. You know that there is tuple with SEX='C' because it was part of the first query's result set. However, in the second query, this row did not show up. Why?

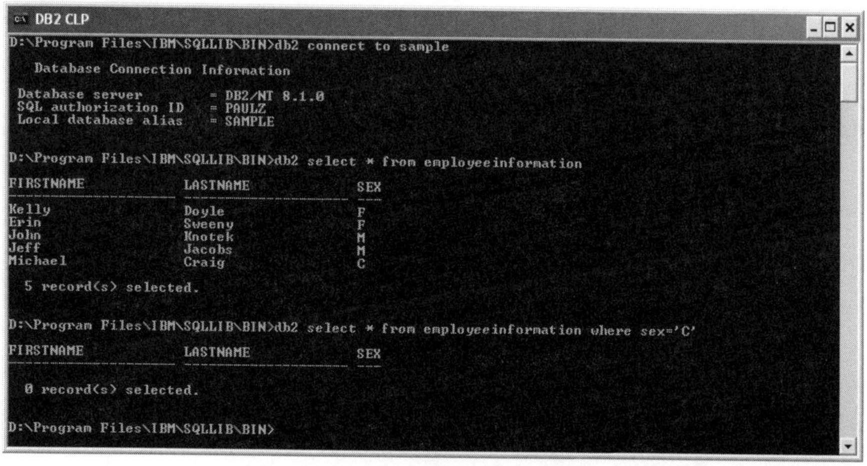

Figure 5.3
Inserts into a table that optimizes for specific data, but does not enforce rules around it.

The EMPLOYEEINFORMATION table was created with the ENABLE QUERY OPTIMIZATION option, which means that DB2 UDB assumes that the only values that exist in the SEX column for optimization purposes are M or F, even though other values exist (more on this in a bit).

Enter the following ALTER statement so that DB2 UDB does not use the information about the SEX column for query optimization with the EMPLOYEEINFORMATION table by entering the following command:

```
db2 alter table employeeinformation
    alter check SEXCHECK disable query optimization
```

Now run the same queries that you ran in Figure 5.3 after running the previous ALTER statement. Notice anything different? This time DB2 UDB returns the results you expected.

> **TIP**
> You may need to run the FLUSH PACKAGE CACHE DYNAMIC statement, or disconnt and reconnect to the database, for the new results to take effect.

Why? After you enter the ALTER statement, DB2 UDB won't optimize a query's access path to this table based on the informational constraints that were initially set up. This means that the value of SEX=C can exist according to the optimizer (even though it always existed, the information constraint caused DB2 UDB to act as if it didn't).

If you wanted to ensure that DB2 would not allow SEX=C to be inserted into the EMPLOYEEINFORMATION table (this would be the normal constraint operation), enter the following command:

```
db2 alter table employeeinformation alter check SEXCHECK enforced
```

In our particular example, this command would return the following error:

```
SQL0544N  The check constraint "SEXCHECK" cannot be added because the
table contains a row that violates the constraint.  SQLSTATE=23512
```

This is because a row, (Michael,Craig,C), exists in the table that violates the constraint. You would have to address this issue before using the table with this constraint. For now, just delete the violating row and enforce the constraint by entering the following commands:

```
db2 delete from employeeinformation where sex='C'
db2 alter table employeeinformation alter check SEXCHECK enforced
```

Now insert the row where SEX='C' that was allowed by the original INSERT statement:

```
db2 insert into employeeinformation values ('Michael','Craig','C')
```

You should receive the following error because DB2 UDB is now enforcing the constraint, not ignoring it like before.

```
SQL0545N  The requested operation is not allowed because a row does
not satisfy the check  constraint
"PAULZ.EMPLOYEEINFORMATION.SEXCHECK". SQLSTATE=23513
```

Usage Considerations

Informational constraints should only be used when the data that is stored in the table is verified to conform to the constraint by some other method than relying on the database manager. For example, an application is only offering the choices of Male or Female via radio buttons for these fields. This interface design would ensure that no other discrete values could be recorded for the SEX attribute, and thus you would be comfortable telling DB2 UDB not to enforce this, but to optimize for it.

If you use the informational constraints feature and incorrectly specify rules to the DB2 UDB server, it could return incorrect results when any data in the table violates the constraint.

Bottom line: Informational constraints are a powerful feature. Ensure that what you tell the database is true.

Connection Concentrator

The introduction of the *connection concentrator* in DB2 UDB v8.1 provides significant performance improvements for database servers that accept many transient connections. The connection concentrator enables database servers to handle more concurrent client database connections and improves the efficiency with which database connections are handled.

CONNECTION MANAGEMENT IMPROVEMENTS

Online transaction processing (OLTP) database systems introduce significant challenges in managing client database connections. Common problems include high volumes of connections with very few transactions and connected applications with significant idle time between transactions. The latter problem is especially common in Internet applications where database transactions are prompted directly by person-driven applications, (e.g., an e-business site selling airline tickets).

In many database servers today, each application connection requires a dedicated database agent. In DB2, a database agent (a process in UNIX and a thread in Windows) performs much of the SQL processing for connected applications. There are a finite number of database agents available, and each represents a resource and dispatch cost to the database server (each agent has its own private memory structures). For database connection sessions with few transactions, the database system spends more time and resources dispatching agents than executing the transactions. For database connection sessions where there is latency between transactions, the coordinator agent and its attendant resources are often idle. Both cases represent significant inefficiencies in the use of database system resources.

In DB2 UDB v8.1, the connection concentrator introduces resource optimizing features that were previously only available in DB2 Connect. In managing client connections to the database, the connection concentrator enables more database connections than there are available coordinating agents. With connection pooling technology, the connection concentrator reduces memory use for each connection and decreases the number of context switches. By managing database connections and reducing connection overhead, this mitigates the negative effects on performance from high-latency applications or applications with few transactions.

Use of the connection concentrator allows users to move from a state in which the number of connected users is constrained by the physical limitations of the underlying hardware to a state in which the limiting factor is based solely on the transaction load and the database server's ability to handle such a load.

ACTIVATING THE CONNECTION CONCENTRATOR

To activate the connection concentrator, set `max_connections` to be greater than `max_coordagents`. For example, if `max_coordagents` has a value of 200, the following commands activate the connection concentrator:

```
db2 update dbm cfg using max_connections 400
db2stop
db2start
```

In this example, the connection concentrator became active once the database manager was reset and the `max_connections` value of 400 was adopted.

CONNECTION CONCENTRATOR OPERATION

After the first connection to a host database, the connection concentrator reduces the connect time for subsequent connections to this database. When an application requests a disconnection from a host database, the connection from the application to the connection concentrator is dropped. Meanwhile, the coordinating agent is put into an agent pool for this host database, with the connection to the database intact. When a new request is made to connect to this host database, DB2 tries to reuse an existing outbound connection from the database's agent pool.

When the connection concentrator is on, there can be more connected applications than there are coordinator agents to service them. A connected application is in an active state only if there is a coordinator agent servicing it and directing its transactions. Otherwise, the application is in an inactive state. Requests from an active application are served by a coordinator agent. Requests from an inactive application are queued until a coordinator agent is assigned to service the application, at which time the application is activated.

Based on the previous example, there can only be as many active transactions as there are coordinating agents. Therefore, the `max_coordagents` database manager configuration parameter can be used to control the load on the database system. For example, in an N-partition system, the maximum number of active transactions in a particular partition would be $N \times$ `max_coordagents`.

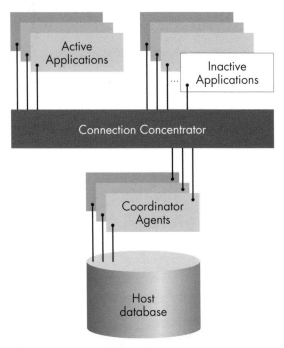

Figure 6.1
The relationship among connected applications, the connection concentrator, and coordinator agents.

When the connection concentrator is on, DB2 uses the num_poolagents configuration parameter to determine how large the agent pool should be when the system workload is low. When an agent finishes its work, it is always returned to the agent pool, regardless of the value of this parameter. If the number of agents in the pool is greater than num_poolagents, the logical agent scheduler can terminate agents. It does this based on the system load and how long agents remain idle in the pool.

CHAPTER 7

User-Maintained Materialized Query Tables

A *materialized query table* (MQT) is a table that has a definition based on the result set of a query. The data in the result set is taken from the one or more tables identified in a query. Judicious use of MQTs can result in tremendous performance improvements, especially for complex queries issued against large tables. MQTs eliminate work for queries by doing computations once, when the MQTs are built and refreshed. They can reuse the updated content for many queries. DB2 UDB v8.1 introduces *user-maintained* MQTs, thus increasing the flexibility with which MQTs can be implemented (these are also known as *user-maintained summary tables*).

The table data in a user-maintained MQT is updated only when users issue UPDATE, INSERT, or DELETE statements against it. Before DB2 UDB v8.1, MQTs could only be defined as *system maintained*. The table data of system-maintained MQTs can be set to be refreshed either automatically, whenever the base tables are updated, or manually, when a user issues a REFRESH TABLE statement. The REFRESH TABLE statement cannot be invoked against user-maintained MQTs. Also, user-maintained MQTs cannot be set to be refreshed automatically.

User-maintained MQTs are particularly useful for database systems in which tables of summary data already exist. Custom applications that maintain such summary tables are quite common. By identifying existing summary tables as user-maintained MQTs, performance for dynamic SQL queries can be dramatically improved. This causes the query optimizer to use the existing summary table to compute result sets for queries against the base tables. Note that the query optimizer does not use user-maintained MQTs in selecting an access plan for static SQL queries.

RESTRICTIONS

For INSERT, UPDATE, and DELETE operations issued against user-maintained MQTs, no validity checking is done against the underlying base tables. The user performing the data changes is responsible for the correctness of the data. Similarly, the utilities LOAD, IMPORT, EXPORT, and

`DPROPR` work with user-maintained MQTs, except no validity checking is done. You also cannot `SET INTEGRITY` to `IMMEDIATE CHECKED` for user-maintained MQTs.

CREATING MATERIALIZED QUERY TABLES

User-maintained MQTs are created with the `CREATE TABLE` statement. For example:

```
DB2 CREATE TABLE example AS (SELECT C1, C2 FROM T1) DATA INITIALLY
DEFERRED REFRESH DEFERRED MAINTAINED BY USER
```

Because this MQT has not yet been populated, it is placed in the `CHECK PENDING NO ACCESS` state. No SQL read or write access is permitted against tables in a `CHECK PENDING NO ACCESS` state.

User-maintained MQTs can only be defined as `REFRESH DEFERRED`. It is the responsibility of the user to ensure that the data in this table is kept up to date.

POPULATING MATERIALIZED QUERY TABLES

You can populate user-maintained MQTs using triggers, insert operations, or the `LOAD`, `IMPORT`, and `DPROPR` utilities. When performing the initial population of a user-maintained MQT, you can avoid logging overhead by using the `LOAD` or `IMPORT` utilities. The following steps represent a typical approach for populating a user-maintained MQT:

1. Make the base tables read only to avoid the creation of new records or changes to existing records.
2. Extract the required data from the base tables and write it to an external file.
3. Import or load the data from the external file into the MQT. You can use the `LOAD` or `IMPORT` utilities on a table in `CHECK PENDING NO ACCESS` state.

> **NOTE**
> If you want to populate the MQT with SQL insert operations, you need to reset the `PENDING NO ACCESS` state. However, optimization must first be disabled via the `DISABLE QUERY OPTIMIZATION` option in the `ALTER TABLE` statement to ensure that a dynamic SQL query does not accidentally optimize to this MQT while the data in it is still in a state of flux. Once the MQT has been populated, optimization needs to be enabled.

4. To issue SQL queries against a newly created MQT, reset the `CHECK PENDING NO ACCESS` state using the following statement. This action indicates that the user has assumed responsibility for data integrity of the materialized view:

```
DB2 SET INTEGRITY FOR example ALL IMMEDIATE UNCHECKED
```

5. Make the base tables read/write.

LEVERAGING MATERIALIZED QUERY TABLES FOR IMPROVED QUERY PERFORMANCE

For the query optimizer to consider a user-maintained MQT in determining an access path, the following conditions must be met:

- The MQT must have ENABLE QUERY OPTIMIZATION set (this is done in the CREATE TABLE or ALTER TABLE statement).
- You must set the following special registers:

```
DB2 SET CURRENT MAINTAINED TABLE TYPES FOR OPTIMIZATION USER
DB2 SET CURRENT REFRESH AGE ANY
```

- The MQT cannot be in a CHECK PENDING NO ACCESS state.
- The query optimization level must be set at Level 2 or at a level greater than or equal to 5:

```
DB2 SET CURRENT QUERY OPTIMIZATION LEVEL 2
```

After creating and populating a user-maintained MQT and setting the appropriate registers, update the query optimization statistics by doing a RUNSTATS. This ensures that the query optimizer is aware of the MQT you created.

Database System Monitoring Enhancements

Database monitoring is a vital activity for the maintenance of the performance and health of your database management system. DB2 UDB v8.1 provides significant improvements in the amount of monitoring information that is collected and the flexibility and ease with which monitoring data can be retrieved, analyzed, and archived.

PREVENTING THE COLLECTION OF TIMESTAMPS

The collection of timestamp data is an expensive monitoring operation. This is especially the case when the collection of a timestamp occurs for a common database operation (e.g., the start or completion of a unit of work).

To control the collection of timestamp monitor data, you can use the TIMESTAMP monitor switch. Setting the TIMESTAMP switch to OFF (it is ON by default) instructs the database manager to skip any timestamp operating system calls when computing time or timestamp-related monitor elements. Turning this switch OFF becomes important when CPU utilization approaches 100%. When this occurs, the performance degradation caused by issuing timestamps increases dramatically.

Unlike all the other monitor switches, the TIMESTAMP monitor switch is not set automatically by event monitors. If the TIMESTAMP switch is OFF, most of the timestamp and time monitor elements collected by event monitors are not collected. These elements are still written to the specified table, file, or pipe, but with a value of zero.

To set the TIMESTAMP monitor switch to OFF at the database manager level, issue the following command:

```
UPDATE DBM CFG USING DFT_MON_TIMESTAMP OFF
```

ENHANCED DEADLOCK MONITORING

With DB2 UDB v8.1, you have access to more information than in prior releases about deadlocks that occur in your database system. To collect detailed database system monitoring data about deadlocks as they occur, create and activate a DEADLOCKS WITH DETAILS event monitor. For example:

```
CREATE EVENT MONITOR dlmon
    FOR DEADLOCKS WITH DETAILS
    WRITE TO FILE 'C:\Temp\DeadLock'
SET EVENT MONITOR dlmon STATE 1
```

DEADLOCKS WITH DETAILS event monitors collect comprehensive information regarding the applications involved, the participating statements (and statement text), and a list of locks being held.

Using a DEADLOCKS WITH DETAILS event monitor instead of a DEADLOCKS event monitor incurs a performance cost when deadlocks occur due to the extra information that is collected.

SQL ACCESS TO EVENT MONITOR DATA

Event monitors log data as specified database events occur. For instance, you can create an event monitor to collect monitor data for deadlocks, transactions, and connections. You can use event monitors to alert you to immediate problems or to track impending problems.

As of DB2 UDB v8.1, DB2 can write event monitor data to tables. Prior to v8.1, users had to write their own applications to parse the event monitor data, organize and filter the data, and then archive it. With the event monitor data being directed into tables, it is already being archived and can easily be filtered and analyzed.

For every event type an event monitor collects, target tables are created for each of the associated logical data groups. The column names for each of these groups correspond to monitor elements. (A monitor element represents a specific attribute of the state of the database system.) The various options for table event monitors are set in the CREATE EVENT MONITOR statement. For assistance in generating CREATE EVENT MONITOR SQL statements for write-to-table event monitors, you can use the db2evtbl command. Here is a sample usage of db2evtbl:

```
db2evtbl -schema SANDRA -evm TableEvMon TABLES
```

The following output is the CREATE EVENT MONITOR statement for a TABLES event monitor, as requested by the preceding db2evtbl command:

```
CREATE EVENT MONITOR TableEvMon
    FOR TABLES
    WRITE TO TABLE
    TABLE (TABLE SANDRA.TABLE_TableEvMon,
      INCLUDES (EVENT_TIME,
```

```
            EVMON_ACTIVATES,
            EVMON_FLUSHES,
            OVERFLOW_ACCESSES,
            PAGE_REORGS,
            PARTIAL_RECORD,
            ROWS_READ,
            ROWS_WRITTEN,
            TABLE_NAME,
            TABLE_SCHEMA,
            TABLE_TYPE )),
     CONTROL (TABLE SANDRA.CONTROL_TableEvMon,
        INCLUDES (EVENT_MONITOR_NAME,
          MESSAGE,
          MESSAGE_TIME ));
```

In the CREATE EVENT MONITOR statement, the specification of all the target tables and their monitor elements is optional. You can simplify the preceding statement as follows:

```
CREATE EVENT MONITOR TableEvMon
    FOR TABLES
    WRITE TO TABLE;
```

There are many instances where a DBA is only interested in a few monitor elements. For some event types, such as DEADLOCKS WITH DETAILS, numerous monitor elements are captured, which introduces storage concerns on systems where database events frequently occur. The db2evtbl utility is particularly useful for these situations, as users can simply delete the lines they do not need, and then issue the statement.

Another means of filtering data can be done after the monitor data has already been captured. You can select only the monitor elements of interest. For example:

```
SELECT conn_time, client_db_alias, auth_id, rows_updated
    FROM connheader_connevmon a, conn_connevmon b
    WHERE a.appl_id = b.appl_id
```

This query was issued against tables maintained by a CONNECTIONS event monitor. Here, the results are correlated based on the application id (the appl_id column).

```
CONN_TIME                    CLIENT_DB_ALIAS AUTH_ID   S_UPDATED
-------------------------    --------------- --------- ---------
2003-06-01-07.10.51.561590 SAMPLE           DDEROOS          18
2003-06-01-07.02.06.591238 SAMPLE           DDEROOS           4
2003-06-01-07.10.51.561590 SAMPLE           DDEROOS          23
```

For further details on write-to-table event monitors and on the monitor elements captured by event monitors, see the *DB2 System Monitor Guide and Reference*.

SQL ACCESS TO SNAPSHOT MONITOR DATA

The snapshot monitor enables you to capture a picture of the state of database activity at a particular point in time (the moment the snapshot is taken). By capturing regular snapshots, you can evaluate the performance of a database system and foresee potential problems.

DB2 UDB v8.1 for UNIX, Linux, and Windows features the capability to capture snapshots using SQL table functions. These *snapshot table functions* return a table of monitor data, where each row represents an instance of the database object being monitored, and each column represents a monitor element. All of the snapshot table functions are described in Chapter 17.

There are two ways you can access monitor data using the snapshot table functions: *direct access* and *file access*. The direct access approach is demonstrated in Chapter 17. With this approach only users with SYSADM, SYSCTRL, or SYSMAINT authority can capture snapshots.

With file access, authorized users call the SNAPSHOT_FILEW stored procedure to make specific collections of snapshot data available for all users. The SNAPSHOT_FILEW stored procedure saves the monitor data into a file on the database server, which any database user can access by using corresponding snapshot table functions. Users only receive results for snapshot table functions for which an authorized user has used the SNAPSHOT_FILEW stored procedure.

Although file access to snapshot monitor data presents a safe approach to making this data available to all users, there are some drawbacks. If authorized users do not update the monitor data files with the SNAPSHOT_FILEW stored procedure, users do not have access to recent data. Also, users without SYSADM, SYSCTR, or SYSMAINT authority cannot identify a database or partition when using the snapshot table functions.

SNAPSHOT_FILEW Snapshot Request Types

When calling the SNAPSHOT_FILEW stored procedure, in addition to identifying the database and partition to be monitored, you need to specify a snapshot request type number. Each of these numbers represents a set of snapshot monitor information that can be accessed by one or more snapshot table functions. Table 8.1 lists the snapshot table functions and their corresponding snapshot request type numbers.

Table 8.1   Snapshot Table Functions, Scopes, and Request Type Numbers

Snapshot Table Function	Scope (all Databases or a Specific Database)	Snapshot Request Type Number
SNAPSHOT_DBM	—	1
SNAPSHOT_DATABASE	All	9
SNAPSHOT_DATABASE	Specific	2
SNAPSHOT_APPL	All	10

Table 8.1 Snapshot Table Functions, Scopes, and Request Type Numbers (Continued)

Snapshot Table Function	Scope (all Databases or a Specific Database)	Snapshot Request Type Number
SNAPSHOT_APPL	Specific	6
SNAPSHOT_APPL_INFO	All	10
SNAPSHOT_APPL_INFO	Specific	6
SNAPSHOT_LOCKWAIT	All	10
SNAPSHOT_LOCKWAIT	Specific	6
SNAPSHOT_STATEMENT	All	10
SNAPSHOT_STATEMENT	Specific	6
SNAPSHOT_TABLE	Specific	5
SNAPSHOT_LOCK	Specific	8
SNAPSHOT_TBS	Specific	13
SNAPSHOT_BP	All	23
SNAPSHOT_BP	Specific	22
SNAPSHOT_DYN_SQL	Specific	36

Capturing a Snapshot to a File with SNAPSHOT_FILEW

Before you can capture a snapshot with SNAPSHOT_FILEW, you must be connected to a database in the instance of the database you need to monitor. Once you have determined the type of snapshot the users need and the database and partition they need to monitor, you can capture the snapshot. The following call captures a snapshot of application information regarding the SAMPLE database for the current connected partition:

```
CALL SNAPSHOT_FILEW(6,'sample',-1)
```

The SNAPSHOT_FILEW stored procedure accepts three parameters. The first is the snapshot request type number, which indicates the kind of snapshot being taken. The second indicates the database for which monitor data is captured. The third parameter indicates the partition. A value of -1 indicates the current connected partition.

Capturing a Snapshot From a File

Once the SNAPSHOT_FILEW call is made, files on the database server become populated with the corresponding monitor data. At this point all users can call snapshot table functions and get result sets of monitor data.

To capture monitor data, users must be connected to any database in the instance of the database they need to monitor. The following snapshot table function invocation captures a snapshot of application information stored in the file populated by the previous SNAPSHOT_FILEW call:

```
SELECT appl_id, agent_id, db_name, appl_status FROM
    TABLE(SNAPSHOT_APPL_INFO(CAST(NULL AS VARCHAR(1)),
        CAST (NULL AS INTEGER))) AS A
```

In this query, only selected monitor element columns are requested. This yields the following output:

```
APPL_ID                     AGENT_ID DB_NAME APPL_STATUS
----------------------      -------- ------- -----------
*LOCAL.DB2.00E5C1124112       23 TRAVEL          2
*LOCAL.DB2.010481111331       16 SAMPLE          3
```

DB2_SNAPSHOT_NOAUTH REGISTRY VARIABLE

To enable all users to capture snapshot monitor data, activate the DB2_SNAPSHOT_NOAUTH registry variable.

Turning on the DB2_SNAPSHOT_NOAUTH registry variable is not recommended, as it introduces the following security risk: Numerous accesses of the snapshot monitor APIs, CLP commands, or SQL table functions can cause serious performance degradation on workloads with high connect–disconnect rates (especially concentrator environments). A user can therefore deliberately slow the database system down by causing excessive latch contention. Also, sensitive information (e.g., the list of connected users and the SQL statements they have submitted to the database) will be available to all users. Note that no actual data from databases or user passwords can be exposed using the snapshot monitor.

A safe alternative to activating the DB2_SNAPSHOT_NOAUTH registry variable is the SNAPSHOT _FILEW stored procedure discussed in the section "SQL Access to Snapshot Monitor Data." With it, you can make selected portions of monitor data available to all users.

PERFORMANCE MONITOR CONTROL CENTER TOOL HAS BEEN DEPRECATED

The performance monitor capability of the Control Center has been removed. Users of the performance monitor should examine the functions of the Health Center (which is part of the Control Center) and the DB2 Performance Expert for Multiplatforms, version 1 (a separate add-on tool) to replace the performance monitoring function.

For further details on the Health Center, see Chapter 12.

Miscellaneous Performance Enhancements

There are multiple minor enhancements in DB2 UDB v8.1 that help performance. In this chapter we will discuss:

- Distributed Catalog Cache
- Prefetching Enhancements with Block-Based Buffer Pools
- Page Cleaner I/O Improvements
- Multithreading of Java-Based Routines
- 64-bit Support
- Automatic Relationship and Association Management (ARAM)
- New Join Variations
- Increased Opportunity for Selection of Bit-Filters

These features don't each warrant their own chapter, but, we cover them each here.

DISTRIBUTED CATALOG CACHE

DB2 UDB v7.2 provides DBAs with a catalog cache that can be leveraged to provide quicker access to a subset of the information stored in SYSTABLES. The information that was cached in DB2 UDB v7.2 was very limited. In DB2 UDB v7.2, there were also issues associated with the catalog cache that were somewhat problematic.

First, when the catalog cache became full and no other information could be purged from it, overflow data from this cache had to be allocated from private memory. Second, when memory allocations occur from private memory, the information is transient and will soon be discarded.

DB2 UDB v8.1 now gives DBAs the ability to distribute the catalog cache across all the database partitions that make up a partitioned database instance, as shown in Figure 9.1. This new distrib-

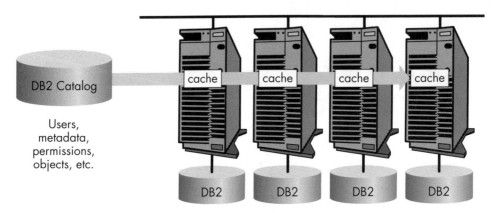

Figure 9.1
Caching catalog information across a partitioned database.

uted catalog cache increases the performance of applications when an application connects to a non-catalog partition. All types of workloads can benefit immensely from this new feature, which gives DBAs more choice in terms of choosing a coordinator partition for their applications without sacrificing performance.

In addition to distributing the catalog cache, more information is stored in it in the DB2 UDB v8.1 release. For example, in addition to caching table and view information, trigger, referential integrity, and check constraint information are also cached.

The information cached helps speed up operations such as SQL compilation, and so on. Specifically, the new caching enhancements improve the overall performance of the following:

- Binding packages and compiling SQL statements, including usage of routines (methods, user-defined functions, and stored procedures)
- Operations that involve checking database-level privileges
- Operations that involve checking execute privileges for routines
- Applications that connect to non-catalog partitions

In DB2 UDB v7.2, the catalog cache was allocated from the database heap. In DB2 UDB v8.1, memory for the catalog cache is allocated from a specially allocated catalog cache heap dedicated to this purpose. In addition, storage allocations from this dedicated heap can temporarily exceed the *catalogcache_sz* limit.

PREFETCHING ENHANCEMENTS WITH BLOCK-BASED BUFFER POOLS

DB2 UDB v8.1 can help the performance of prefetching algorithms through the use of a new block-based buffer pool.

When a block-based buffer pool is available to DB2 UDB, the prefetching code recognizes this and uses block I/Os to read multiple pages into the buffer pool in a single I/O operation. This significantly improves the performance of prefetching. The *blocksize* parameter of the CREATE and ALTER BUFFERPOOL statements defines the size of the blocks, and hence the number of pages read from disk in a block I/O.

By default, the buffer pools are page-based, which means that contiguous pages on disk are prefetched into noncontiguous pages in memory. Sequential prefetching can be enhanced if contiguous pages can be read from disk into contiguous pages within a buffer pool. You can create block-based buffer pools for this purpose. A block-based buffer pool consists of both a page area and a block area. The page area is required for non-sequential prefetching workloads. The block area consists of blocks, each containing a specified number of contiguous pages, which is referred to as the block size.

DB2 UDB v8.1.2 adds to the DB2 UDB v8.1 prefetching enhancements with an initial redesign to certain aspects of the prefetchers to reduce contention and context switching. This enhancement should help with query-reporting type workloads.

PAGE CLEANER I/O IMPROVEMENTS

Transaction workloads, characterized by high amounts of INSERT, UPDATE, and DELETE activity, change a lot of pages (makes them dirty) in the buffer pool. For performance reasons, it is essential that these pages are flushed from the buffer pools and hardened to disks efficiently.

DB2 UDB technology has long employed the use of *page cleaners* that write dirty pages in the buffer pool to disk. Efficient page cleaning reduces the chance that a DB2 UDB agent looking for space in the buffer pool has to incur the cost of writing dirty pages to disk.

DB2 UDB v8.1.2 enhances the performance of these page cleaners by making them aware of the underlying complexities of the I/O subsystems (both hardware and software). The page cleaner algorithms now take into account these I/O subsystems. This level of environment understanding involves considerations such as what I/O primitives are the best for use in page cleaning and how they can be applied to DB2 UDB. This new feature is transparent to applications and DBAs and is used by DB2 UDB when available.

MULTITHREADING OF JAVA-BASED ROUTINES

In DB2 UDB v7.2, Java routines were run in fenced mode by most customers and independent software vendor applications enabled for DB2 UDB. The process-based model is expensive not only from a startup perspective, but also from a memory and operation system dispatch perspective.

In DB2 UDB v8.1.2, routines (stored procedures, user-defined functions, and methods) are now implemented using a thread-based model that results in a dramatic performance increase for database servers running numerous routines. This allows resource sharing of the Java virtual machine (JVM) for Java routines and reduces the amount of context switching in general for users that run large numbers of fenced-mode routines.

Routines that are defined as thread-safe will run in a single fenced-mode process. There is one process for Java routines and another process for non-Java routines to reduce the amount of context switching for users that run a large numbers of fenced-mode routines. For Java routines, this also allows resource sharing of the JVM.

DB2 UDB assumes that non-Java routines that are migrated to DB2 UDB v8.1 are not thread-safe. Java routines are migrated with the assumption that they are thread-safe.

If you want to modify preexisting routines, you need to drop and re-create them or use the appropriate ALTER SQL statement. New routines are created with the aforementioned defaults if the *no thread-safe* or *non-thread-safe* value is specified at creation time.

C-based routines are still fenced by default because there are threading issues that must be dealt with. As well, SQL/PL procedures are not fenced because they are self-written.

64-BIT SUPPORT

64-bit computing allows for the creation of larger buffer pools, sort heaps, and other memory-intensive resources. When applications can exploit 64-bit features, they most often see a performance improvement as more data can be moved in a single CPU cycle.

DB2 UDB v7.2 included support for 64-bit computing and DB2 instances on HP-UX, Sun, and AIX systems. Core support was part of the DB2 UDB v7.2 release for these platforms, but other features were missing (e.g., there was no "vanilla" connectivity mechanism for a 32-bit client connecting to a 64-bit server, there were no GUI tools, etc.).

DB2 UDB v8.1 completes the support picture for 64-bit computing and DB2 UDB servers. Details for Linux and Windows 64-bit support are discussed in Chapter 1. Because this is not a new feature to the product, just a completion of features, we do not cover it any further in this book.

AUTOMATIC RELATIONSHIP AND ASSOCIATION MANAGEMENT (ARAM)

This new feature to DB2 UDB v8.1.2 performs "Automatic Relationship and Association" detection. DB2 UDB has an internal utility that, when automatically invoked through the RUNSTATS utility, will automatically discover relationships between columns (the performance impact to RUNSTATS is unoticeable). These relationships could be referential integrity (RI) relationships or correlation information. The discovery process uses DB2 UDB v8.1.2's new sampling techniques to minimize the resources consumed to do the discovery. The way that these relationships are specified to DB2 UDB for future usage is through MQTs. The main difference from a typical MQT is that DB2 UDB in this case stores exception data. A typical ARAM created MQT will have little or no data. What is important is the definition of the MQT where the predicates reveal valuable information about the relationships and correlation between column values. This is all transparent to users and applications, but provides more information to the DB2 UDB optimizer which in turn allows it to potentially come up with more efficient access plans.

NEW JOIN VARIATIONS

DB2 UDB v8.1.2 introduces three new join variations to the current run-time joins. They are:

- *Reverse outer join* (or right outer join)—an outer join that has the inner table as the row preserving side.
- *Reverse early out*—an inner join that a tuple of the inner table only need to match the first matched tuple of the outer table.
- *Anti join*—an outer join that returns only tuples from the row preserving side (can be either inner table or outer table) that have no match to tuples from the null producing side.

The new variations are exposed from various Explain tools via two existing flags: outer join flag and early out flag.

INCREASED OPPORTUNITY FOR SELECTION OF BIT-FILTERS

DB2 UDB v8.1.2 includes improved performance for hash joins by selecting bit filters more often (in situations where they will help). This "behind-the-scenes" feature will also improve performance of larger hash joins due to the addition of a 32-bit hash code.

P A R T **3**

Manageability

- Logging
- Load Enhancements
- DB2 Tools
- Container Operations
- Dynamic Memory Allocation and Online Reconfiguration
- Online Utilities
- Miscellaneous Manageability Enhancements

Logging

There are two distinct kinds of logging that are discussed in this chapter: *transactional logging* and *diagnostic logging*. DB2 engages in transactional logging to keep records of database changes for run-time rollbacks, crash recovery, and backup recovery. Diagnostic logging involves the capturing and recording of data when database errors occur.

TRANSACTIONAL LOGGING IMPROVEMENTS

There are a number of improvements to the transactional logging capabilities of DB2. Logging capacity has been increased, along with logging performance. Meanwhile, configuration parameters have been added that enable DBAs to closely control the logging activity of transactions.

Increased Log Space

The maximum amount of log space that can be defined has been increased from 32 GB to 256 GB. This provides support for large numbers of concurrent transactions and database applications that require large transactions.

Infinite Active Log Space

In addition to the increase in the maximum amount of log space, you can enable *infinite active log space*. In this state, transaction logs are able to span the primary logs and archive logs. Therefore, transaction logs can exceed the limit identified in the *logprimary* database configuration parameter, and for that matter, the available disk space in the active log path. Infinite active log space can be used to support database applications that require extremely large transactions or an exceedingly high amount of concurrent transactions.

To enable infinite active log space, set the *logsecondary* database configuration parameter to a value of -1. With no limit to the number of files in the archive log, transactions can write to an infinite number of log files in the archive log once all the primary log files are consumed. Infinite active log space can only be enabled when the *userexit* database configuration parameter is enabled.

When infinite active log space is enabled, you still need to consider values for the *logprimary* and *logfilsiz* database configuration parameters. The number and size of log files in the active log path is an important factor in run-time rollback and database recovery performance. If DB2 needs to read data from a log file that is not in the active log path, DB2 invokes a userexit program to retrieve the log file from the archive log back to the active log path. Once this is retrieved, DB2 caches the retrieved log file so other reads of log data from the same log file will be faster.

Controlling the Consumption of Log Space

In DB2 UDB v8.1.2, two configuration parameters were introduced to enable you to set limits on an application's consumption of active log space. In previous versions of DB2, a single application could use all the available logging resources. These database configuration parameters can prevent this and prevent long-running applications from holding up excessive amounts of active log space.

The *max_log* database configuration parameter indicates the percentage of primary log space that can be consumed by one transaction. If the value is set to 0, there is no limit to the percentage of total primary log space that one transaction can consume.

You can override this behavior by setting the DB2_FORCE_APP_ON_MAX_LOG registry variable to false. This causes transactions that violate the *max_log* database configuration parameter to fail and return an SQL0964N error. The application can still commit the work completed by previous statements in the transaction, or it can roll back the completed work to undo the transaction.

The *num_log_span* database configuration parameter indicates the number of active log files that an active transaction can span. If the value is set to 0, there is no limit to how many log files one transaction can span.

If an application violates the *max_log* or the *num_log_span* settings, the application is forced to disconnect from the database, the transaction is rolled back, and an SQL1224N error is returned.

The following DB2 commands are excluded from the limitations imposed by the *max_log* and *num_log_span* database configuration parameters: ARCHIVE LOG, BACKUP DATABASE, LOAD, REORG TABLE (online), RESTORE DATABASE, and ROLLFORWARD DATABASE.

Transactional Logging Performance Improvements

The performance of transaction logging has been improved because the logger no longer issues log writes asynchronously. This enables the logger to make more optimal use of I/O and processing resources. The performance benefits are most noticeable in SMP workstations with log mirroring enabled.

Log Mirroring

For backup and crash recovery, transaction logs are essential in maintaining the integrity of a database. By enabling *log mirroring*, you can help protect the transaction logs against hardware failure or the accidental deletion of an active log. When you enable log mirroring, the database writes an identical second copy of log files to a different path.

The concept of log mirroring was first introduced in DB2 UDB v7.2 as *dual logging*. Dual logging was only supported on UNIX database servers and did not allow users to configure a custom path for the mirrored log files. Log mirroring is now provided on all platforms supported by DB2 UDB v8.1. Also, the DB2NEWLOGPATH2 registry variable that enabled dual logging is not supported in DB2 UDB v8.1. By using a database configuration parameter instead of a registry variable, you can now enable log mirroring on selected databases within an instance.

To enable log mirroring, assign a path for the mirrored logs to the database configuration parameter, *mirrorlogpath*. It is recommended that you assign *mirrorlogpath* a path on a physically separate disk (preferably one that is also on a different disk controller). Also, the mirror log files (or any log files, for that matter) should be on a physical disk that does not have high I/O. The *mirrorlogpath* database configuration parameter is not supported if the primary log path is a raw device and the value specified for this parameter cannot be a raw device.

When *mirrorlogpath* is first enabled, it is not used until the next database startup.

If there is an error writing to either the active log path or the mirror log path, the database marks the failing path as bad, writes a message to the administration notification log, and writes subsequent log records to the remaining good log path only. DB2 does not attempt to use the bad path again until the current log file is completed. When DB2 needs to open the next log file, it verifies that this path is valid, and if so, begins to use it. If not, DB2 does not attempt to use the path again until the next log file is accessed for the first time. There is no attempt to synchronize the log paths, but DB2 keeps information about access errors that occur so that the correct paths are used when log files are archived. If a failure occurs while writing to the remaining good path, the database shuts down.

To turn the *mirrorlogpath* database configuration parameter off, set its value to default.

Blocking Transactions When the Logs Are Full

By default, transactions fail with disk full errors when DB2 cannot create a new log file in the active log path. To prevent this, you can set the *blk_log_dsk_ful* database configuration parameter to YES.

Instead of having the transactions fail with disk full errors, DB2 attempts to create the log file every five minutes until it succeeds. After each attempt, DB2 writes a message to the administration notification log.

If DB2 cannot create a new log file in the active log path, no applications are able to commit transactions. The applications hang until log space is made available. As a result, any read-only queries accessing locked data also hang. You can confirm that your application is hanging because of a log disk full condition by monitoring the administration notification log.

The *blk_log_dsk_ful* database configuration parameter replaces the DB2_BLOCK_ON_LOG _DISK_FULL registry variable. This enables you to implement transaction blocking when logs are full for selected databases within an instance.

Diagnostic Logging Improvements

With the introduction of the *administration notification log*, the usability of DB2's diagnostic logs has been greatly improved. DB2 writes information to the administration notification log when database errors and other significant database events occur. This information is in the form of meaningful messages useful to database and system administrators.

The *db2diag.log* text log file records memory dumps and internal messages when database errors occur. This information is intended for DB2 customer support.

On UNIX platforms, the administration notification log is a text file called *<instance-name>*.nfy. This file is located in the directory specified by the *diagpath* database manager configuration parameter (along with the *db2diag.log*, dump files, and trap files). On Windows NT, Windows 2000, and Windows XP systems, the DB2 administration notification log is found in the event log and can be examined through the Windows Event Viewer.

The scope of database system information recorded in the administration notification log is determined by the *notifylevel* database manager configuration parameter. The following are possible *notifylevel* values. Each value includes the information and messages in the preceding levels.

- 0—No administration notification messages captured
- 1—Only fatal and unrecoverable errors are logged
- 2—Conditions are logged that require immediate attention from the system administrator or the DBA
- 3—Conditions are logged that are nonthreatening and do not require immediate action but may indicate a nonoptimal system
- 4—Informational messages are logged

User applications can write to the notification file or Windows Event Log by calling the db2AdminMsgWrite API.

Load
Enhancements

S everal enhancements have been made to the LOAD utility in DB2 UDB v8. The new features improve data availability through better management of increasing data volumes despite shrinking maintenance windows.

ONLINE LOAD

Load operations now take place at the table level. This means that the load utility no longer requires exclusive access to the entire table space, and concurrent access to other table objects in the same table space is possible during a load operation. The LOAD utility locks only the table objects that are associated with the load operation. During a load insert (but not a load replace) operation, read access to data existing in the table prior to the load operation is permitted. This access is permitted for the entire duration of the load operation, except for a brief period just before the data is commited, when the LOAD utility must lock the table in exclusive mode. The loaded data cannot be read until the load operation has completed. As usual, if constraints are defined on the table, the SET INTEGRITY statement must be used to check the constraints before the loaded data can be read.

To illustrate ALLOW READ ACCESS behavior, consider the following scenario.

User U1 initiates an ALLOW READ ACCESS load append operation on the SALES table:

```
DB2 LOAD FROM newsales.del OF DEL INSERT INTO sales ALLOW READ ACCESS
```

Meanwhile, unknown to User U1, User U2 issues:

```
DB2 SELECT sales_date, sales FROM sales
  WHERE region = 'Ontario-South' AND sales_person = 'LEE'

SALES_DATE SALES
---------- -----------
12/31/1995           3
03/29/1996           2
03/30/1996           7
03/31/1996          14
04/01/1996           8

  5 record(s) selected.
```

User U3 issues:

```
DB2 EXPORT TO D:\Temp\export.del OF DEL
  SELECT sales_date, sales FROM sales
  WHERE region = 'Ontario-South' AND sales_person = 'LEE'
```

The export file contains this:

```
19951231,3
19960329,2
19960330,7
19960331,14
19960401,8
```

When the load operation has finished, User U2 again issues:

```
DB2 SELECT sales_date, sales FROM sales
  WHERE region = 'Ontario-South' AND sales_person = 'LEE'

SALES_DATE SALES
---------- -----------
12/31/1995           3
03/29/1996           2
03/30/1996           7
03/31/1996          14
04/01/1996           8
02/11/1997           5
04/21/1997           8
07/15/1997           4
08/09/1997          12

  9 record(s) selected.
```

LOCKING BEHAVIOR

The new LOCK WITH FORCE option (see Figure 11.1) permits you to force applications to release the locks they have on a table, allowing a load operation to proceed. Either SYSADM or SYSCTRL authority is required to use the LOCK WITH FORCE option. Table 11.1 summarizes locking behavior under different access modes with and without the LOCK WITH FORCE option.

Table 11.1 Behavior Under Different Access Modes with and without the LOCK WITH FORCE Option if an Attempt to Acquire a Lock Is Unsuccessful

Access Mode	Table Lock	LOCK WITH FORCE	
		Yes	**No**
Exclusive (ALLOW NO ACCESS)	Superexclusive (for the entire load operation)	Applications holding table locks are forced off and load operation proceeds	Possible timeout and failed load operation
Read access (ALLOW READ ACCESS)	Share initially, then superexclusive prior to the commit	*Unsuccessful share*: Applications holding table locks are forced off and load operation proceeds; *Unsuccessful superexclusive*: Applications holding table locks are forced off and load operation proceeds	*Unsuccessful share*: Possible timeout and failed load operation; *Unsuccessful superexclusive*: LOAD utility waits indefinitely

NEW TABLE STATES

The v8.1 LOAD utility does not use table space states (QUIESCED_EXCLUSIVE, LOAD_PENDING, DELETE_PENDING) to gain exclusive access to a table space. In fact, table spaces that are involved in the load operation are not quiesced. Instead, there are two new persistent *table states*: LOAD IN PROGRESS and READ ACCESS.

- The LOAD IN PROGRESS table state restricts access to a partially loaded table. Except for the backup utility, no utility, command, or SQL statement can operate on a table that is in LOAD IN PROGRESS state and not in READ ACCESS state. No utility, command, or SQL statement can update a table that is in LOAD IN PROGRESS state. This state is reset at load commit time or during the commit of a load restart or a load terminate operation following a load failure or a system crash.
- The READ ACCESS table state allows other applications and utilities to have read access to data existing in the table prior to the load operation. If the ALLOW READ ACCESS option is specified (see Figure 11.1), the table is placed in READ ACCESS state in addition to LOAD IN PROGRESS state. If indexes are being rebuilt as part of the online load operation, a shadow copy of these indexes can be built in a system temporary table space and copied to the index table space when the loaded data becomes accessible. A

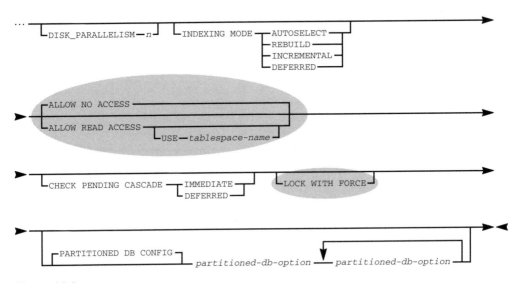

Figure 11.1
Partial syntax of the LOAD command showing the new ALLOW READ ACCESS and the LOCK WITH
FORCE clauses.

> system temporary table space can be specified for this purpose with the new USE
> *tablespace-name* option. If this option is not specified, you must ensure that there is
> enough space available in the index table space to create a second copy of all the table
> indexes during the index rebuild phase of an online load operation. This leaves index
> table spaces underutilized most of the time, wasting space. Physically copying the index
> tables from the system temporary table space can have a performance impact. (The
> indexes are copied while the table is offline at the end of the load operation.)

Because the load utility no longer quiesces table spaces that are involved in a load operation, the
LOAD command option HOLD QUIESCE is no longer supported. If desired, you can manually quiesce the table spaces prior to a load operation (using the QUIESCE TABLESPACES FOR TABLE
command); these table spaces remain quiesced after the load operation has completed.

The load query utility has been enhanced to include in its output the table state of the table into
which data is being loaded. The LOAD QUERY command can be used to query table states while a
load operation is in progress or after it has aborted.

LOADING DATA INTO PARTITIONED DATABASES

You can now use the DB2 LOAD command or the db2Load API (instead of the AutoLoader utility, db2atld) to load data in partitioned database environments. The load utility does not use a
configuration file, as was the case with the AutoLoader. The configuration parameters have
become new parameters in the extended db2Load API, and can be specified using the new

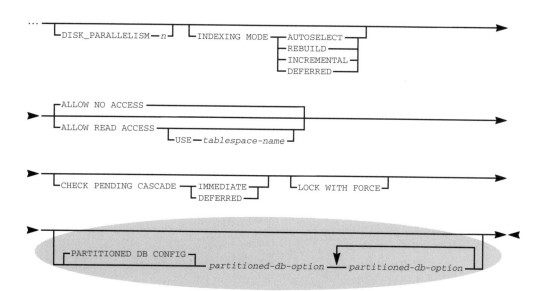

Figure 11.2
Partial syntax of the LOAD command showing the new PARTITIONED DB CONFIG
partitioned-db-option clause.

PARTITIONED DB CONFIG *partitioned-db-option* clause of the LOAD command (Figure
11.2). Valid values for *partitioned-db-option* are as follows:

- HOSTNAME *x*
- FILE_TRANSFER_CMD *x*
- PART_FILE_LOCATION *x*
- OUTPUT_DBPARTNUMS *x*
- PARTITIONING_DBPARTNUMS *x*
- MODE *x*
- MAX_NUM_PART_AGENTS *x*
- ISOLATE_PART_ERRS *x*
- STATUS_INTERVAL *x*
- PORT_RANGE *x*
- CHECK_TRUNCATION
- MAP_FILE_INPUT *x*
- MAP_FILE_OUTPUT *x*
- TRACE *x*
- NEWLINE
- DISTFILE *x*
- OMIT_HEADER

For example, the keyword MODE can be specified with one of the following options (represented by *x* in the preceding list):

- PARTITION_AND_LOAD—Data is partitioned and loaded simultaneously on the corresponding database partitions.
- PARTITION_ONLY—Data is partitioned and the output is written to files in a specified location on each loading partition.
- LOAD_ONLY—Data is assumed to be partitioned and is loaded simultaneously on the corresponding database partitions.
- LOAD_ONLY_VERIFY_PART—Data is assumed to be partitioned and is loaded simultaneously on the corresponding database partitions. During the load operation, each row is checked to verify that it is on the correct partition.
- ANALYZE—A partitioning map with even distribution across all database partitions is generated.

The database partition to which you connect to perform a load operation is called the *coordinator partition*. In the PARTITION_AND_LOAD, PARTITION_ONLY, and ANALYZE modes, it is assumed that the data file resides on this partition, unless the CLIENT option of the load command is specified, indicating that the data to be loaded resides on a remotely connected client.

The DB2 UDB v8 LOAD utility uses terminology that differs from that associated with the Auto-Loader. The process that does the work of the splitter is called a *partitioning agent*, and a split file (the output of the splitter) is called a *partition file*. The input data file is now *partitioned*, not split. Instead of a SPLIT_ONLY mode, there is now a PARTITION_ONLY mode, and instead of a SPLIT_NODES option, there is a PARTITIONING_NODES option. (The db2split executable is no longer shipped as part of the DB2 product. Use the PARTITION_ONLY mode of the v8 load utility instead.) The AutoLoader FORCE option has been replaced with the new ISOLATE_PART_ERRS option, which lets you specify one of four different types of partition error isolation, one of which is similar to the isolation type that was offered by the AutoLoader FORCE option. The ISOLATE_PART_ERRS option lets you control how errors occurring on individual partitions affect the entire load operation.

If a load failure occurs on one or more partitions, the data on all partitions will not be visible, even on those partitions that succeeded. If a load restart operation is invoked, the data on partitions that succeeded is immediately committed and becomes visible, and the load utility attempts to load on those partitions that failed.

If the new registry variable DB2_PARTITIONEDLOAD_DEFAULT is set to NO, you can load data into a single partition in a partitioned database environment without specifying any of the new partitioning options. The partition that is specified in the most recent SET CLIENT CONNECT_NODE operation determines which node is loaded. The DB2_PARTITIONEDLOAD _DEFAULT registry variable, which defaults to YES, is provided only in support of backward compatibility with previous versions of the load utility.

LOADING DATA FROM A CURSOR

The new CURSOR file type (see Figure 11.3) allows you to load the result set from an SQL query into a table without first exporting the data to a file. You can even use this method to load data from another database by specifying a nickname in the query.

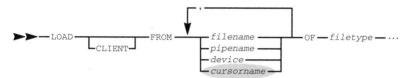

Figure 11.3
Partial syntax of the LOAD command showing that data can now be loaded from a cursor.

A load from cursor operation requires that the specified cursor be declared, using the SQL DECLARE CURSOR statement. To illustrate this, consider the following command line processor (CLP) command script:

```
CONNECT TO sample;
CREATE TABLE myorg LIKE org;
DECLARE mycurs CURSOR FOR
   SELECT deptnumb, deptname, manager, division, location FROM org;
LOAD FROM mycurs OF CURSOR INSERT INTO myorg;
COMMIT WORK;
CONNECT RESET;
TERMINATE;
```

This script creates a MYORG table in the SAMPLE database, using the table definition for the existing ORG table. The DECLARE CURSOR statement specifies a cursor called MYCURS. The SELECT statement of the cursor in this example specifies all of the columns in the ORG table. The load utility then copies all of the data in the ORG table to the MYORG table.

LOAD WIZARD

The Control Center has a new Load wizard to help you set up complex load operations for which there could be many options to configure (see Figures 11.4 through 11.13).

You can even copy a saved load task and then modify the setting values of the existing task for your new load task. If you have saved at least one load task, the wizard contains a Task page, which is the first page of the Load wizard. You can select an existing load task, which causes the wizard to be prefilled with the setting values from that task. You can change any of these values on the appropriate page of the wizard.

The Operation page and the Partitions page appear if your table resides in a partitioned database. The Operation page lets you specify whether the operation is to be a split operation, a load operation, or a split and load operation. You can also use this page to generate an optimized partition map. The Partitions page lets you specify whether the data is to be loaded to all partitions or only selected partitions.

Figure 11.4
The Load wizard. The Type page lets you specify whether the load operation is to append or replace existing data in the table. If data is to be appended, you can specify that users are to have read access to the table during the load operation.

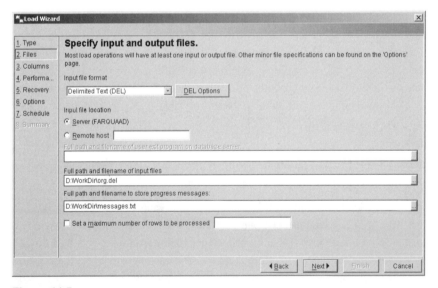

Figure 11.5
The Files page of the Load wizard lets you specify the location of your input and output files, and the input file format (ASC, DEL, IXF, or CURSOR).

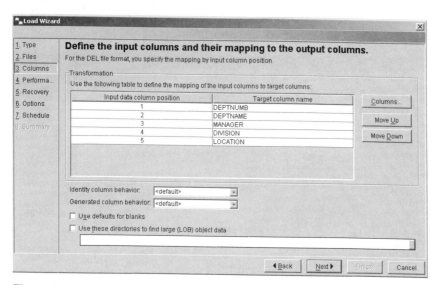

Figure 11.6
The Columns page of the Load wizard lets you specify column options and map input column positions to target column names.

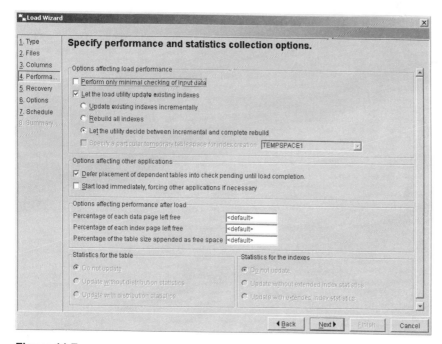

Figure 11.7
The Performance page of the Load wizard lets you specify performance and statistics options for the load task.

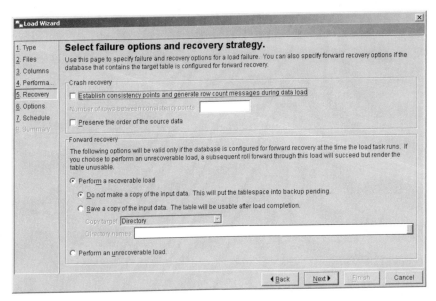

Figure 11.8
The Recovery page of the Load wizard lets you specify recovery options for the load task.

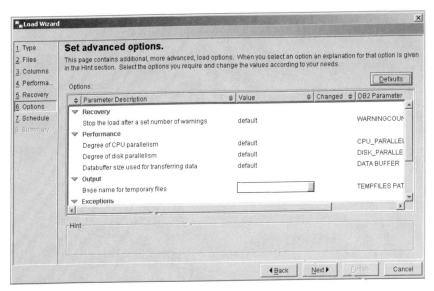

Figure 11.9
The Options page of the Load wizard lets you specify additional options for the load task.

If you have not already created a scheduling database, the Schedule page of the Load wizard lets you enable the scheduling function by creating a database for the DB2 tools catalog. Before you can use the scheduling function, you must create a database for the DB2 tools catalog to store task and schedule information.

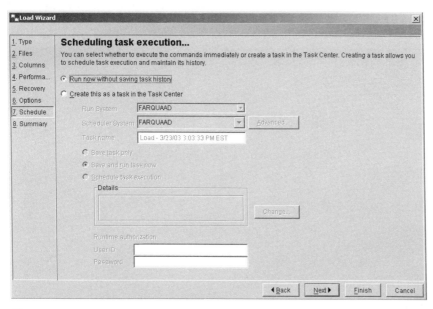

Figure 11.10
The Schedule page of the Load wizard lets you specify when you want DB2 to perform the load task. You can run the task immediately, save the task to the Task Center, or schedule the task to run later.

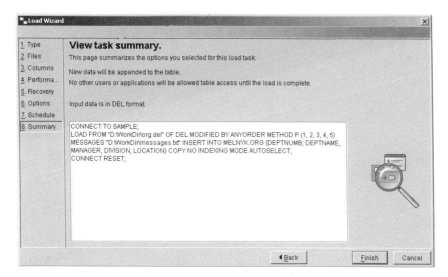

Figure 11.11
The Summary page of the Load wizard shows information about the load task. If you elected to run the task immediately, this page shows the options that you selected. You can go back and make any necessary changes, and then click Finish to run the task. If you elected to save the task to the Task Center, the Summary page shows the task name, task script, and other information about the task. You can also launch the Task Center from this page.

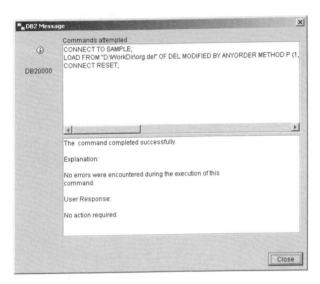

Figure 11.12
The DB2 Message window that appears following the load operation displays both script details and execution status.

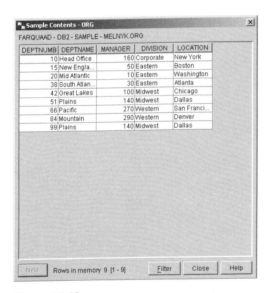

Figure 11.13
Viewing sample table contents through the Control Center provides quick confirmation that the ORG table has been loaded with new data.

DB2 Tools

CONFIGURATION ASSISTANT

The new Configuration Assistant (CA) replaces the pre-v8 Client Configuration Assistant (CCA). Each database that you or your applications need to access must first be properly configured at your DB2 client. The CA makes it easy for you to do this. It includes wizards and provides hints to help you along the way. It also preserves the familiar discovery feature, so useful in the CCA, which you can use to add a database object whose exact name you might not know. The CA offers you improved response times for discovery requests, as well as the option to refresh the list of discovered objects at any time.

The CA can be opened from:

- The Start menu on Windows operating systems by selecting Start ➤ Programs ➤ IBM DB2 ➤ Set-up Tools ➤ Configuration Assistant
- The command line by issuing the db2ca command

The CA's main window displays a list of the databases that are available to you (Figure 12.1). You can use the Add Database wizard to add databases to this list, or you can use the Change Database wizard to alter database directory information that is associated with a database in the list. Of course, you can remove databases from the list as well.

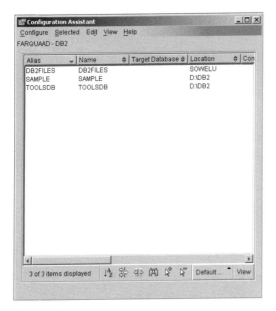

Figure 12.1
The Configuration Assistant main window.

You can also use the CA to do the following:

- Alter the bind options associated with a particular database
- Verify the integrity of your database connections
- Change the connection password for a database
- Configure CLI settings for a data source
- Set or reset database manager configuration parameters (see Figure 12.2)
- Set DB2 registry variables (that define DB2's operating environment; see Figure 12.3)
- Configure another local instance or an instance on a remote system
- Import, export, or edit a configuration profile

The CA also has an advanced view that organizes tasks by object: Systems, Instance Nodes, Databases, Database Connection Services (DCS), and Data Sources (Figure 12.4). In addition to the tasks just outlined, you can use the CA advanced view to do the following:

- Add, change, or remove a system
- Add, change, or remove entries from the node directory
- Add, change, or remove entries from a DCS (host database) directory
- Add, change, or remove a data source

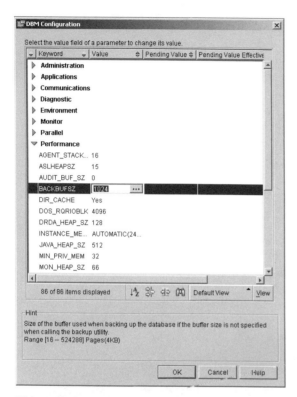

Figure 12.2
Using the Configuration Assistant to set database manager configuration parameters.

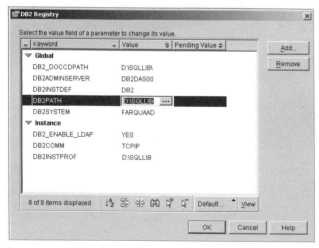

Figure 12.3
Using the Configuration Assistant to set DB2 registry variables.

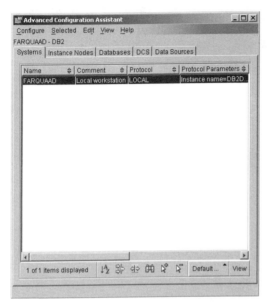

Figure 12.4
The Configuration Assistant advanced view.

HEALTH CENTER

The new DB2 Health Center makes it easy to monitor the "health" of your system. It provides you with key information about the resources that your instance uses. The *health monitor* is a server-side tool that continually monitors the health of your instance by comparing actual system status to defined health indicator thresholds. If thresholds for any of these indicators are exceeded, the health monitor raises alerts that enable you to address health issues before they become significant performance problems.

You can enable or disable the health monitor by updating the value of the database manager configuration parameter *health_mon*.

The Health Center is the graphical interface to the health monitor. You can use the Health Center to configure the health monitor and to examine the alert states of your instances and database objects (see Figure 12.5).

The Health Center can be opened from:

- The Start menu on Windows operating systems by selecting Start ➤ Programs ➤ IBM DB2 ➤ Monitoring Tools ➤ Health Center
- The Control Center by clicking the Health Center icon in the toolbar
- The command line by issuing the db2hc command

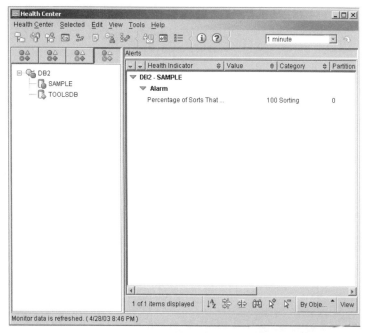

Figure 12.5
The Health Center, showing an object tree for the default instance named DB2. The filter button with the green diamond has been selected; this displays objects in alarm, warning, attention, and normal state. The refresh frequency has been set to 1 minute. The contents pane shows that an alarm has been triggered for a particular health indicator (Percentage of Sorts that Overflowed).

The health monitor comes with a set of predefined thresholds for the health indicators. You can customize these settings and define who should be notified, what script should be run, or what task should be performed if an alert is raised.

To start the health monitor on a particular instance, right-click the instance in the Health Center object tree, and select Start Health Monitor.

To change health indicator thresholds, right-click your database and select Configure ➤ Database Object Health Indicator Settings. Select a health indicator for which you want to change warning or alarm threshold values. Select the check box in the Evaluate column to enable evaluation of the specific health indicator. Click a column in the highlighted row to edit its contents (e.g., to change a threshold value; see Figure 12.6). You can also click the Action column to open the Select Actions window. This window lets you specify and enable the actions that are to be taken if an alert is raised. Apply the changes and click OK to close the Configure Database Object Health Indicator Settings window.

By right-clicking an alert and selecting Show Details, you can retrieve details about the alert and get a list of recommended actions (see Figures 12.7 through 12.9).

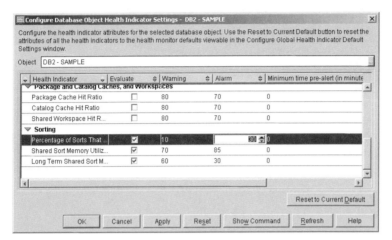

Figure 12.6
Changing a health indicator threshold setting.

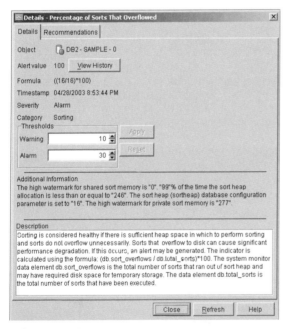

Figure 12.7
Alert details pertaining to the Percentage of Sorts that Overflowed health indicator.

You can then follow the recommended actions to address the alert.

If the recommended action is to make a configuration change, you can do so on the spot (Figure 12.8).

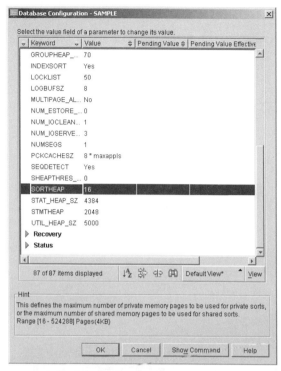

Figure 12.8
Changing the value of a configuration parameter to address an alert.

The recommended action might be to address the problem further by launching a tool, such as the Design Advisor, to tune the workload (Figures 12.9 through 12.11).

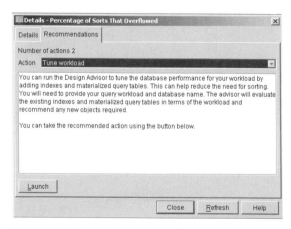

Figure 12.9
Launching the Design Advisor to address an alert.

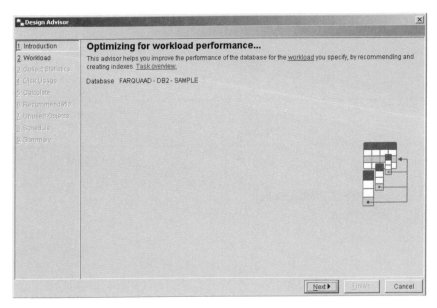

Figure 12.10
The Design Advisor analyzes your workloads.

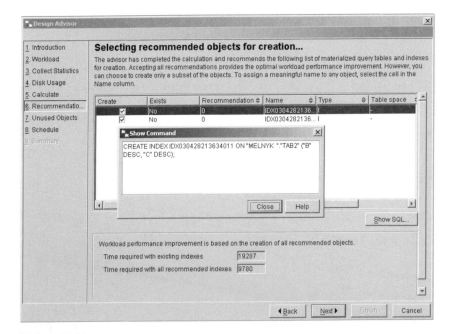

Figure 12.11
The Design Advisor makes recommendations regarding new indexes that could significantly improve performance.

You can also use new DB2 commands (or administrative APIs) to retrieve health information from the health monitor (see Table 12.1), thereby integrating DB2 health monitoring tools with your existing system monitoring solutions.

Table 12.1

CLP Command	Description
Example	
ADD CONTACT	Adds an entry to the contact list.
db2 add contact 'Dirk Deroos' type email address dderoos@ca.ibm.com	
ADD CONTACTGROUP	Adds an entry to the contact group list. A contact group is a list of users to whom the health monitor can send messages.
db2 add contactgroup Jets contact 'Paul Zikopoulos'	
DROP CONTACT	Removes an entry from the contact list.
db2 drop contact 'Dirk Deroos'	
DROP CONTACTGROUP	Removes an entry from the contact group list.
db2 drop contactgroup Jets	
GET ALERT CONFIGURATION	Returns the alert configuration settings for health indicators associated with a particular instance.
db2 get alert cfg for dbm	
GET CONTACTGROUP	Returns the contacts in a particular contact group.
db2 get contactgroup Jets	
GET CONTACTGROUPS	Returns a list of defined contact groups.
db2 get contactgroups	
GET CONTACTS	Returns a list of defined contacts.
db2 get contacts	
GET DESCRIPTION FOR HEALTH INDICATOR	Returns a description for the specified health indicator.
db2 get description for health indicator db.spilled_sorts	

Table 12.1

CLP Command	Description
Example	
GET HEALTH NOTIFICATION CONTACT LIST	Returns the list of contacts that are to be notified in the event of an alert. The health notification contact list is a subset of the contact list; it stores references to contacts that are defined in the contact list.
db2 get health notification contact list	
GET HEALTH SNAPSHOT	Returns health status information for the database manager or databases.
db2 get health snapshot for all on sample show detail	
GET RECOMMENDATIONS	Returns recommendations for improving the health of the database system pertaining to a specified health indicator.
db2 get recommendations for health indicator db.spilled_sorts	
RESET ALERT CONFIGURATION	Resets the health indicator settings for specific objects to default values.
db2 reset alert cfg for dbm	
UPDATE ALERT CONFIGURATION	Updates the alert configuration settings for health indicators.
db2 update alert cfg for dbm using db2.sort_privmem_util set warning 80	
UPDATE CONTACT	Updates the attributes of a defined contact.
db2 update contact 'George Baklarz' using address baklarz@us.ibm.com	
UPDATE CONTACTGROUP	Updates the attributes of a defined contact group.
db2 update contactgroup Jets add contact 'Roman Melnyk'	
UPDATE HEALTH NOTIFICATION CONTACT LIST	Updates the list of contacts that are to be notified in the event of an alert.
db2 update notification list add contact 'George Baklarz'	

MEMORY VISUALIZER

The Health Center provides vital status information about the resources that your instance uses. One of the most important resource groups being monitored is memory. If health indicators for the memory resource group suggest that there is some problem that needs to be addressed, you can use the new Memory Visualizer tool to analyze the problem further (see Figure 12.12). The Memory

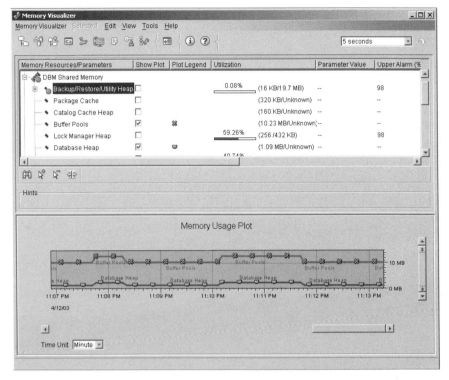

Figure 12.12
The Memory Visualizer, showing part of the tree view and the history view. Increases in memory utilization shown correspond to a database backup operation, followed by a database connection and a query workload applied to that database.

Visualizer shows details of memory allocation and utilization for a particular instance and all of its databases. It displays information about sort heaps, buffer pools, and caches. Such information, conveniently displayed, makes it easy for you to troubleshoot memory resource problems.

The Memory Visualizer window can be opened from:

- The Start menu on Windows operating systems by selecting Start ➤ Programs ➤ IBM DB2 ➤ Monitoring Tools ➤ Memory Visualizer
- The Control Center by right-clicking the instance that you want to view and selecting View memory usage from the shortcut menu
- The command line by issuing the db2memvis command

You can run the Memory Visualizer continuously while DB2 is running to observe the relationships among various memory resources as they respond to different types of workload. You can also use this tool to dynamically change the values of memory-related configuration parameters in response to identified problems, and then to observe the effects of those changes (see Figure 12.13).

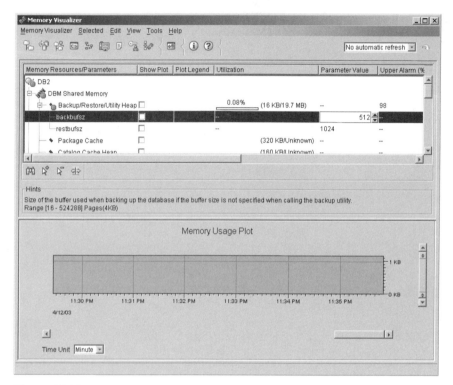

Figure 12.13
You can use the Memory Visualizer to dynamically change the values of memory-related configuration parameters.

The Memory Visualizer tree view mirrors the hierarchical nature of DB2 memory resources. The high-level memory components include Database Manager Shared Memory, Database Global Memory, Application Global Memory, and Agent Private Memory. Each of these memory components contains other components that are also organized in a hierarchical manner. Low-level components, called leaf-level memory components, are the real memory components, whereas the high-level components are logical groupings of the leaf-level components. The leaf-level components are allocated and deallocated at different times, and they acquire memory resources from different areas of the database system.

Icons in the tree view are color-coded to indicate the utilization severity status for memory components. The thresholds that determine these severities are shown in the warning and alert columns as both percentage and absolute values. Upper and lower warning and alert columns (showing percentage values) are editable. This allows you to change the default settings, which are 90% and 10% for upper and lower warning levels, respectively, and 98% and 2% for upper and lower alert levels, respectively.

Included in the tree view are items representing the configuration parameters that affect memory utilization on the system. The location of these parameters in the tree is intended to match the memory resources with which they are most closely associated. This proximity makes it easy for you to locate the configuration parameters, determine their current values, and update them on the spot.

The history view displays a history of memory resource allocation and utilization in a multiline graph, where each line corresponds to a particular memory resource. The history can be captured for as long as the tool is running. You can select from the tree view which memory resources are to be plotted on this graph. You can also use a slider to set the scaling factor for the graph. The history view also shows the time at which you make updates to any of the configuration parameters, including the updated values. Scroll bars on the time dimension enable you to quickly access a particular point in the history.

Historical data for memory allocation and utilization can be saved to and retrieved from files (with an .mdf extension) for offline examination or reporting.

Memory Tracker

The Memory Tracker provides the memory allocation and utilization data for the Memory Visualizer. Data for all memory resources belonging to an instance is collected by the Memory Tracker, which can also return maximum values instead of actual usage values. You can invoke the Memory Tracker by issuing the db2mtrk command. For example, to display instance and database-level memory on Windows operating systems, issue the following command:

```
db2mtrk -i
```

On UNIX-based systems, the same command would be:

```
db2mtrk -i -d
```

The following is sample output from this command:

```
Tracking Memory on: 2003/04/12 at 16:00:11

Memory for instance

    utilh      pckcacheh catcacheh bph       bph       bph       bph
    16.0K      320.0K    160.0K    7.9M      1.1M      592.0K    336.0K


    bph        bph       lockh     dbh       monh      other
    208.0K     144.0K    256.0K    1.1M      176.0K    5.7M
```

The memory codes in this output represent values that are defined in the following legend:

```
appctlh - Application Control Heap    apph      - Application Heap
bph      - Buffer Pool Heap           catcacheh - Catalog Cache Heap
dbh      - Database Heap              dlfmh     - DFM Heap
fcmbp    - FCMBP Heap                 ip        - Import Pool
lockh    - Lock Manager Heap          monh      - Database Monitor Heap

other    - Other Memory               pckcacheh - Package Cache
queryh   - Query Heap                 stath     - Statistics Heap
stmth    - Statement Heap             utilh     - Backup/Restore/Util Heap
```

"Other Memory" represents overhead associated with running the database management system.

STORAGE MANAGEMENT

A storage management tool is now available through the Control Center. You can use this tool to periodically capture storage snapshots at the database, database partition group, or table space level. To access the storage management tool, right-click a database object.

Database-level snapshots contain information about all the database partition groups in the database. This information spans all the table spaces defined in the specified database or database partition group. Table space information is captured from the system catalogs and the database monitor for any tables, indexes, and containers that are defined under the scope of the given table space.

The Storage Management view (the graphical interface to the storage management tool) can then be used to monitor space usage, data skew in database partition groups, and cluster ratios for indexes.

- *Space usage* indicates the percentage of available storage space that is used by an object.
- *Data skew* indicates the percentage deviation from the average data level among the database partitions in a database partition group. Data skew can range from –100 to 100. A negative value means that the data level in a particular database partition is less than the average data level for the database partition group. The value shown is the maximum skew for the database partition group.
- *Cluster ratio* indicates the degree to which the rows in a table are arranged in the order specified by an index. Cluster ratio is represented as a percentage. A higher cluster ratio indicates that the data rows are stored in a similar physical sequence to that of the index.

You can use the Specify Threshold Settings notebook to set thresholds for these parameters. Threshold settings are used to warn you of potential storage problems with your database; a warning or alarm flag is raised if a target object exceeds a specified threshold. Default thresholds for a database object are set at database creation time, but can be overridden later. Objects within the database's scope (its children) inherit the default or changed threshold values.

The Specify Threshold Settings notebook is initially accessed from the Storage Management Setup Launchpad, which also provides access to the Specify Snapshot Schedule window. Before you can use either of these tools, however, you must select a table space to store database snapshot data; you can do this through the Specify Snapshot Storage window, which is also accessed from the Storage Management Setup Launchpad (see Figures 12.14 through 12.23).

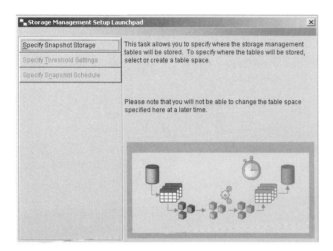

Figure 12.14
The Storage Management Setup Launchpad, showing an introduction to the Specify Snapshot Storage notebook.

Figure 12.15
The Specify Snapshot Storage window.

Figure 12.16
You can click the Show Command button in the Specify Snapshot Storage window to review the script that will create the storage management tables.

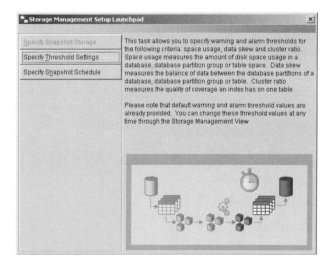

Figure 12.17
The Storage Management Setup Launchpad, showing an introduction to the Specify Threshold
Settings notebook.

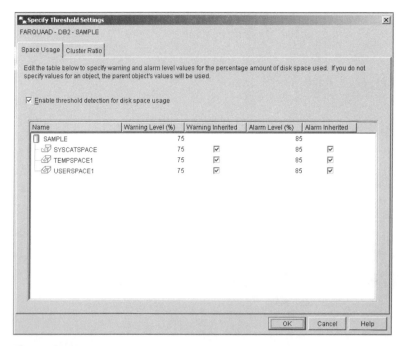

Figure 12.18
The Space Usage page of the Specify Threshold Settings notebook.

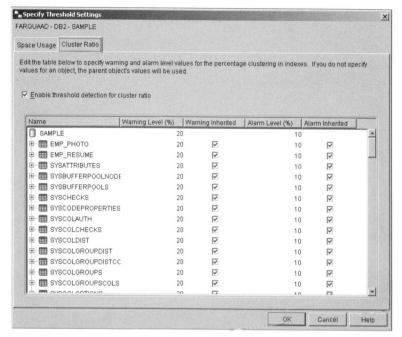

Figure 12.19
The Cluster Ratio page of the Specify Threshold Settings notebook.

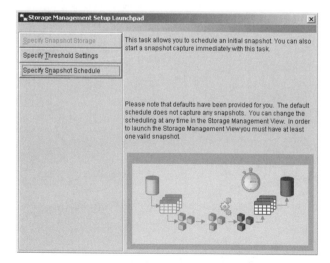

Figure 12.20
The Storage Management Setup Launchpad, showing an introduction to the Specify Snapshot Schedule notebook.

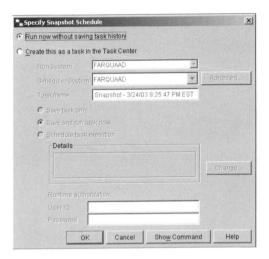

Figure 12.21
The Specify Snapshot Schedule notebook lets you schedule an initial storage snapshot or start a snapshot capture immediately.

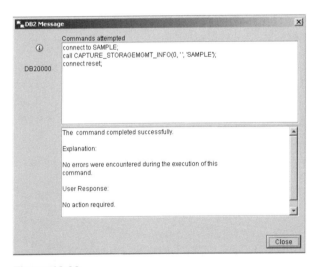

Figure 12.22
The DB2 Message window that appears following the snapshot capture operation displays both script details and execution status.

The Storage Management view shows which (if any) database objects have exceeded their specified warning or alarm threshold settings for space usage, data skew, or cluster ratio (see Figure 12.23).

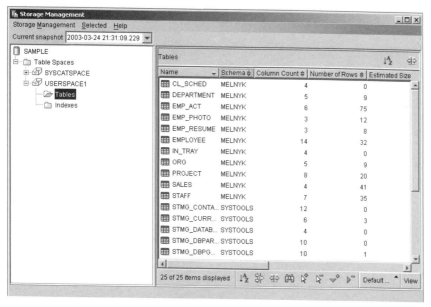

Figure 12.23
The Storage Management view, showing table snapshot data for the `SAMPLE` database.

Storage Management View Columns

In a partitioned database system, the Storage Management view contains the following database partition columns:

- Partition Number
- Host (the host system name of the database partition)
- Estimated Data Size (an estimate of the amount of system space used by this database partition)
- Log File Size (the amount of log space available on the database partition)
- In Use Status (indicates whether or not the partition is in use)

The Storage Management view contains the following database partition group columns:

- Name
- Partition Count (the number of database partitions in the database partition group)
- Avg. Data Level (the amount of storage space used by all partitions in this database partition group)
- Skew (%)
- Skew Warning Threshold (%)
- Skew Alarm Threshold (%)
- Total Size (the total amount of storage available to the database partition group)
- Data Size (the total amount of storage used by the database partition group)

- Percent Used (the percentage of available storage space used by the database partition group)
- Space Warning Threshold (%)
- Space Alarm Threshold (%)

The Storage Management view contains the following table space columns:

- Name
- Data Type (index, long, or regular)
- Managed By (DMS or SMS)
- Allocated Size
- Percent Used
- Data Size (the total amount of storage used by the table space)
- Data Pages (the number of pages used by the data)
- Page Size
- Extent Size
- Prefetch Size
- Overhead (an estimate of the time required by the container before any data is read into memory)
- Transfer Rate (the time it takes to read one page into the buffer)
- Bufferpool (the table space buffer pool ID)
- Space Warning Threshold (%)
- Space Alarm Threshold (%)

The Storage Management view contains some or all of the following table columns:

- Name
- Schema
- Column Count (the number of columns in each table)
- Number of Rows (the row count for each table, or the average row count across all partitions)
- Data Skew in Rows (the row count difference for each database partition with respect to the average row count across all database partitions in the database partition group; displays the maximum data skew for all the partitions)
- Percentage Data Skew (a calculated value based on Data Skew in Rows for each database partition divided by the average shown in the Number of Rows column)
- Skew Warning Threshold (%)
- Skew Alarm Threshold (%)
- Estimated Size (an estimate of the total amount of storage used by the table)
- NPages (the total number of pages on which the rows of the table exist)
- FPages (the total number of pages)
- Overflow (the total number of overflow records in the table)
- Table Space (the main table space for the table)

- Index Table Space
- Long Data Table Space

The Storage Management view contains the following index columns:

- Table Schema
- Table Name
- Index Schema
- Index Name
- Cluster Ratio
- Cluster Warning Threshold (%)
- Cluster Alarm Threshold (%)
- Cluster Factor (the percentage of data rows that are stored in the same physical sequence as the index)
- Column Count (the number of columns in the key plus the number of include columns, if any)
- Number of Leaf Pages
- Sequential Pages (the number of leaf pages located on disk in index key order with few or no large gaps between them)
- Number of Index Levels
- Number of Distinct First Key Values
- Number of Two-Column Distinct Keys (the number of distinct keys using the first two columns of the index)
- Number of Three-Column Distinct Keys
- Number of Four-Column Distinct Keys
- Number of Distinct Full Keys
- Page Density (ratio of sequential pages to number of pages in the range of pages occupied by the index, expressed as a percentage)

INDOUBT TRANSACTION MANAGER

An indoubt transaction is a transaction that has been prepared, but not yet committed or rolled back; it has, in fact, been left in an uncertain state. An indoubt transaction can occur when the transaction manager (TM) or at least one resource manager (RM) becomes unavailable after the first phase (the prepare phase) of the two-phase commit protocol has been successfully completed. The RM is one of the databases participating in the transaction, but it is not the TM database. The RM will not know whether to commit or to roll back its branch of the transaction until the TM can reconcile its log with the RM logs.

To make it very easy to process indoubt transactions, DB2 UDB v8 introduces the Indoubt Transaction Manager user interface (see Figure 12.24). The Indoubt Transaction Manager lists all the indoubt transactions for a selected database and one or more selected partitions.

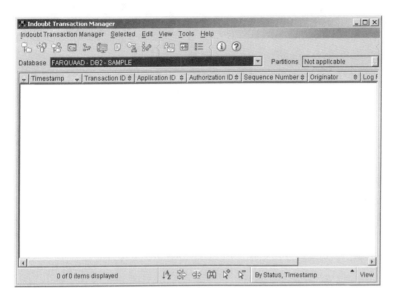

Figure 12.24
The DB2 Indoubt Transaction Manager.

This window can be opened from:

- The Start menu on Windows operating systems by selecting Start ➤ Programs ➤ IBM DB2 ➤ Monitoring Tools ➤ Indoubt Transaction Manager
- The command line by issuing the db2indbt command

A Database selection field and a Partitions selection field allow you to select a database and, in a partitioned database environment, those partitions for which you want to process indoubt transactions.

Details about those indoubt transactions appear in the Indoubt Transaction container, which takes up the majority of the Indoubt Transaction Manager window. When a new database is selected, information in the container is refreshed accordingly. The container lists all the current indoubt transactions for the selected database. It is empty when no database is selected, or when there are no indoubt transactions associated with the database.

The container contains the following columns:

- *Status*. Indoubt status. Valid values are committed (c), ended (e), indoubt (i), missing commit acknowledgment (m), and rolled back (r).
- *Timestamp*. Time at which the transaction entered the indoubt state.
- *Transaction ID*. XA identifier assigned by the TM to uniquely identify a global transaction.

- *Application ID.* Application identifier assigned by the database manager for this transaction.
- *Authorization ID.* ID of the user who ran the transaction.
- *Sequence Number.* Sequence number assigned by the database manager as an extension to the application ID.
- *Partitions.* The partitions on which the indoubt transaction exists. (This column appears only when a partitioned database has been selected.)
- *Originator.* Indicates whether the transaction was originated by XA or by DB2 in a partitioned database environment.
- *Log Full.* Indicates whether the transaction caused a log full condition.
- *Type.* The role of the database in each indoubt transaction. Valid values are TM (the indoubt transaction is using the database as a TM), and RM (the indoubt transaction is using the database as an RM).

The indoubt transaction information in the container can be displayed according to one of several selectable views. When the database is not partitioned, the available views are as follows:

- *By Status and Timestamp.* This is the default view. Columns are sorted and rolled up by status in ascending order, and then sorted by timestamp in ascending order.
- *By Timestamp.* Columns are sorted by timestamp in ascending order.
- *By Application ID and Timestamp.* Columns are sorted and rolled up by application ID in ascending order, and then sorted by timestamp in ascending order.

When the database is partitioned, the available views are as follows:

- *By Status and Timestamp.* This is the default view. Columns are sorted and rolled up by status in ascending order, and then sorted by timestamp in ascending order.
- *By Timestamp.* Columns are sorted by timestamp in ascending order.
- *By Partition, Status, and Timestamp.* Columns are sorted and rolled up by partition in ascending order, then sorted and rolled up by status in ascending order, and then sorted by timestamp in ascending order.
- *By Partition and Timestamp.* Columns are sorted and rolled up by partition in ascending order, and then sorted by timestamp in ascending order.
- *By Application ID and Timestamp.* Columns are sorted and rolled up by application ID in ascending order, and then sorted by timestamp in ascending order.

The following possible actions are available for each indoubt transaction that is displayed:

- *Commit.* This action is available if the transaction status is in doubt or missing commit acknowledgment.
- *Rollback.* This action is available if the transaction status is in doubt or ended.
- *Forget.* This action is available if the transaction status is committed or rolled back.

FAULT MONITOR

DB2 UDB v8 for UNIX-based systems introduces a fault monitor facility to improve the availability of nonclustered DB2 environments. This facility works to ensure that DB2 is running. A fault monitor coordinator (FMC) monitors fault monitors that, in turn, monitor DB2. The FMC starts one fault monitor for each DB2 instance. If a DB2 instance stops prematurely, its fault monitor restarts it. Normally, a fault monitor can only be stopped through invocation of the db2stop command.

A fault monitor registry file is created for a specific machine when the fault monitor daemon starts. Information in this file—which is located in the *sqllib* subdirectory, and which is named fm.<*machine_name*>.reg—governs the behavior of the fault monitors with which it is associated, and can be altered by invoking the db2fm command. The following is an example of a fault monitor registry file, named *fm.elk.reg*:

```
FM_ON = yes # updated by db2fm
FM_ACTIVE = yes # default
START_TIMEOUT = 600 # default
STOP_TIMEOUT = 600 # default
STATUS_TIMEOUT = 20 # default
STATUS_INTERVAL = 20 # default
RESTART_RETRIES = 3 # default
ACTION_RETRIES = 3 # default
NOTIFY_ADDRESS = db2idad@elk # default
```

The fault monitor registry variables are defined as follows:

- FM_ON specifies whether or not the fault monitor is to be started.
- FM_ACTIVE specifies whether or not the fault monitor is active. If FM_ON is set to YES and FM_ACTIVE is set to NO, the fault monitor daemon starts, but is not active; it does not try to start a stopped instance.
- START_TIMEOUT specifies the amount of time within which the fault monitor must start its instance.
- STOP_TIMEOUT specifies the amount of time within which the fault monitor must stop its instance.
- STATUS_TIMEOUT specifies the amount of time within which the fault monitor must get the status of the instance it is monitoring.
- STATUS_INTERVAL specifies the minimum time between two consecutive calls to obtain the status of the instance that is being monitored.
- RESTART_RETRIES specifies the number of times the fault monitor tries to obtain the status of the instance that is being monitored after a failed attempt. Once this number has been reached, the fault monitor takes action to bring the instance back online.

- `ACTION_RETRIES` specifies the number of times the fault monitor attempts to bring the instance back online.
- `NOTIFY_ADDRESS` specifies the e-mail address to which the fault monitor sends notification messages. The default value is *<instance_name>@<machine_name>*.

You can use the `db2fm` command to bring the fault monitor daemon up (`-U`) or down (`-D`), or to query the status of the fault monitor daemon (`-S`). For example:

```
db2fm -U
db2fm -D
db2fm -S
```

You can also use the `db2fm` command to update the fault monitor registry file; that is, to configure a specific fault monitor. For example:

Turn off fault monitoring for instance `DB2IDAD`:

```
db2fm -i db2idad -f off
```

When this option is set to `OFF`, the fault monitor daemon is brought down if it was previously available.

Activate fault monitoring for instance `DB2IDAD`:

```
db2fm -i db2idad -a on
```

Update the `START_TIMEOUT` value for instance `DB2IDAD`:

```
db2fm -i db2idad -T 100
```

Update the `STOP_TIMEOUT` value for instance `DB2IDAD`:

```
db2fm -i db2idad -T /200
```

Update the `START_TIMEOUT` value to 100 seconds and the `STOP_TIMEOUT` value to 200 seconds for instance `DB2IDAD`:

```
db2fm -i db2idad -T 100/200
```

Update the `STATUS_INTERVAL` value to 40 seconds and the `STATUS_TIMEOUT` value to 10 seconds for instance `DB2IDAD`:

```
db2fm -i db2idad -I 40/10
```

Update the `ACTION_RETRIES` value for the default instance:

```
db2fm -R /2
```

Update the `NOTIFY_ADDRESS` value for instance `DB2IDAD`:

```
db2fm -i db2idad -n melnyk@ca.ibm.com
```

C H A P T E R **13**

Container Operations

DB2 UDB v8 introduces three important new database managed space (DMS) container operations, which feature the ability to do the following:

- Drop containers from a table space
- Reduce the size of containers in a table space
- Add new containers to a table space without rebalancing

These operations are accessible through enhancements to the ALTER TABLESPACE statement (see Figure 13.1).

TABLE SPACE MAPS

Pages in a DMS table space are logically numbered from 0 to N–1, where N is the number of usable pages in the table space. This addressing scheme is called *pool relative addressing*, and these page numbers are referred to as *pool page numbers*.

The pages in a table space are grouped into extents. An *extent* is container space (measured in pages) that is allocated to a single database object. When a container is created, some space is used to hold the container tag, and this space cannot be used to hold data. For simplicity, the following examples do not take the space that these tags occupy into consideration.

If a DMS table space contains a single container, pool pages are simply mapped to disk in numerical order. If there are several containers of equal size, the first extent in the table space (containing pool pages 0 to extent size –1) is located in the first container, the second extent is located in the second container, and so on. After the last container, the process repeats in a round-robin fashion, starting with the first container (see Figure 13.2). A layer of extents across the set of the containers is called a *stripe*. If, for example, a table space has three containers, each

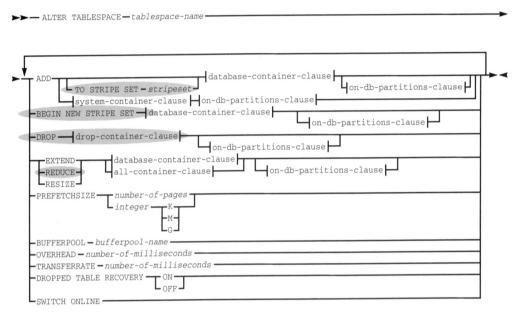

Figure 13.1
Partial syntax of the ALTER TABLESPACE statement highlighting enhancements that impact table space container operations.

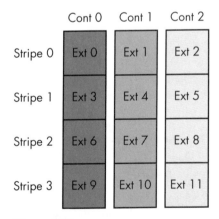

Figure 13.2
Location of extents in DMS containers. In this example, there are three containers of equal size. The extents are grouped into logical units called stripes.

container contains 80 pages, and the extent size for the table space is 20, each container will have 4 extents (80/20), for a total of 12 extents. Because all of the stripes (0 to 3) contain the same set of three containers (0, 1, and 2), this particular configuration is considered to represent a single *range*. Multiple ranges are typical of table spaces that have containers of different sizes.

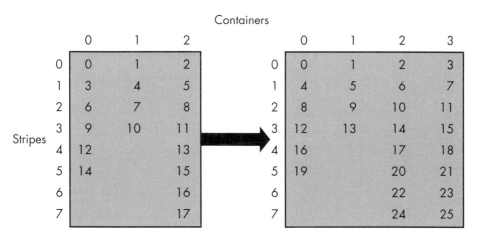

Figure 13.3
Table space rebalancing. In this example, a table space starts with 3 containers and has an extent size of 10 pages. The containers are 60, 40, and 80 pages (6, 4, and 8 extents) in size, respectively. An 80-page container is being added. Assuming that the high-water mark is within extent 14, the rebalancer starts at Extent 0 and moves extents up to and including Extent 14. Extents 0, 1, and 2 do not need to be moved because they have the same location in both table space maps.

When a table space is created, all of its containers are lined up to start in stripe 0. The data is striped evenly across all of the table space containers until they fill up.

When a container is added to an existing table space, its starting position in the table space map depends on its size. If the container is large enough to start in stripe 0 and end at or past the largest stripe in the map, that is how it is positioned. If it is not large enough to do this, it is placed in such a way that it ends in the last stripe of the map. It does not start in stripe 0. With this approach, if rebalancing is needed, not all of the data has to be rebalanced. If more than one container is added, the new smaller containers are lined up with the end stripe of the existing containers, and not with any new end stripe that results from adding a new large container.

When existing containers are extended, their start stripe in the map does not change, but their end stripe does.

When new containers are added to a table space, or existing containers are extended, a rebalancing of the table space data might occur. *Rebalancing* is the process of moving table space extents from one location to another in an attempt to keep the data striped (see Figure 13.3).

DROPPING CONTAINERS FROM A DMS TABLE SPACE

With DB2 UDB v8, you have the ability to drop containers from a DMS table space. This operation is only allowed if the number of extents being dropped is less than or equal to the number of free extents above the high-water mark in the table space. The *high-water mark* is the page number of the highest allocated page in the table space. This restriction is necessary because pool page numbers cannot be allowed to change as a result of the drop operation. All extents up to and including the high-water mark must remain in the same logical position within the table space, and the altered table space must have enough space to hold all of the data up to and including the high-water mark.

In the following example, a new regular table space (TS1) is created in the SAMPLE database. Two file containers (TSC1 and TSC2) are created for this table space, and then container TSC2 is dropped.

```
db2 connect to sample
db2 create tablespace ts1 managed by database
  using (file 'D:\tsc1' 1024)
db2 alter tablespace ts1 add (file 'D:\tsc2' 1024)
db2 list tablespace containers for 3
db2 alter tablespace ts1 drop (file 'D:\tsc2')
db2 connect reset
```

REDUCING THE SIZE OF CONTAINERS IN A DMS TABLE SPACE

You now also have the ability to reduce the size of existing table space containers. Prior to v8, you could use the RESIZE option on the ALTER TABLESPACE statement to increase the size of one or more containers in a DMS table space, but you could not reduce the size of table space containers. Now you can reduce their size to a specified value (using the enhanced RESIZE option), or by a specified value (using the new REDUCE option). For example:

```
db2 connect to sample
db2 list tablespace containers for 3 show detail
db2 alter tablespace ts1 reduce (file 'D:\tsc1' 100)
db2 alter tablespace ts1 resize (file 'D:\tsc1' 512)
db2 list tablespace containers for 3 show detail
db2 connect reset
```

You cannot increase the size of some containers and decrease the size of others in the same statement, nor can you add containers and drop containers in the same statement, because the rebalancing operations associated with either of these scenarios result in the overwriting (loss) of data.

You can, however, add containers and extend existing containers in the same statement, and you can also drop containers and reduce existing containers in the same statement. For example:

```
db2 connect to sample
db2 list tablespace containers for 3 show detail
db2 alter tablespace ts1 add (file 'D:\tsc2' 1024)
    extend (file 'D:\tsc1' 1536)
db2 list tablespace containers for 3 show detail
```

```
db2 alter tablespace ts1 drop (file 'D:\tsc2')
    reduce (file 'D:\tsc1' 1024)
db2 list tablespace containers for 3 show detail
db2 connect reset
```

ADDING CONTAINERS TO A DMS TABLE SPACE WITHOUT REBALANCING

Rebalancing a large table space can take a very long time; in some cases, it can take hours or even days. The process can also have a significant negative impact on performance.

Fortunately, you can now add new containers to a DMS table space without invoking the rebalancer. This process is accomplished through the creation of stripe sets. A *stripe set* is similar to a table space map. Each stripe set is independent of the other stripe sets in the table space. Because all of the table space data can be found in the existing stripe sets, adding a new stripe set does not require rebalancing, and the new space is available for use immediately (see Figure 13.4).

The following example shows how to add a table space container without rebalancing, by specifying the BEGIN NEW STRIPE SET option:

```
db2 connect to sample
db2 list tablespace containers for 3 show detail
db2 alter tablespace ts1 begin new stripe set (file 'D:\tsc2' 1024)
db2 list tablespace containers for 3 show detail
db2 connect reset
```

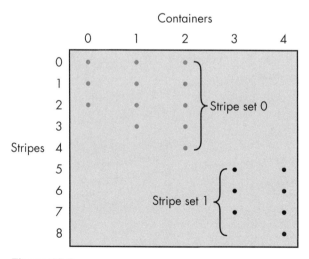

Figure 13.4
Adding containers to a DMS table space without rebalancing. In this example, a table space starts with 3 containers and has an extent size of 10 pages. The containers are 30, 40, and 50 pages (3, 4, and 5 extents) in size, respectively. Two new containers are being added using the new BEGIN NEW STRIPE SET option. These new containers are 30 and 40 pages (3 and 4 extents) in size, respectively. A new set of ranges, called a stripe set, is created.

If you were to add more containers to the table space later, but did not specify the BEGIN NEW STRIPE SET option, those containers would become part of the new stripe set, and their starting position in the table space map would depend on their size, as described in the earlier section "Table Space Maps." If you were then to add even more containers, and this time you *did* specify the BEGIN NEW STRIPE SET option, a new stripe set would be created, and those containers would be part of that new stripe set.

You can use the ADD option, along with the TO STRIPE SET clause, to add a container to the current (most recently created) stripe set or to another existing stripe set. For example:

```
db2 connect to sample
db2 list tablespace containers for 3 show detail
db2 alter tablespace ts1 add to stripe set 0 (file 'D:\tsc3' 512)
db2 list tablespace containers for 3 show detail
db2 connect reset
```

If you do not specify the TO STRIPE SET clause, the current stripe set is assumed.

If a container that is not in the current stripe set is extended to a degree that would cause it to grow out of its stripe set, all of the following stripe sets are moved down so that the container will not become part of the stripe set that follows it in the map.

Dynamic Memory Allocation and Online Reconfiguration

In DB2 UDB v8, you can change how DB2 uses memory without stopping database activity. You can change your buffer pool allocations and alter database or database manager configuration parameters that affect memory use while DB2 is running.

You can dynamically add a new buffer pool or alter the size of an existing buffer pool. New options have been added to the CREATE BUFFERPOOL statement and the ALTER BUFFERPOOL statement:

- IMMEDIATE, the default, attempts to make the changes while DB2 is running.
- DEFERRED allows you to defer the changes to the next database activation.

Here is the partial syntax of these statements, showing the new options:

```
                                        .-IMMEDIATE-.
>>-CREATE BUFFERPOOL--bufferpool-name--+-----------+------------- ...
                                        '-DEFERRED--'


>>-ALTER BUFFERPOOL--bufferpool-name------------------------------>

    .-IMMEDIATE-.
>--+-+-----------+--+----------------------+--SIZE--numpages-+->< 
   | '-DEFERRED--'  '-DBPARTITIONNUM--dbpnum-'               |
   +-+-NOT EXTENDED STORAGE-+--------------------------------+
   | '-EXTENDED STORAGE-----'                                |
   +-ADD DATABASE PARTITION GROUP--dbpartgrpname-------------+
   +-NUMBLOCKPAGES--numpages--+--------------------+---------+
   |                          '-BLOCKSIZE--numpages-'        |
   '-BLOCKSIZE--numpages-------------------------------------'
```

In v8, the memory is made available to the database shared memory immediately and can be reused for other memory allocations.

With the ability to change your buffer pool allocations and update configuration parameters online, you can now customize memory usage to the task. For example, if you have a daytime memory allocation that is optimized for query performance (a large buffer pool), you could use a script to optimize nighttime memory usage for a load operation. For example:

```
db2 connect to sample
db2 update db cfg for sample using dbheap 2400 deferred
db2 get db cfg for sample show detail
```

Output from the GET DATABASE CONFIGURATION SHOW DETAIL command shows both the current value and the (deferred) new value of the *dbheap* configuration parameter:

```
                Database Configuration for Database sample

Description                Parameter   Current Value        Delayed Value
--------------------------------------------------------------------------
Database configuration                 = 0x0a00
  release level
Database release level                 = 0x0a00

Database territory                     = US
Database code page                     = 819
Database code set                      = ISO8859-1
Database country/                      = 1
  region code
. . .
Database heap (4KB)        (DBHEAP) = 1200                   2400
. . .
```

Two new configuration parameters are used to reserve memory at the instance or database level:

- INSTANCE_MEMORY specifies the amount of memory that is to be reserved for instance management. If you set this parameter to AUTOMATIC, DB2 calculates the amount required for the current configuration automatically.
- DATABASE_MEMORY specifies the amount of shared memory that is to be reserved for the database shared memory region. If you set this parameter to AUTOMATIC, DB2 calculates the amount required automatically. This parameter can be used, for example, to reserve additional memory for creating new buffer pools or increasing the sizes of existing buffer pools.

Two new administrative APIs simplify the process of viewing or changing entries in a database manager configuration file or a database configuration file. Table 14.1 shows the pre-v8 APIs to which these new APIs map.

Table 14.1 Old to New API Mappings

V7 API	Descriptive Name	V8 API
sqlfddb	Get Database Configuration Defaults	db2CfgGet
sqlfdsys	Get Database Manager Configuration Defaults	db2CfgGet
sqlfrdb	Reset Database Configuration	db2CfgSet
sqlfrsys	Reset Database Manager Configuration	db2CfgSet
sqlfudb	Update Database Configuration	db2CfgSet
sqlfusys	Update Database Manager Configuration	db2CfgSet
sqlfxdb	Get Database Configuration	db2CfgGet
sqlfxsys	Get Database Manager Configuration	db2CfgGet

The following database manager configuration parameters are configurable online:

```
catalog_noauth
comm_bandwidth
conn_elapse
cpuspeed
dft_account_str
dft_monswitches
dftdbpath
diaglevel
diagpath
discover_inst
fcm_num_buffers
fed_noauth
health_mon
indexrec
max_connretries
max_querydegree
notifylevel
start_stop_time
use_sna_auth
```

The following database configuration parameters are configurable online:

```
autorestart
avg_appls
blk_log_dsk_ful
catalogcache_sz
dbheap
dft_degree
dft_extent_sz
dft_loadrec_ses
dft_prefetch_sz
dft_queryopt
discover_db
dlchktime
dl_expint
dl_num_copies
dl_time_drop
dl_token
dl_upper
dl_wt_iexpint
indexrec
locklist
logsecond
maxappls
maxfilop
maxlocks
mincommit
num_db_backups
num_freqvalues
num_quantiles
pckcachesz
seqdetect
sortheap
stmtheap
tsm_mgmtclass
tsm_nodename
tsm_owner
tsm_password
util_heap_sz
```

The following DB2 Administration Server (DAS) configuration parameters are configurable online:

```
contact_host
das_codepage
das_territory
db2system
discover
jdk_path
smtp_server
```

Online Utilities

ONLINE REORGANIZATION

DB2 UDB v8 has the capability of reorganizing both tables and indexes online; that is, while users have full read or write access to these objects. Along with an enhanced REORG TABLE command, there is a new REORG INDEXES command.

Table Reorganization

The performance of your database is significantly impacted by the physical distribution of the table data. After many transactions, logically sequential data might no longer reside on physically sequential data pages, making additional read operations to access data necessary. Table reorganization corrects this problem while reclaiming space.

There are two main approaches that you can use to determine whether a table needs to be reorganized:

- *Invoke the runstats utility*, which collects a variety of statistics pertaining to data distribution, space utilization, prefetch efficiency, indexes, and so on. Because the optimizer uses these statistics when determining access paths to the data, simply invoking the RUNSTATS command to refresh statistical information could improve performance. If you regularly invoke the RUNSTATS command and analyze the resulting statistics (by querying the database catalog), you can determine whether table or index reorganization is necessary.
- *Invoke the reorgchk utility*, which returns some of the catalog statistics and recommendations about whether tables or indexes need to be reorganized.

You can query the database catalog to determine whether a table needs to be reorganized:

- Query the OVERFLOW column in SYSCAT.TABLES to monitor the number of rows that no longer fit on their original data page.

- Query the FPAGES and NPAGES columns in SYSCAT.TABLES to estimate the number of empty pages in a table. Subtract the NPAGES value (the number of pages that contain rows) from the FPAGES value (the number of pages that are in use) to obtain an estimate of the number of empty pages in the table.

- Query the CLUSTERRATIO column in SYSCAT.INDEXES to determine how well the data in the table is clustered.

- Query the AVERAGE_SEQUENCE_FETCH_PAGES column, the AVERAGE_RANDOM _FETCH_PAGES column, and the AVERAGE_SEQUENCE_FETCH_GAP column in SYSCAT.INDEXES to determine the effectiveness of the prefetchers when the table is accessed in index order.

- Query the NUM_EMPTY_LEAFS column in SYSCAT.INDEXES to determine the number of leaf pages on which all RIDs are marked as deleted (but not removed). Alternatively, query the NUMRIDS_DELETED column to determine the total number of logically deleted RIDs on leaf pages that have RIDs not all marked as deleted.

Once you have determined that your table needs reorganizing, the actual decision to do so might depend on your assessment of the relative importance of degrading query performance and the costs associated with reorganizing the table. The latter have been significantly reduced with the introduction, in v8, of *online table reorganization*, which promotes database availability by allowing the reorganization process to take place while applications have both read and write access to the table.

Online table reorganization can be paused and then resumed later. In v8, you can reorganize tables in a single partition, a set of partitions, or all partitions in a database partition group.

Online table reorganization can only be performed on a table that has type-2 indexes defined on it.

Type-2 Indexes

DB2 UDB v8 introduces *type-2 indexes*, which enhance concurrency through the elimination of most next-key locking behavior: Keys are marked deleted instead of being physically removed from the index page. A type-2 index can be created on columns that are more than 255 bytes long. Type-2 indexes are also required for MDC.

Any new index that you create is a type-2 index unless your table already has older indexes defined on it. In this case, your new index is also a type-1 index, because you cannot have both type-1 and type-2 indexes defined on the same table. You can use the REORG INDEXES command to convert type-1 indexes to type-2 indexes, using the following syntax:

```
db2 reorg indexes all for table <table-name> convert
```

Although you can use the INSPECT command to find out what type of index a table has, it's faster to just run the conversion (if that's what you ultimately want to do). If the table already has type-2 indexes, the command has no effect.

Index Reorganization

After many transactions against a table, the performance of indexes defined on that table declines. Leaf pages become fragmented and poorly clustered, and sequential prefetching is compromised, causing more leaf pages to be read when table pages are fetched. The resulting increases in I/O waits are expensive. The solution to this problem is index reorganization. You can accomplish this by dropping and then re-creating the indexes that require reorganization, or by invoking the REORG TABLE command to reorganize a table and its indexes offline. These approaches work, but they are impractical and costly in a production environment.

Version 8 introduces the REORG INDEXES command, which enables you to reorganize indexes online. Online index reorganization means that users can read from and write to a table while its indexes are being rebuilt. The REORG INDEXES command reorganizes all indexes defined on a table by rebuilding them into unfragmented, physically contiguous pages.

Table updates that affect the indexes and that occur during index reorganization are logged. These changes are then processed and applied while the indexes are being rebuilt.

Renaming an Existing Index

A radical form of index reorganization is the replacement of one index with another, perhaps better, one with the same name. Prior to v8, the process for doing this was somewhat convoluted. You had to first drop the old index and then create a new one. Because creating an index can take a significant amount of time, particularly with very large tables, this approach could be costly in terms of the performance hit to users while the process is underway.

With v8, you can rename an existing index. This enables you to create a new index, remove the old index, and then change the name of the new index so that it can be used in place of the old index.

You can rename an existing index using the following syntax:

```
db2 rename index <schema-name>.<index-name> to <new-name>
```

The schema name of the source object is used to qualify the new name for the object.

ONLINE DATABASE INSPECTION TOOL

The new INSPECT command (or the db2Inspect API) allows you to inspect the architectural integrity of table spaces and tables while your database remains online. This is a significant improvement over the db2dart utility, which could only be used offline. The tool checks whether the structures of table objects and table spaces are valid. If done offline, such integrity checking of large databases could take a considerable amount of time, a period in which the database is unavailable for use. The inspect utility is integrated into the DB2 UDB engine and, as such, can take advantage of buffer pools and prefetchers for better performance.

Inspection of a whole database includes the processing of all table objects, including index, long field, or LOB objects located in other table spaces. Inspection of a single table space includes only the processing of objects that reside in that table space.

You can specify the type of objects to be processed; the default behavior is to process all objects. Specifying the NONE keyword with an object excludes that object from processing.

SYSADM, DBADM, SYSCTRL, or SYSMAINT authority is required for inspect check processing. CONTROL privilege on a table is required for processing of that table. A connection to the database must exist before you can invoke the inspect utility.

Online inspect processing accesses database objects using the uncommitted read (UR) isolation level, and runs in the current unit of work. COMMIT processing is done during inspect processing, and it is a good idea to end the previous unit of work by issuing a COMMIT or a ROLLBACK statement before invoking the inspect utility.

This shows part of the syntax for the new INSPECT command:

```
>>-INSPECT--CHECK------------------------------------------------->

>----+-+-DATABASE--+--------------------------------------+------------+-+-->
     | |             '-BEGIN TBSPACEID--n--+-------------+-'           | |
     | |                                   '-OBJECTID--n-'             | |
     | '-TABLESPACE--+-NAME--tablespace-name-+---+------------------+-' |
     |               '-TBSPACEID--n----------'   '-BEGIN OBJECTID--n-'  |
     '-TABLE--+-NAME--table-name--+--------------------+-+-------------'
              |                   '-SCHEMA--schema-name-' |
              '-TBSPACEID--n--OBJECTID--n----------------'

                              .-LIMIT ERROR TO DEFAULT--.
>--+--------------------+--+-------------------------+---------->
   '-FOR ERROR STATE ALL-'  '-LIMIT ERROR TO--+-n---+-'
                                              '-ALL-'

>--+------------------+--RESULTS--+------+--filename----------->
   '-| Level Clause |-'          '-KEEP-'

>--+---------------------------------+----------------------><
   '-| On Database Partition Clause |-'
```

The RESULTS *file-name* clause specifies a result file that is created in the diagnostic data directory path. If the inspect utility finds no errors during processing, the result file is erased at the end of the inspect operation, unless the optional KEEP keyword is specified.

You can choose from among a number of options to customize error reporting by the inspect utility. Normally, if a table object has an internal status that indicates an error state, the inspect utility reports this status but does not scan through the object. Specifying the FOR ERROR STATE ALL option, however, instructs the utility to scan through an object even if its internal status indicates an error state. The LIMIT ERROR TO *n* option specifies the number of pages in error that an object must have before inspect processing on the rest of that object is to stop. The LIMIT ERROR TO DEFAULT option specifies that inspect processing on an object is to stop when an extent size number of pages in error has been reached for that object. The LIMIT ERROR TO ALL option specifies that there is to be no limit on the number of pages in error reported on an object.

The Level Clause allows you to specify the level of processing (normal, low, or none) that is to be done on various table objects, including extent map, data, block map, index, long, or LOB objects. The On Database Partition Clause allows you to specify one or more database partitions on which inspect processing is to be done. Details about these options are provided in the DB2 product documentation.

The inspect utility writes unformatted inspection data to a specified results file. In a partitioned database environment, each database partition generates its own results file with an extension corresponding to its node number. The results file is written to the database manager diagnostic data directory path. Use the db2inspf utility to format this data so that it can be read. This is the command syntax for db2inspf:

```
                              .-,----------.
                              V            |
>>-db2inspf--data-file--out-file----+--------+-+---------------><
                                    +-tsi--n-+
                                    +-ti--n--+
                                    +-e------+
                                    +-w------+
                                    '-s------'
```

You must specify an unformatted inspection results file and a file for the formatted output. The -tsi option specifies that only the table space with ID equal to *n* is to be processed. The -ti option specifies that only the table with ID equal to *n* is to be processed; in this case, the table space ID must also be provided. The -e, -w, and -s options specify that only error, warning, or summary data, respectively, is to be formatted.

The following example, based on the SAMPLE database, shows how these utilities can be used. After connecting to the SAMPLE database, an application issues an INSPECT command requesting inspection of the entire database. The results file, *inspect.res*, is not to be erased following the inspect operation. The application then queries the system catalog to obtain the internal identifiers for the DEPARTMENT table and its associated table space; this information is used to filter the formatted output from the db2inspf utility. To do this, the application issues a db2inspf command, specifying the qualified name of the unformatted inspection results file. (In this example, the file is located in the db2dump subdirectory of the sqllib directory, which represents the diagnostic data directory path on UNIX-based systems.) The name of the file to which the formatted output will be written and the table space and table identifiers are also specified.

```
db2 connect to sample

db2 inspect check database results keep inspect.res

db2 "select name, tid as table_space_id, fid as table_ID
  from sysibm.systables
  where name='DEPARTMENT'"


NAME                      TABLE_SPACE_ID TABLE_ID
------------------------- -------------- --------
DEPARTMENT                             2        4
  1 record(s) selected.


db2inspf sqllib/db2dump/inspect.res inspect.for -tsi 2 -ti 4


DATABASE: SAMPLE
VERSION : SQL08010
2002-09-18-14.09.28.459109
INSPECT CHECK DATABASE

    Table phase start (ID Signed: 4, Unsigned: 4; Tablespace ID: 2) :

      Data phase start. Object: 4  Tablespace: 2
      The index type is 1 for this table.
       DAT Object Summary: Total Pages 1 - Used Pages 1 - Free Space 56 %
      Data phase end.
    Table phase end.

db2 connect reset
```

INCREMENTAL MAINTENANCE OF MATERIALIZED QUERY TABLES

An MQT is a table with a definition based on the result of a query (a fullselect). Such a table is populated with precomputed results taken from one or more tables on which the MQT definition is based. A *summary table* is a type of MQT with a fullselect that contains a GROUP BY clause that summarizes data from the tables that are referenced in the fullselect. A summary table is a descendent of a parent table.

The following statement creates a summary table named AVG_SAL, which has two columns, JOB and AVG_SALARY. The AVG_SALARY column is computed from the SALARY column of the parent table, STAFF:

```
db2 create table avg_sal as
    (select job, avg(salary) as avg_salary
        from staff group by job)
    data initially deferred refresh deferred
```

The DATA INITIALLY DEFERRED clause indicates that data will not be inserted into the table as part of the CREATE TABLE statement; instead, the MQT will be populated with data through the invocation of a REFRESH TABLE statement. The REFRESH DEFERRED clause specifies that the MQT data can be refreshed at any time by invoking a REFRESH TABLE statement. Specifying the REFRESH IMMEDIATE clause, on the other hand, would have requested that changes to the parent table resulting from delete, insert, or update operations be automatically cascaded to the MQT. In this example, specifying the REFRESH IMMEDIATE clause would have created an automatic summary table (AST). With an *AST*, changes made to the underlying (parent) tables are cascaded to the summary table immediately and without the need for a REFRESH TABLE statement.

There are certain restrictions on what the fullselect can include, depending on whether the table is defined as a refresh deferred or a refresh immediate MQT. For details on those restrictions, see the description of the CREATE TABLE statement in the *DB2 Universal Database Version 8 SQL Reference, Volume 2.*

Prior to v8, refreshing an MQT meant completing a *full refresh* of the MQT; in effect, a recomputation of the MQT definition. If a parent table entered check pending state (e.g., following a load insert operation), all of its descendents (including descendent refresh immediate summary tables) would also enter check pending state. Once a table entered check pending state, it was offline and unavailable for select, delete, insert, or update operations.

With v8, the MQT can remain available during a load insert operation on the underlying table. When the load operation is complete, the MQT can be refreshed *incrementally*, using only the appended data, which significantly reduces the time required to update the MQT.

Following is the syntax of the REFRESH TABLE statement, showing the new INCREMENTAL option:

```
                    .-,----------.
                    V            |
>>-REFRESH TABLE----table-name-+--+-----------------+----------><
                                  +-INCREMENTAL-----+
                                  '-NOT INCREMENTAL-'
```

If a refresh deferred MQT is to be incrementally maintained, it must have a staging table associated with it. A *staging table* is used to save data before that data is replicated to a target database; it is used as an intermediate source for updating data to a target table. You can use a CREATE TABLE statement to define the staging table that is to be associated with a specific MQT.

When delete, insert, or update operations modify the underlying tables of an MQT, changes resulting from those operations are automatically propagated to the staging table.

The SET INTEGRITY statement can be used to do the following:

- Turn off or turn on the immediate refreshing of data in refresh immediate MQTs or in propagate immediate staging tables. This can be done either with or without first performing deferred integrity checking.
- Move tables from normal (no data movement) state to normal (full access) state.
- Prune the contents of one or more staging tables.

You can also use the SET INTEGRITY statement to incrementally refresh MQTs or incrementally propagate staging tables with the load-appended portions of underlying tables.

Version 8 introduces three new table states to facilitate higher data availability following load insert operations:

- *Check Pending No Access state.* This new table state replaces the pre-v8 check pending state. Select, delete, insert, and update operations are not allowed on a table in this state.
- *Check Pending Read state.* This table state does not allow write access, but does allow read access to pre-existing data.
- *Normal (No Data Movement) state.* This table state allows both read and write access to a parent table that has been checked for constraints violations, but prevents data movement operations that might invalidate RIDs associated with descendent refresh immediate summary tables.

To understand how these new table states can work, consider a simple scenario in which load insert operations are performed on a single parent table (T) that has a single descendent refresh immediate summary table (S). Assume that table T has a referential integrity relationship with table C, and that table T also has a check constraint defined on it. Initially, tables T, S, and C are in normal state.

After a load insert operation (specifying CHECK PENDING CASCADE DEFERRED and ALLOW READ ACCESS) into T from *source*:

- T enters check pending read state. Read access to T (for data other than that contained in *source*) is allowed.
- S and C are still in normal state.

After a set integrity operation (specifying IMMEDIATE CHECKED) for T, in which table T is incrementally checked for constraints violations (only newly inserted rows from *source* are checked):

- T enters normal (no data movement) state. Queries and updates against T are allowed. Data movement operations that could affect descendent refresh immediate ASTs are not allowed.
- S enters check pending no access state.
- C is still in normal state, because rows appended to a parent table should not affect the validity of data in child tables.

After a refresh table operation against S (during which table S is incrementally checked):

- S enters normal state.
- T enters normal state, because the last (and in this case the only) descendent refresh immediate AST is now in normal state.
- C is still in normal state.

Miscellaneous Manageability Enhancements

T here are multiple manageability enhancements in DB2 UDB v8. In this chapter we will discuss:

- Throttling Utilities
- New Administration Notification Log
- Table Space Change History File
- `QUIESCE` Command
- `RUNSTATS` Command Enhancements
- Point-in-Time Rollforward Recovery to Local Time
- XBSA Support
- Data Movement Enhancements for Original Equipment Manufacturer Databases
- Trace Facility Enhancements
- Multiple Service Level Install for UNIX
- New Tivoli-focused Options
- LDAP Support on Linux
- Dynamic LPAR Support for AIX5.2B
- Dynamic System Domain Support
- Transaction Log Space Usage
- `ALTER TABLE VARGRAPHIC`
- Command History Support and CLP Roundtrip Editing

THROTTLING UTILITIES

An ongoing challenge faced by DBAs has been to minimize the performance impact of online utilities on production workloads, while ensuring that system resources are maximally utilized when the workloads diminish.

The throttling utilities enhancement introduced in DB2 UDB v8 is designed to let you run DB2 utilities aggressively when the workload is light and run them conservatively when the workload is heavy. This eliminates the need to schedule large utility runs at off-peak hours, or to plan for actual down time.

There is a new database manager configuration parameter, *util_impact_lim*, which allows you to define an *impact policy*, or limit the cumulative performance degradation caused by all throttled utilities (currently the backup and rebalance utilities only) running on the system. This configuration parameter can be updated dynamically, enabling you to throttle a utility after it has been started. This is particularly useful if you have invoked the utility and then realize that the workload performance has been unacceptably degraded. You can use the UPDATE DATABASE MANAGER CONFIGURATION command to change the value of *util_impact_lim*. For example:

```
db2 update dbm cfg using util_impact_lim 10
```

The default value of this configuration parameter is 100 (percent), meaning that all utilities are to run unthrottled. Normal practice would be to specify a very low impact limit, unless there are utility jobs that are considered critical and of sufficiently high priority to justify a higher impact on production workloads.

The *utility priority* represents the importance of one throttled utility relative to another. For example, a utility with a priority of 10 consumes twice the resources of a utility with a priority of 5. If only one utility is throttled, its priority value has no meaning.

There is a new option on the BACKUP DATABASE command, UTIL_IMPACT_PRIORITY, which enables you to specify the initial priority of a backup operation. Valid values for this parameter range from 1 to 100. For example:

```
db2 backup db sample util_impact_priority 5
```

A lower priority value results in a higher degree of throttling. The default priority value is 50. The utility runs unthrottled if:

- The UTIL_IMPACT_PRIORITY clause is omitted.
- The clause is specified, but the value of the *util_impact_lim* database manager configuration parameter is 100.

A utility can be throttled or reprioritized after it has started by invoking the SET UTIL_IMPACT_PRIORITY command, as follows:

```
db2 set util_impact_priority for <utility-id> to <priority>
```

The utility ID can be determined by issuing the GET SNAPSHOT FOR DATABASE MANAGER command while the utility is running.

The rebalancer (invoked as part of an ALTER TABLESPACE operation) can only be throttled after it has started.

NEW ADMINISTRATION NOTIFICATION LOG

DB2 now writes event information to two different logs, the new administration notification log (*<instance_name>*.nfy) and the customary diagnostic log (*db2diag.log*).

- DB2 writes information to the DB2 notification log when significant events occur. This information is intended to be useful to DBAs and system administrators who are trying to resolve minor issues. The type of event and the level of detail provided are determined by the current value of the *notifylevel* database manager configuration parameter.
- Detailed diagnostic information about errors is recorded in the DB2 diagnostic log. This information is used for problem determination and is intended for DB2 customer support. The level of detail provided is determined by the current value of the *diaglevel* database manager configuration parameter.

The db2AdminMsgWrite API, which is now available on all DB2 platforms, allows users and the DB2 replication utility to write information to the *db2diag.log* file and the administration notification log. With Windows NT, messages are written to the Event Log. With other platforms and Windows NT Satellite Edition, messages are written to the DB2 administration notification log. On UNIX-based systems, the administration notification log is located in the same directory as the *db2diag.log* file (/home/*<instance>*/sqllib/db2dump). A user application must call the db2AdminMsgWrite API to be able to write to the notification log or the Windows Event Log.

The *notifylevel* database manager configuration parameter specifies the type of administration notification messages that are to be written to the administration notification log. Errors can be written by DB2, the Health Monitor, the Capture and Apply programs, or user applications.

Valid values for this parameter are:

- 0 (No messages captured)
- 1 (Fatal or unrecoverable errors)
- 2 (Errors that require immediate action)
- 3 (Default: Important information that requires no immediate action)
- 4 (Informational messages)

The administration notification log contains messages with a severity level up to and including the value of *notifylevel*. For example, setting *notifylevel* to 3 specifies that messages at Levels 1, 2, and 3 are to be written to the administration notification log.

The following are sample contents from an administration notification log:

```
2002-09-26-13.33.55.712003    Instance:db2idad    Node:000
PID:19922(db2star2)    TID:1    Appid:none
base sys utilities    startdbm Probe:911


ADM7513W   Database manager has started.
```

```
-
2002-09-28-20.51.51.860123   Instance:db2idad   Node:000
PID:21936(db2agent (SAMPLE))   TID:1   Appid:*LOCAL.db2idad.018079005013
base sys utilities  sqleDatabaseQuiesce Probe:1   Database:SAMPLE

ADM7506W  Database quiesce has been requested.
-
2002-09-28-20.51.52.800119   Instance:db2idad   Node:000
PID:21936(db2agent (SAMPLE))   TID:1   Appid:*LOCAL.db2idad.018079005013
base sys utilities  sqleDatabaseQuiesce Probe:2   Database:SAMPLE

ADM7507W  Database quiesce request has completed successfully.
-
2002-09-28-20.59.32.329856   Instance:db2idad   Node:000
PID:21936(db2agent (SAMPLE))   TID:1   Appid:*LOCAL.db2idad.018079005013
base sys utilities  sqleDatabaseUnquiesce Probe:1   Database:SAMPLE

ADM7510W  Database unquiesce  has been requested.
-
2002-09-28-20.59.32.489549   Instance:db2idad   Node:000
PID:21936(db2agent (SAMPLE))   TID:1   Appid:*LOCAL.db2idad.018079005013
base sys utilities  sqleDatabaseUnquiesce Probe:2   Database:SAMPLE

ADM7509W  Database unquiesce request has completed successfully.
-
2002-09-30-13.27.59.564794   Instance:db2idad   Node:000
PID:24134(db2agent (SAMPLE))   TID:1   Appid:*LOCAL.db2idad.061310172759
data protection  sqlufrol Probe:980   Database:SAMPLE

ADM1602W  Rollforward recovery has been initiated.
-
2002-09-30-13.28.02.162342   Instance:db2idad   Node:000
PID:24134(db2agent (SAMPLE))   TID:1   Appid:*LOCAL.db2idad.061310172759
data protection  sqlufrol Probe:8180   Database:SAMPLE

ADM1611W  The rollforward recovery phase has been completed.
```

TABLE SPACE CHANGE HISTORY FILE

Prior to v8, a table space rollforward recovery operation required the processing of all log files that had accumulated since the backup image was created, even if there were no transactions in the log files associated with the specified table space. This is no longer the case. Now only log files that are required to recover the table space are processed; log files that are not required are skipped. If the log files are being retrieved from the archive, the user exit program is asked to retrieve only the needed log files. (If, for some reason, you want all of the log files to be processed, set the new DB2_COLLECT_TS_REC_INFO registry variable to NO.)

A new history file, the table space change history file (*db2tschg.his*), keeps track of which logs should be processed for each table space. This file is created when it is needed for the first time, and is located in the database directory. There is one file associated with each database partition that is backed up during each database backup operation and restored during a database restore operation. The file is updated during run time (when log files become full), as well as during database rollforward and crash recovery operations.

You can use the db2logsForRfwd utility (located in sqllib/bin) to view the contents of *db2tschg.his* (useful if you want to know which logs are needed to recover a particular table space) and delete entries from it using the PRUNE HISTORY command. The file is pruned whenever the recovery history file is pruned.

The syntax for the db2logsForRfwd command is as follows:

```
>>-db2logsForRfwd--path--+-------+------------------------------><
                         '--all-'
```

The *path* parameter specifies the fully qualified name of the *db2tschg.his* file. Specifying -all returns more detailed information. For example:

```
elk /home/db2idad>db2logsForRfwd db2idad/NODE0000/SQL00001/DB2TSCHG.HIS
-------------------------------------------------------------
Extent               : 0
Pools                : 2
-------------------------------------------------------------
Extent               : 1
Pools                : 2


elk /home/db2idad/db2idad/NODE0000/SQL00001>db2logsForRfwd DB2TSCHG.HIS -all
-------------------------------------------------------------
Extent               : 0
First New Record LSN : 000003E8000C
Log Extent Tail LSN  : 000004268000
Backup End Time Stamp : 0
Flags                : 7
pID                  : 0
cID                  : 1033401182 2002-09-30-15.53.02.000000 GMT
Pools                : 2
```

```
----------------------------------------------------------
Extent                   : 1
First New Record LSN     : 00000426800C
Log Extent Tail LSN      : 000004650000
Backup End Time Stamp    : 0
Flags                    : 7
pID                      : 1033401182 2002-09-30-15.53.02.000000 GMT
cID                      : 1033406881 2002-09-30-17.28.01.000000 GMT
Pools                    : 2
```

If information about a particular log file is unavailable (because of overpruning, or because information has been lost before it could be written to disk following a crash), the log is treated as though it were required for the recovery of every table space. The only consequence is that more log files than necessary are processed during table space rollforward recovery.

QUIESCE COMMAND

The new QUIESCE command allows you to force all users off an instance or a database, and to put the instance or the database into a quiesced mode. Users with the correct authority have exclusive access to the quiesced instance or database and can perform system administration or database maintenance activities. (Users with *sysadm*, *sysmaint*, or *sysctrl* authority always have access to a quiesced instance, and users with *sysadm* or *dbadm* authority always have access to a quiesced database.) After these activities are completed, you can use the UNQUIESCE command to restore user access to the instance or the database without a shutdown and subsequent database restart.

You do not have to stop users from attaching to a quiesced instance or connecting to a quiesced database by, for example, shutting down all transaction managers.

The syntax for the new QUIESCE command is as follows:

```
                                        .-FORCE CONNECTIONS-.
>>-QUIESCE--+-DATABASE-+--+-IMMEDIATE-+--+-------------------+-><
            '-DB-------'  '-DEFER-----'


>>-QUIESCE INSTANCE--instance-name--+-------------------+-->
                                    +-USER--user-name---+
                                    '-GROUP--group-name-'


                   .-FORCE CONNECTIONS-.
>-+-IMMEDIATE-+---+-------------------+--------------------><
  '-DEFER-----'
```

The IMMEDIATE keyword specifies that any uncommitted transactions are to be rolled back when the QUIESCE command executes. This is currently the only supported option; the DEFER keyword is not yet operational. The USER *user-name* parameter specifies the name of a user who is to be allowed access to the quiesced instance, and the GROUP *group-name* parameter specifies the name of a group that is to be allowed access to the quiesced instance. The QUIESCE_CONNECT option on the GRANT (Database Authorities) statement grants the authority to access a database when it is quiesced to specific users, groups, or PUBLIC. A similar option on the corresponding REVOKE statement revokes the authority to access a database when it is quiesced from specific users, groups, or PUBLIC.

In the following example, a connection is made to the SAMPLE database, which is then quiesced, preventing access by all users except those with *sysadm*, *sysmaint*, *sysctrl*, or *dbadm* authority. User access is then restored to the database, and the connection to it is reset.

```
db2 connect to sample
db2 quiesce db immediate
db2 unquiesce db
db2 connect reset
```

RUNSTATS COMMAND ENHANCEMENTS

Runstats is a DB2 utility that collects statistics on a table or its indexes. The RUNSTATS command in v8 has new options and performs significantly better during statistics collection.

The new ON COLUMNS clause allows you to specify a list of columns on which statistics are to be collected. You can specify the ON KEY COLUMNS clause to collect statistics on columns that make up all of the indexes defined on the table. If the WITH DISTRIBUTION clause is specified together with the ON COLUMNS clause, distribution statistics are collected on the specified columns only (with the exception of columns, such as CLOB and LONG VARCHAR columns, on which distribution statistics cannot be gathered). If the ON COLUMNS clause is not specified, distribution statistics are collected on all columns of the table.

You can now specify the distribution statistics limits, NUM_FREQVALUES and NUM_QUANTILES, at the table level. You no longer need to change the *num_freqvalues* or the *num_quantiles* database configuration parameters, disconnect all users, and then connect again to do this. You can also specify individual column values for NUM_FREQVALUES or NUM_QUANTILES. NUM_FREQVALUES specifies the maximum number of frequency values to collect. NUM_QUANTILES specifies the maximum number of distribution quantile values to collect. If a value for an individual column is not specified, the value that was specified in the DEFAULT clause is used. If a default value is not specified, the value specified in the database configuration file is used.

The RUNSTATS command now accepts a list of index names, a feature that previously was available only with the db2Runstats API.

Because all of the information needed to collect index statistics is available at index creation time, you now have the option of collecting index statistics as part of the CREATE INDEX statement; you no longer need to invoke the runstats utility every time you create a new index on a table. The following partial syntax diagram for the CREATE INDEX statement shows the new parameters:

```
>>-CREATE--+---------+---INDEX--index-name-----------------------------> 
           '-UNIQUE-'
   .


   .


   .

>--+----------------------------------------------------------+---------->< 
   '-COLLECT--+-----------------------------+--STATISTICS-'
              '-+----------+--DETAILED-'
                '-SAMPLED-'
```

The DETAILED keyword specifies that extended index statistics (CLUSTERFACTOR and PAGE_FETCH_PAIRS) for large indexes are to be gathered. The SAMPLED keyword, when specified with the DETAILED keyword, requests that a CPU sampling technique be used when compiling extended index statistics. This option results in better performance: If the SAMPLED keyword is not specified, every entry in the index must be examined when extended index statistics are gathered.

MDC introduces a new type of index called a *block index*. The v8 runstats utility supports statistics collection for this type of index and introduces new statistics that enable the DB2 query optimizer to utilize this new index type. For example, ACTIVE_BLOCKS, which records the total number of active blocks in an MDC table, helps the query optimizer better estimate the block I/O cost.

New index and table prefetching-related statistics have been introduced in v8. These statistics will eventually be used to help the query optimizer take into account the prefetching capabilities of DB2 when costing an access plan.

POINT-IN-TIME ROLLFORWARD RECOVERY TO LOCAL TIME

A new USING LOCAL TIME clause on the ROLLFORWARD DATABASE command allows you to roll logs forward to a point in time that represents the server's local time rather than Greenwich Mean Time (GMT). This feature eliminates potential user errors in conversion of local time to GMT. Returned messages are also based on local time. Time conversions occur on the server and, on partitioned database systems, on the catalog database partition.

XBSA SUPPORT

The DB2 UDB v8 backup utility is compatible with storage solutions that implement the X/Open Backup Services API (XBSA) industry standard interface.

DATA MOVEMENT ENHANCEMENTS FOR ORIGINAL EQUIPMENT MANUFACTURER DATABASES

An Original Equipment Manufacturer (OEM) uses product components from other companies to build a product that it sells under its own company name and brand. DB2 UDB v8 includes enhancements that enable the data movement utilities to accept the Sybase Bulk Copy Program (BCP) text file format.

Rather than handle the BCP native file format, the DB2 export utility uses file type modifiers (*nochardel* and *timestampformat*) to produce a delimited (DEL) file that is an acceptable BCP text file. It is able to do so because the BCP text file format is quite similar to the DEL file format. Similarly, the DB2 import and load utilities use the corresponding file type modifiers to interpret BCP text files.

The BCP text file format supports column and row delimiters, but not character delimiters. The *nochardel* file type modifier (for DEL files) prevents the export utility from surrounding column data with character delimiters and doubling existing character delimiters. This modifier also bypasses the logic that causes the import and load utilities to expect column data to be surrounded by character delimiters and character delimiters to be doubled.

The following is an example of a BCP timestamp:

```
May 13 2003 10:32:15:007PM
```

The equivalent exported DEL timestamp looks like this:

```
2003-05-13-22.32.15.007000
```

To bring these timestamp formats into closer alignment, the *timestampformat* file type modifier (for DEL files) is now recognized by the DB2 export utility. This modifier, previously recognized by the DB2 import and load utilities (for both DEL and ASC files), has also been updated to accept three-digit microsecond values (UUU) and three-character month names (MMM, representing Jan, Feb, Mar, Apr, May, Jun, Jul, Aug, Sep, Oct, Nov, or Dec).

TRACE FACILITY ENHANCEMENTS

The DB2 trace facility is used to capture events, dump trace data to a file, and format the data into a readable form. The trace facility can be invoked by issuing the `db2trc` command. The facility has been significantly improved for v8.

Prior to v8, enabling a trace could severely impact DB2's performance. This made using the facility in many production environments—or for extended periods of time—impractical. More complex problems could, in certain cases, be difficult to diagnose, because the facility's performance impact had the potential to alter a problem's behavior. Moreover, the trace buffer often proved to be too small and filled up too quickly.

V8 enhancements to the DB2 trace facility include:

- *Greatly improved performance.* The impact to production systems has been minimized. A given DB2 operation with trace enabled should require no more than 5% to 10% of additional time to complete.
- *Improved filtering.* Trace can now be enabled for a specific process or thread.
- *A larger trace buffer.*

MULTIPLE SERVICE LEVEL INSTALL FOR UNIX

Prior to DB2 UDB v8, UNIX or Linux FixPak installations replaced existing DB2 UDB files with updated files. This meant that after a FixPak installation, there would only be one version, point release, and modification level of the DB2 UDB server on the system. (In a UNIX or Linux environment, multiple DB2 UDB versions—but not point releases or modification levels—can coexist on the same machine.)

Today's business environments demand the flexibility of multiple point releases or modification levels for a specific version of a DB2 UDB server because:

- The production side of the business might be running a particular level of the code, and they do not want to switch to a FixPak level until it can be thoroughly tested. This could create the need for separate production- and test-level code on the same machine.
- Different lines of business or teams within an enterprise might require different release or modification levels. They might not want to move to a different code level once they have become accustomed to the current level, which could be well suited to their needs. Perhaps an appropriate switch cannot be synchronized among the groups. Perhaps they are using ISV applications that are only certified at specific version, release, and modification levels.

You now have the option of installing different maintenance levels of the same version of a DB2 UDB ESE server on UNIX- or Linux-based workstations. FixPaks and updates are now delivered in two different formats:

- *Regular.* This format works the same way that previous fixes have worked: It installs on top of the existing code.
- *Alternate.* This format is a fully installable image at a specific modification level. It could be independently installed on a workstation that does not have a previous DB2 UDB installation at the same release level. This means that if you install the Alternate FixPak (FP1) code, the DB2 UDB server in this separate installation image is DB2 UDB v8.1+FP1. The GUI tools recognize this as a separate installation. A command line-based utility is provided to install Alternate FixPak code. This feature is only supported for DB2 UDB ESE, and not for any of the other DB2 UDB server products.

NEW TIVOLI-FOCUSED OPTIONS

DB2 UDB v8.1.2 adds support for new Tivoli-focused options that can be used with the backup and restore utilities. These new options simplify a DBA's requirements when restoring a backup written to Tivoli Storage Manager (TSM) from one machine (node A) to another (node B).

Before DB2 UDB v8.1.2, if a DBA wanted to restore a backup taken on node A to node B, the target node (node B) would have to masquerade as the source node (node A). The DBA would have to know the TSM password on both nodes, change node A's TSM configuration file (setting PASSWORDACCESS to PROMPT), and change the database configuration file too (the *tsm_nodename*, *tsm_owner*, and *tsm_password* parameters). These DBA requirements are not flexible enough for many customer environments for security reasons. The new Tivoli GRANT and REVOKE features in DB2 UDB v8.1.2 provide access to DB2 UDB objects stored on the TSM server.

Prior to this feature being implemented, if the *tsm_owner* parameter was set, all DB2 UDB backup objects would be TSM-owned by this name. If this parameter was not set, the objects would be owned by an "unnamed" TSM-owner. As well, if the *tsm_nodename* parameter was set, the DB2 UDB backup objects would be owned by this TSM node name. TSM does not allow the *tsm_owner* or the *tsm_nodename* parameter to be set when it is in PASSWORDACCESS GENERATE mode.

Now, if the *tsm_nodename* parameter is set to the node corresponding to the current host (or not set at all), the backup objects are owned by the user name; otherwise, the backup will fail. If the *tsm_owner* parameter is set, its value is ignored, and the backup objects are saved on the current node owned by the user name. Restore operations will only work if the proper authorizations are set according to GRANT or REVOKE functionality provided by the db2adutl utility.

This utility is used to manage DB2 UDB objects on the TSM server. In DB2 UDB v8.1.2, this has been extended so that it can also manage access rights for DB2 UDB objects. New GRANT or REVOKE features with the db2adult utility are used to add or remove access rights to files on the current node to other users on other nodes. When a DBA grants access, access is granted for all files related to that database (granularity is not at the file level). This operation grants or revokes access to all files (both existing and future) related to the specified database. You can use a query to retrieve the access status for a database.

These new Tivoli integration features in DB2 UDB v8.1.2 enhance the integration of TSM and DB2 UDB environments, and reduce administrative complexity.

LDAP SUPPORT ON LINUX

Lightweight Directory Access Protocol (LDAP) directories greatly simplify the deployment of client-server applications. Each client workstation must know the location of the DB2 databases that its applications must access. Traditionally, this has been accomplished by cataloging node (network address) and database information on every client workstation. This creates a high management cost: Whenever a new database is added, each and every client catalog must be updated.

LDAP offers an easier alternative: A central location contains all catalog information, and any changes or additions to the catalog are made in that one central location. All of the client work-stations refer to the LDAP directory for information about the databases they need. It is impor-tant to note here that only the connection information is stored on the LDAP server; the connection is still made from the client.

LDAP support has been in the DB2 product since DB2 UDB v7.1. In DB2 UDB v8.1.2, IBM's LDAP v3.2.2 client has been enhanced to allow:

- DB2 UDB and DB2 Connect servers running on 32-bit Linux on Intel/AMD or 31-bit Linux zSeries servers to publish their database connection information in an LDAP directory
- DB2 clients running on these operating systems to refer to the LDAP directory to find the databases to which they need to connect

DYNAMIC LPAR SUPPORT FOR AIX5.2B

Dynamic LPAR (DLPAR) capabilities are starting to appear in today's operating and hardware systems; for example, AIX v5.2B running on a POWER4-based pSeries system, such as Regatta p690. LPARs makes it possible to run multiple, independent operating system images on a single server. Using DLPAR, you can dynamically add or remove resources (memory and CPUs) from active partitions without the need to reboot the machine.

When using DLPARs for new resource assignments, a script must be run to handle the:

- removal of resources such as CPU and memory, while ensuring that the DB2 UDB server can continue to operate without crashing.
- reconfiguration of the DB2 UDB server based on the new system resources. If DB2 UDB cannot operate after a resource is removed, dynamic allocation is rejected.

Sample scripts, provided for DLPAR allocations on AIX, are located in the ../sqllib/samples/ DLPAR/ directory.

DYNAMIC SYSTEM DOMAIN SUPPORT

Dynamic System Domain (DSD) capabilities have been available for a while with Solaris-based hardware. DSDs allow you to change the availability of hardware resources to the operating sys-tem and applications. This enables you to upgrade, downgrade, or exchange components without having to reboot the system.

A script must be run when using DSD support for new resource assignments. This script handles:

- the approval or rejection of any hardware reconfiguration request from the perspective of DB2.
- an orderly shutdown and restart of DB2, in case of approved or forced reconfiguration.

Sample scripts, provided for Solaris, are located in the ../sqllib/samples/DLPAR/ directory.

TRANSACTION LOG SPACE USAGE

DB2 UDB v8.1 introduced a new concept called log chaining, which allows in-flight live transactions to be archived. DB2 UDB v8.1.2 adds new database configuration parameters to handle transactions that either consume large amounts of log space without committing, or issue a small number of updates and do not commit in an infinite logging environment. If a transaction exceeds specified limits, it is terminated and rolled back. This feature can also be used without infinite logging to control transaction-focused environments.

The new *maxlog* database configuration parameter can be used to prevent a transaction from taking up all of the active log space in a multi-user environment. If an application exceeds the *maxlog* threshold, the application is forced off of the database, and the transaction is rolled back. This behavior can be overridden by setting the DB2_FORCE_APP_ON_MAX_LOG registry variable to FALSE. If you set this registry variable to TRUE, and an application exceeds the defined threshold, the current statement fails, but the application can still issue a COMMIT or a ROLLBACK statement to complete the work done by previous statements in the unit of work.

The new *numlogspan* database configuration parameter can be used to limit an application's consumption of the active log space and prevent long-running transactions. If an application exceeds the *numlogspan* threshold, the application is forced off of the database, and the transaction is rolled back.

Both configuration parameters are useful in preventing incorrectly written applications (with missing COMMIT or ROLLBACK statements, or incorrect conditions specified for the WHERE clause of INSERT, DELETE, or UPDATE statements) from using up all of the active log space.

ALTER TABLE VARGRAPHIC

DB2 UDB v8.1.2 extends DB2's capability to alter the length of a VARCHAR column to the VARGRAPHIC data type. You can now extend the length of VARGRAPHIC columns in an existing table without dropping and then recreating the table using the new VARGRAPHIC column length. This also saves having to export the data from the old table, import the data into the new table, and recreate all the objects (such as indexes, views, and triggers) that were dependent on that table.

COMMAND HISTORY SUPPORT AND CLP ROUNDTRIP EDITING

DB2 UDB v8.1.2 adds support for command retention to CLP interactive mode. Command history support is implemented through two new commands: HISTORY and RUNCMD.

The HISTORY command displays the 20 most recent commands in the command history list, along with numbers that represent the order in which the commands were run.

The RUNCMD command runs the command corresponding to a specified number in the command history list. If you do not specify a command number, the most recent command runs.

A new DB2 interactive CLP command called EDIT, which invokes the operating system's native integrated editor, allows you to edit a previously run DB2 command, and then to run the edited command. You can specify the number of a command in the command history list. If you do not specify a command number, the most recently run command is loaded into the editor. When you exit the editor and save your changes, the command is updated at the CLP interactive prompt, and you have the option of running it immediately.

The size of the command history list can be controlled using the DB2_CLPHISTSIZE registry variable, which accepts values between 1 and 500 inclusive.

The command history is not persistent, and is lost when a CLP session ends. If you start two separate interactive CLP sessions, each session maintains its own command history.

Development

- SQL Enhancements
- Application Development Enhancements
- DB2 in the Microsoft Environment

SQL Enhancements

The standard language of relational database access is Structured Query Language (SQL). In this chapter we examine the new enhancements to DB2's implementation of SQL.

SQL INSERT THROUGH UNION ALL

Views with tables connected through the use of UNION ALL have been supported for a number of releases. SELECT, DELETE, and UPDATE operators have been allowed as long as DB2 could determine the table to which the corresponding command was applied.

In DB2, support for the INSERT operator has been extended to views with UNION ALL, as long as the following conditions hold:

- The expressions have the same data types.
- A constraint exists on at least one column that can be used to uniquely identify where a row should be inserted and the constraint ranges are nonoverlapping.
- Views defined in this fashion also support UPDATE operations as long as the column being changed does not violate the constraint for that column. In this case, the user must first DELETE and then INSERT the record.

The following examples demonstrate this concept.

Consider four tables that have been created to represent the sales for each quarter of the year. The tables all have the same definition, as shown here.

```
CREATE TABLE Q1SALES
  (
  store    int    not null,
  tx_date  date   not null,
  item     int    not null,
  quantity int    not null
  );
CREATE TABLE Q2SALES LIKE Q1SALES;
CREATE TABLE Q3SALES LIKE Q1SALES;
CREATE TABLE Q4SALES LIKE Q1SALES;
```

These tables can be UNIONed together to create a single view of the entire year as shown here:

```
CREATE VIEW ALLQ AS
  (
  SELECT * FROM Q1SALES
  UNION ALL
  SELECT * FROM Q2SALES
  UNION ALL
  SELECT * FROM Q3SALES
  UNION ALL
  SELECT * FROM Q4SALES
  )
```

Even though you can issue SELECT, UPDATE, and DELETE statements against this view, these statements will not be handled efficiently. For instance, consider the SELECT shown here:

```
SELECT * FROM ALLQ WHERE
  item = 142 AND
  tx_date between '2002-05-14' AND '2002-07-21'
```

When DB2 optimizes this statement, it has no information about where the data might reside in the four tables. A visual EXPLAIN of this SELECT shows the work that DB2 must do to satisfy this request (Figure 17.1).

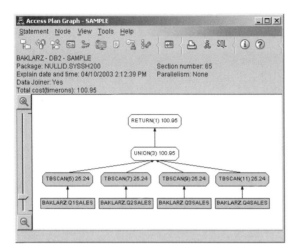

Figure 17.1
EXPLAIN statement of SELECT across UNION ALL.

To give DB2 better information on how to handle these rows, a check constraint needs to be added to the original table definition. This can be accomplished at either table creation time or through the use of the ALTER table statement. For the existing tables defined earlier, the ALTER table statement would be similar to that shown here:

```
ALTER TABLE Q1SALES
   ADD CONTRAINT Q1_DATES
CHECK (tx_date BETWEEN '2002-01-01' AND '2002-03-31');
```

Each table would have its own range of dates in the tx_date field. With this additional constraint added, the query is now executed using the explain plan shown in Figure 17.2.

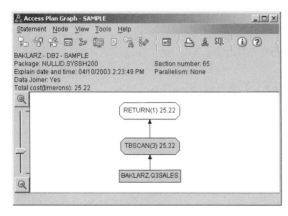

Figure 17.2
Explain plan after addition of check constraints.

Note how DB2 is able to eliminate two tables (Q1SALES and Q4SALES) from the access logic because the constraints tell DB2 that only Q2SALES and Q3SALES have the ranges of dates that we are interested in.

When a user issues an INSERT, DELETE, UPDATE, or SELECT against the ALLQ view, DB2 can use this new constraint information to direct the transaction to the proper table. This is especially important for queries where tables not appropriate to the query can be eliminated from the search. Note that for proper handling of this view, the check constraints (range) must not over-lap. In addition, modification to the column defined in the check constraint must not be updated outside the range. For instance, consider the UPDATE statements found here:

```
UPDATE ALLQ
   SET    STORE = 4
   WHERE STORE = 1;

UPDATE ALLQ
   SET    TX_DATE = '2002-02-26'
   WHERE TX_DATE = '2002-02-27';

UPDATE ALLQ
   SET    TX_DATE = '2002-04-01'
   WHERE TX_DATE = '2002-03-30';
```

The first update does not change any value in the check constraint, so it will run successfully. Note that because we don't define a date range, all tables will have store number 4 changed to store number 1.

The second update runs successfully because we have changed a date from the 27th to the 26th and the date is still within the check constraint (2002-01-01 to 2002-03-31).

The last update will not complete successfully due to the updated value being outside the check constraint range. To update this record, the user must first delete the record and then insert it. This restriction will probably be removed from DB2 in some future release.

USING TABLE SPACES WITH UNION ALL

A UNION ALL in a view can be used to circumvent some restrictions in DB2 and allow for more flexible maintenance in time-series data.

Tables in DB2 can only occupy 64 GB of storage if a 4 K data page is specified. Increasing the page size to 8 K, 16 K, or 32 K can result in larger table sizes, but the restriction of 255 rows per page could still limit the amount of data that you can store.

A user could overcome this space limitation by breaking a table into smaller units and placing each of these units into a separate table space. Consider the quarterly sales data tables found earlier, where each table was placed into the default table space. This design limited all tables to a limit of 64 GB of data. Instead of using the default table space for these tables, the user could create a separate table space for each individual table, as shown here:

```
CREATE REGULAR TABLESPACE Q1_2002
   PAGESIZE 4 K MANAGED BY SYSTEM
   USING('Q1_2002') EXTENTSIZE 2;
CREATE REGULAR TABLESPACE Q2_2002
   PAGESIZE 4 K MANAGED BY SYSTEM
   USING('Q2_2002') EXTENTSIZE 2;
CREATE REGULAR TABLESPACE Q3_2002
   PAGESIZE 4 K MANAGED BY SYSTEM
   USING('Q3_2002') EXTENTSIZE 2;
CREATE REGULAR TABLESPACE Q4_2002
   PAGESIZE 4 K MANAGED BY SYSTEM
   USING('Q4_2002') EXTENTSIZE 2;
```

Once these table spaces have been created, each table can be placed into its own table space. Only one table definition is shown here:

```
CREATE TABLE Q1SALES
   (
   store    int    not null,
   tx_date  date   not null,
   item     int    not null,
   quantity int    not null
   ) in Q1_2002;
```

At this point, each quarterly sales table can take up to 64 GB of space using a 4 K page size. All transactions against this view, including INSERTs, are directed to the appropriate table. Applications could still be written that directed their transactions to the appropriate quarterly sales table, but the view makes the handling of queries much easier. In addition, by designing the view as a UNION ALL of four separate tables, it is possible for the user to load new data into the database without impacting current workloads and then making the new data "live" with a minimum of administration.

If data is continually being refreshed on a monthly or quarterly basis, a user could create a separate table and table space and load the information into that table first. When the load is complete, then only a few commands need to be issued to make this data available to all users. In the case of the quarterly updated data, assume that a new set of data comes in for the first quarter of 2003 and you want to include it as part of the four quarters of information, replacing the first quarter of 2002. A new table for the first quarter of 2003 has to be created that mimics the same table design as the prior four quarters of information, as given here:

```
CREATE REGULAR TABLESPACE Q1_2003
  PAGESIZE 4 K MANAGED BY SYSTEM
  USING('Q1_2003') EXTENTSIZE 2;

CREATE TABLE Q1SALES_2003
  (
  STORE    INT    NOT NULL,
  TX_DATE  DATE   NOT NULL,
  ITEM     INT    NOT NULL,
  QUANTITY INT    NOT NULL
  ) IN Q1_2003;
```

We need to change the name of the table because Q1SALES already exists in our database. Once the table is loaded with data from Quarter 1, the existing Q1SALES table needs to be dropped and the view re-created to include the new Q1SALES_2003 table, as shown here:

```
DROP TABLESPACE Q1_2002;
CREATE VIEW ALLQ AS
  (
  SELECT * FROM Q1SALES_2003
  UNION ALL
  SELECT * FROM Q2SALES
  UNION ALL
  SELECT * FROM Q3SALES
  UNION ALL
  SELECT * FROM Q4SALES
  )
```

When a DROP statement is issued against a table space, typically no logging occurs. This means that a user can eliminate these rows from the database without the overhead associated with logging row deletes. An added benefit of separating the tables is the ability to manage loads and other activities on this new quarterly information without affecting production data.

There are some maintenance issues that a user must be aware of when separating tables into different table spaces. Although select processing can be relatively efficient, INSERT statements running against these tables require some additional overhead to determine which base table the transaction needs to be directed to. This might only amount to a few milliseconds of additional optimization time, but this could make a difference on a heavily loaded system. Finally, DB2 does not recognize the relationship between the tables that make up the view from a recovery perspective. Normal logging and transaction rollbacks are handled the same as any other SQL statement. However, the table spaces that make up the various tables need to be backed up at the same time (if doing individual table space backups) so that they are recovered as one complete unit. If the table spaces are not recovered based on the same unit, transactions across the tables might not be synchronized.

INSTEAD OF TRIGGERS

In many installations, views are used as a way of limiting access to base tables. With a view, a DBA can restrict both the columns and sets of rows that a user can access. However, the use of views causes some difficulties when data modification commands need to be applied to rows in the base table. For instance, a user might have created a customer reference table with the following definition:

```
CREATE TABLE CUSTOMERS
  (
  CUSTNO       INT          NOT NULL,
  CUSTNAME     VARCHAR(20)  NOT NULL,
  PHONE        CHAR(12)     NOT NULL,
  CREDIT_CARD VARCHAR(20)   FOR BIT DATA NOT NULL,
  YTD_SALES    DECIMAL(15,2) NOT NULL
  )
```

This table needs to be made available to a variety of people in the company, including salespeople, the order desk, customer service, and accounts receivable. However, some of this information is not relevant to all users, and from a security perspective you might not want all users to see everything in the table. A possible solution is to create a view for each group of users. The customer service staff might have the following view defined for them:

```
CREATE VIEW CUSTOMER_SERVICE AS
  (
  SELECT CUSTNO, CUSTNAME, PHONE, CREDIT_CARD
  FROM CUSTOMERS
  )
```

Now the customer service staff can select from this table and retrieve all of the contact information without seeing the yearly sales numbers. Although this fixes the security problem, it raises new issues when the service staff has to add new records. Based on their knowledge of the view that they have access to (CUSTOMER_SERVICE), adding a new customer to their table would look like this:

```
INSERT INTO CUSTOMER_SERVICE VALUES
  (1234, 'ZIKOPOULOS CARWASH','887-555-1212','3922 1111 2222');
```

Unfortunately, DB2 returns the error message shown next because this insert violates a constraint on the base table. In this case, the YTD_SALES column is not included as part of the INSERT statement and it must be supplied according to the original table definition (NOT NULL):

```
SQL0407N  Assignment of a NULL value to a NOT NULL column "TBSPACEID=5,
TABLEID=61, COLNO=4" is not allowed.  SQLSTATE=23502
```

To get around this problem, the DBA can take one of the following measures:

- Create a better database design to avoid this error
- Allow NULL values in the YTD_SALES field or set the default to zero
- Create an INSTEAD OF trigger

You can argue that the database should be redesigned to avoid this problem, but if we are forced to use the current table definitions, an INSTEAD OF trigger can help solve the problem.

An INSTEAD OF trigger is used only on views, not base tables. It has characteristics similar to a normal trigger except for the following restrictions:

- Only allowed on views
- Always FOR EACH ROW
- DEFAULT values get passed as NULL
- Cannot use positioned UPDATE/DELETE on cursor over view with INSTEAD OF UPDATE/DELETE trigger

For the CUSTOMER_SERVICE view, we can create an INSTEAD OF trigger to handle the missing field during an INSERT operation:

```
CREATE TRIGGER I_CUSTOMER_SERVICE
  INSTEAD OF INSERT ON CUSTOMER_SERVICE
  REFERENCING NEW AS CUST
  FOR EACH ROW MODE DB2SQL
BEGIN ATOMIC
  INSERT INTO CUSTOMERS VALUES (
    CUST.CUSTNO,
    CUST.CUSTNAME,
    CUST.PHONE,
    CUST.CREDIT_CARD,
    0);
END
```

When an INSERT is executed against this view, DB2 invokes this INSTEAD OF trigger and the record is successfully inserted into the table. Although this is a trivial example, the INSTEAD OF trigger can be used for a variety of purposes, including encrypting and decrypting fields in the table. For instance, the credit card information in this table could be encrypted for security reasons. If we decide to use a fixed password for the encryption and decryption, we can create the following view to select decrypted credit card values:

```
CREATE VIEW CUSTOMER_SERVICE AS
  (
  SELECT CUSTNO, CUSTNAME, PHONE,
    DECRYPT_CHAR(CREDIT_CARD,'SECRET') AS CREDIT_CARD
```

```
      FROM CUSTOMERS
   )
```

The INSTEAD OF trigger also needs to be modified to encrypt the values and insert the zero sales for the year, as shown here:

```
CREATE TRIGGER I_CUSTOMER_SERVICE
   INSTEAD OF INSERT ON CUSTOMER_SERVICE
   REFERENCING NEW AS CUST
   DEFAULTS NULL
   FOR EACH ROW MODE DB2SQL
BEGIN ATOMIC
   INSERT INTO CUSTOMERS VALUES (
      CUST.CUSTNO,
      CUST.CUSTNAME,
      CUST.PHONE,
      ENCRYPT(CUST.CREDIT_CARD,'SECRET'),
      0);
END
```

When a user does a select from the CUSTOMER_SERVICE table, he or she would see the following results:

```
SELECT * FROM CUSTOMER_SERVICE;
CUSTNO        CUSTNAME              PHONE         CREDIT_CARD
----------- --------------------- ------------ -----------------------
      1234 ZIKOPOULOS CARWASH   887-555-1212 3922 1111 2222

   1 record(s) selected.
```

Note what happens if another user selected from the base table instead:

```
CUSTNO   CUSTNAME              PHONE         CREDIT_CARD
-------- --------------------- ------------ ----------------------------
    1234 ZIKOPOULOS CARWASH    887-555-1212 '08B749FFE404A5D553755D1C...'

   1 record(s) selected.
```

Because the decryption is not occurring on the base table, any other user accessing this field will not see the results.

In summary, the INSTEAD OF trigger can give you greater flexibility in the use of views and allow you to handle situations with INSERTs, UPDATEs, and DELETEs that DB2 cannot handle on its own.

ORDER BY ENHANCEMENTS

The results from an SQL statement are retrieved in an undetermined order if no ORDER BY clause is specified in SQL. The ORDER BY clause specifies an ordering of the rows of a result table. Normally this ordering is based on a series of columns and the entire answer set is sorted.

Two additional features have been added to the ORDER BY clause to give the user more flexibility in how the sort is done and how many records should be returned by the sort.

FETCH FIRST Clause

The result set from a SELECT can be limited through the use of the FETCH FIRST ... ROWS clause. This same clause can be applied to an ORDER BY clause to reduce the size of the sorted result table. A good example would be a query that retrieves the top five marks in an exam.

To limit the number of rows sorted in a select, the FETCH FIRST ... ROWS must be added to the end of the ORDER BY, as shown here:

```
SELECT EMPNO, LASTNAME, WORKDEPT FROM EMPLOYEE
  ORDER BY EMPNO DESC FETCH FIRST 5 ROWS ONLY
```

The result table from this SQL statement is shown here:

```
EMPNO   LASTNAME          WORKDEPT
------  ----------------  --------
000340  GOUNOT            E21
000330  LEE               E21
000320  MEHTA             E21
000310  SETRIGHT          E11
000300  SMITH             E11


  5 record(s) selected.
```

ORDER BY ORDER OF

The ORDER BY ORDER OF clause specifies that the ordering used in a prior table designator should be applied to the result table of the subselect. The following select statement illustrates how this is used:

```
SELECT E.EMPNO, E.LASTNAME, PAY FROM EMPLOYEE E,
   (SELECT EMPNO, SALARY+BONUS AS PAY FROM EMPLOYEE
    WHERE (SALARY+BONUS)>40000
    ORDER BY PAY DESC) AS TOTAL_PAY
WHERE
   E.EMPNO = TOTAL_PAY.EMPNO
ORDER BY ORDER OF TOTAL_PAY;
```

The SELECT statement specifies four columns that are to be returned in the answer set: employee number, last name, pay, and the total pay column as a combination of pay and bonus columns. This subselect within the select list further restricts the records to only those employees who make more than $40,000 in total pay.

The WHERE clause restricts the employee records to those that meet the minimum total pay as defined in the subselect.

Finally, the ORDER BY ORDER OF statement tells DB2 to sort the result set in the same order as that returned in the subselect. The results from this statement are shown here:

```
EMPNO   LASTNAME          PAY
------  ----------------  ------------
000010  HAAS                 53750.00
000110  LUCCHESSI            47400.00
000020  THOMPSON             42050.00
000050  GEYER                40975.00

   4 record(s) selected.
```

Changing the sort order of the subselect to ORDER BY PAY ASC results in the following answer:

```
EMPNO   LASTNAME          PAY
------  ----------------  ------------
000050  GEYER                40975.00
000020  THOMPSON             42050.00
000110  LUCCHESSI            47400.00
000010  HAAS                 53750.00

   4 record(s) selected.
```

FETCH FIRST

The FETCH FIRST clause is used to limit the amount of output returned from a SELECT statement, or from an ORDER BY clause. This can result in much faster processing when the application must retrieve only a few records instead of the entire answer set.

The FETCH FIRST clause can also be used within subselects to allow for proper equality tests. For instance, the following SQL is attempting to select all employees whose last name starts with S:

```
SELECT EMPNO, FIRSTNME, LASTNAME FROM EMPLOYEE
  WHERE
     EMPNO = (SELECT EMPNO FROM EMPLOYEE WHERE LASTNAME LIKE 'S%' )

SQL0811N  The result of a scalar fullselect, SELECT INTO statement, or VALUES
INTO statement is more than one row.  SQLSTATE=21000
```

This SELECT statement cannot run because of the SQL restriction that only one value can be compared with the equal sign. The subselect has returned more than one value, so to avoid this problem, you can use the FETCH FIRST ROW ONLY clause to force only one row to be returned:

```
SELECT EMPNO, FIRSTNME, LASTNAME FROM EMPLOYEE
   WHERE
      EMPNO = (SELECT EMPNO FROM EMPLOYEE WHERE LASTNAME LIKE 'S%'
                  FETCH FIRST ROW ONLY);


EMPNO   FIRSTNME      LASTNAME
------  ------------  ----------------
000060  IRVING        STERN

   1 record(s) selected.
```

SQL FUNCTIONS

DB2 contains a large number of built-in column and scalar functions that can add flexibility to the type of calculations you can perform against the data. These functions can be broken down into the following categories:

- Trigonometric functions (COS, SIN, TAN, COT, TANH, COSH, SINH, ATAH, ATAN2)
- Math functions (INTEGER, FLOOR, CEILING, TRUNC, SQRT, LN, EXP)
- String functions (RTRIM, LTRIM, INSTR, TRANSLATE, REPEAT, REPLACE, CONCAT, SUBSTR, LENGTH, LOWER, UPPER)
- Statistical functions (CORRELATION, STDDEV, VARIANCE)
- Date functions (DATE, TIME, TO_CHAR, TO_DATE, DAYNAME, DAYOFWEEK)
- Logic functions (COALESCE, NULLIF)
- Specialty functions (MQPUBLISH, MQREAD, ENCRYPT, REC2XML)

There are many more functions available within DB2 that you can use. For a complete listing of available functions, refer to the *DB2 UDB v8.1 SQL Reference*. Some specific functions that have been introduced in DB2 UDB v8.1 are described next.

VARCHAR_FORMAT and TIMESTAMP_FORMAT

The DB2 family has been extending SQL in an effort to ease the migration or conversion of applications coded for competitive databases to the DB2 family. There are two new built-in functions, VARCHAR_FORMAT and TIMESTAMP_FORMAT, to support conversion capability provided by other vendors' formatting functions.

These formatting options are in the form of templates that tell the function what the input looks like (TIMESTAMP_FORMAT) or what the output should look like (VARCHAR_FORMAT). The DB2 functions currently only support one format pattern.

The syntax of the TIMESTAMP_FORMAT function is shown here:

```
TIMESTAMP_FORMAT (string-expression, format-string)
```

TIMESTAMP_FORMAT returns a timestamp from a character string that has been interpreted using format-string. String-expression is a character representation of a timestamp. Format-string must be the constant character string YYYY-MM-DD HH24:MI:SS. An example of this function is shown here:

```
VALUES TO_DATE('2002-02-28 23:30:23', 'YYYY-MM-DD HH24:MI:SS');
```

TO_DATE can be specified as a synonym for TIMESTAMP_FORMAT.

The syntax of the VARCHAR_FORMAT function is the following:

```
VARCHAR_FORMAT (timestamp-expression, format-string)
```

VARCHAR_FORMAT returns a character representation of a timestamp. The returned character string is formatted according to the format-string. Format-string must be the constant character string YYYY-MM-DD HH24:MI:SS. An example of this function is shown here:

```
VALUES TO_CHAR(CURRENT TIMESTAMP, 'YYYY-MM-DD HH24:MI:SS');
'2002-02-28 23:30:23'
```

TO_CHAR can be specified as a synonym for VARCHAR_FORMAT.

If you needs to do additional formatting on a date value, you can take advantage of user-defined functions (UDFs) and build your own function. The following UDF converts a date field into the format MM-DD-YYYY:

```
CREATE FUNCTION FORMAT_DATE(DATE_IN DATE) RETURNS VARCHAR(10)
   LANGUAGE SQL READS SQL DATA
   BEGIN ATOMIC
      DECLARE C_MM   VARCHAR(2);
      DECLARE C_DD   VARCHAR(2);
      DECLARE C_YYYY VARCHAR(4);
      DECLARE C_DATE VARCHAR(10);

      SET C_DATE = VARCHAR(DATE_IN);
      SET C_MM   = SUBSTR(C_DATE,6,2);
      SET C_DD   = SUBSTR(C_DATE,9,2);
      SET C_YYYY = SUBSTR(C_DATE,1,4);
      RETURN(C_MM || '-' || C_DD || '-' || C_YYYY);
   END
```

XML Publishing

DB2 has provided support for XML structures for a number of releases. These functions allow a developer to store and retrieve XML information from a DB2 database. Within SQL, a number of XML functions are supported that allow for formatting of the data in an XML format. These functions are described in Table 17.1.

Table 17.1 XML Functions

Function	Purpose
XML2CLOB	The XML2CLOB function returns the argument as a CLOB value. The argument must be an expression of data type XML. The result has the CLOB data type.
XMLAGG	The XMLAGG function returns the concatenation of a set of XML data. If the XMLAGG function is applied to an empty set, the result is a null value. Otherwise, the result is the concatenation of the values in the set.
XMLELEMENT	Constructs an XML element from the arguments. This function takes an element name, an optional collection of attributes, and zero or more arguments that make up the element's content. The result data type is XML.
XMLATTRIBUTES	XMLATTRIBUTES constructs an XML element from the arguments. This function takes an element name, an optional collection of attributes, and zero or more arguments that make up the element's content. The result data type is XML.
REC2XML	The REC2XML function returns a string formatted with XML tags and containing column names and column data.
COLATTVAL COLATTVAL_XML	This is a format value for the REC2XML function that returns a string with columns as attribute values.

In addition to these built-in functions, there is an XML Extender available that can extend DB2's ability to deal with XML objects. For more information on the XML Extender, see the *DB2 Universal Database XML Extender Administration and Programming Reference*. These XML functions are also described in detail in the *DB2 UDB v8.1 SQL Reference*.

The following example shows how the REC2XML function can be used to return data in an XML format for either browsing on the Web or for sending to another application that can interpret this information. The following example shows the standard output that would be retrieved by using a SELECT statement:

```
SELECT EMPNO, FIRSTNME, LASTNAME, WORKDEPT FROM EMPLOYEE
    WHERE WORKDEPT = 'E11'

EMPNO   FIRSTNME      LASTNAME          WORKDEPT
------  ------------  ----------------  --------
000090  EILEEN        HENDERSON         E11
000280  ETHEL         SCHNEIDER         E11
000290  JOHN          PARKER            E11
```

```
000300 PHILIP        SMITH           E11
000310 MAUDE         SETRIGHT        E11
```

To format this information in an XML format, the REC2XML (or XML2CLOB) functions can be used to extract information. The following SQL is used to generate an XML record for each row in the table:

```
SELECT REC2XML (1.0,'COLATTVAL','EMPLOYEE',
        EMPNO,FIRSTNME,LASTNAME,WORKDEPT)
FROM EMPLOYEE
        WHERE WORKDEPT='C01'

<EMPLOYEE>
  <column name="EMPNO">000030</column>
  <column name="FIRSTNME">SALLY</column>
  <column name="LASTNAME">KWAN</column>
  <column name="WORKDEPT">C01</column>
</EMPLOYEE>
<EMPLOYEE>
  <column name="EMPNO">000130</column>
  <column name="FIRSTNME">DOLORES</column>
  <column name="LASTNAME">QUINTANA</column>
  <column name="WORKDEPT">C01</column>
</EMPLOYEE>
<EMPLOYEE>
  <column name="EMPNO">000140</column>
  <column name="FIRSTNME">HEATHER</column>
  <column name="LASTNAME">NICHOLLS</column>
  <column name="WORKDEPT">C01</column>
</EMPLOYEE>
```

This is an extremely simple example, but it shows some of the power of using XML functions within DB2. The other XML functions give you more control over the formatting and output of the records. The REC2XML function simplifies the creation of XML output, but doesn't have as much flexibility as the other XML functions. Note that the XML functions are considered part of the SELECT statements and are not shown as scalar or column functions.

Snapshot API

DB2 has a number of table functions that return data on internal objects that are normally only accessible via an API call. The advantage of using SQL to retrieve this information is that scripts can be written to extract this information rather than writing C++ programs to do the same thing. In addition, Java developers can also take advantage of these SQL calls rather than having to link C routines into their applications.

These snapshot functions return information on a variety of objects within DB2 (see Table 17.2).

Table 17.2 Snapshot Functions

Function	Purpose
SNAPSHOT_AGENT	The SNAPSHOT_AGENT function returns information about agents from an application snapshot.
SNAPSHOT_APPL	The SNAPSHOT_APPL function returns general information from an application snapshot.
SNAPSHOT_APPL_INFO	The SNAPSHOT_APPL_INFO function returns general information from an application snapshot.
SNAPSHOT_BP	The SNAPSHOT_BP function returns information from a buffer pool snapshot.
SNAPSHOT_CONTAINER	The SNAPSHOT_CONTAINER function returns container configuration information from a table space snapshot.
SNAPSHOT_DATABASE	The SNAPSHOT_DATABASE function returns information from a database snapshot.
SNAPSHOT_DBM	The SNAPSHOT_DBM function returns information from a snapshot of the DB2 database manager.
SNAPSHOT_DYN_SQL	The SNAPSHOT_DYN_SQL function returns information from a dynamic SQL snapshot. It replaces the SQLCACHE_SNAPSHOT function, which is still available for compatibility reasons.
SNAPSHOT_FCM	The SNAPSHOT_FCM function returns database manager level information regarding the fast communication manager (FCM).
SNAPSHOT_FCMPARTITION	The SNAPSHOT_FCMPARTITION function returns information from a snapshot of the FCM in the database manager.
SNAPSHOT_LOCK	The SNAPSHOT_LOCK function returns information from a lock snapshot.
SNAPSHOT_LOCKWAIT	The SNAPSHOT_LOCKWAIT function returns lock wait information from an application snapshot.
SNAPSHOT_QUIESCERS	The SNAPSHOT_QUIESCERS function returns information about agents that are trying to quiesce the database.
SNAPSHOT_RANGES	The SNAPSHOT_RANGES function returns information from a range snapshot.
SNAPSHOT_STATEMENT	The SNAPSHOT_STATEMENT function returns information about statements from an application snapshot.
SNAPSHOT_SUBSECT	The SNAPSHOT_SUBSECT function returns information about subsections of access plans from an application snapshot.

Table 17.2 Snapshot Functions (Continued)

Function	Purpose
SNAPSHOT_SWITCHES	The SNAPSHOT_SWITCHES function returns information about the database snapshot switch state.
SNAPSHOT_TABLE	The SNAPSHOT_TABLE function returns activity information from a table snapshot.
SNAPSHOT_TBS	The SNAPSHOT_TBS function returns activity information from a table space snapshot.
SNAPSHOT_TBS_CFG	The SNAPSHOT_TBS_CFG function returns configuration information from a table space snapshot.
SQLCACHE_SNAPSHOT	The SQLCACHE_SNAPSHOT function returns the results of a snapshot of the DB2 dynamic SQL statement cache.

The general form of a snapshot function is shown here:

```
SELECT *
  FROM TABLE(SNAPSHOT_FUNCTION(database, partition)) AS S;
```

The SNAPSHOT_FUNCTION is replaced with the appropriate snapshot command, and the DATA-BASE field contains the name of the database you want the snapshot to be taken against. The partition should be set to –1 to return information for the current partition and –2 for all partitions. If this field is not included or set to null, the command only works against the current partition.

A DBA can use these commands to monitor the status of various objects within DB2 from within a script. For instance, the following SQL retrieves information on all table spaces in the SAMPLE database:

```
SELECT TABLESPACE_ID, TABLESPACE_NAME, TOTAL_PAGES
  FROM TABLE(SNAPSHOT_CONTAINER('SAMPLE',-2)) AS S;


TABLESPACE_ID TABLESPACE_NAME                    TOTAL_PAGES
------------- ---------------------------------- -----------
            0 SYSCATSPACE                               3644
            1 TEMPSPACE1                                   1
            2 USERSPACE1                                4150
            3 DB2DEMO                                      1
            4 TEMPSESSION                                  1
            5 MDC                                        458
            6 ORVRTS                                     108
            8 Q2_2001                                     22
```

```
        9 Q3_2001                                       23
       10 Q1_2002                                        2
       11 Q4_2001                                       22


   11 record(s) selected.
```

Health Snaphots

In DB2 UDB v8.1, DB2 provided access to health snapshot data via DB2 C APIs and the DB2 CLP. Although this is useful, some high level programming languages cannot leverage these APIs directly. These languages can use SQL, so DB2 also provides an SQL interface into this data via a UDF that is callable from the SQL API.

This new feature is an extension of the GET HEALTH SNAPSHOT monitor data. DB2 introduces 12 new UDFs that can be used to retrieve health snapshot information for the database manager, database, table spaces, and containers.

The implemented UDFs call the db2GetSnapshot() API. These UDFs can be used in a partitioned environment as well as using the *partition* input parameter. The UDF converts the self-defining data stream returned from the API into a virtual table for SQL manipulation.

For each tracked group (database manager, database, table spaces, and containers) there are three categories of UDFs: INFO, HI (Health Indicator), and HI_HIS (Health Indicator HIStory). As a general rule of thumb:

- INFO captures the global information for the specific logical group (e.g., the server instance name for the database manager).
- HI UDF contains the latest health indicator information.
- HI_HIS UDF contains the health indicator history information.

You can use this UDF as follows:

```
select *|<columnname>[,<columnname>] from
   table( <udfname>( [<database>,] <partition> )) as <aliasname>
```

The <partition> field has the following values:

- 1..n—Partition number
- –1—Currently connected partition
- –2—All partitions

The current supported functions are listed in Table 17.3.

Table 17.3 Health Snapshot Functions

Function	Purpose
HEALTH_DBM_INFO	Returns information from a health snapshot of the DB2 database manager.
HEALTH_DBM_HI	Returns health indicator information from a health snapshot of the DB2 database manager.
HEALTH_DBM_HI_HIS	Returns health indicator history information from a health snapshot of the DB2 database manager.
HEALTH_DB_INFO	Returns information from a health snapshot of a database.
HEALTH_DB_HI	Returns health indicator information from a health snapshot of a database.
HEALTH_DB_HI_HIS	Returns health indicator history information from a health snapshot of a database.
HEALTH_TBS_INFO	Returns table space information from a health snapshot of a database.
HEALTH_TBS_HI	Returns health indicator information for table spaces from a health snapshot of a database.
HEALTH_TBS_HI_HIS	Returns health indicator history information for table spaces from a health snapshot of a database.
HEALTH_CONT_INFO	Returns container information from a health snapshot of a database.
HEALTH_CONT_HI	Returns health indicator information for containers from a health snapshot of a database.
HEALTH_CONT_HI_HIS	Returns health indicator history information for containers from a health snapshot of a database.

The following SQL statement retrieves health information about the status of the SAMPLE database:

```
SELECT SNAPSHOT_TIMESTAMP,
       DB_NAME,
       ROLLED_UP_ALERT_STATE_DETAIL
FROM TABLE(HEALTH_DB_INFO('SAMPLE',-2)) AS S;

SNAPSHOT_TIMESTAMP         DB_NAME  ROLLED_UP_ALERT_STATE_DETAIL
-------------------------- -------- ----------------------------
2003-04-24-14.31.35.488293 SAMPLE   Normal

  1 record(s) selected.
```

A DBA can use these health center snapshots to write scripts that check on the status of databases and send appropriate alerts or invoke corrective actions. This type of functionality is also available in the Health Center, but the ability to get information through SQL gives the user more flexibility in retrieving the information.

IDENTITY COLUMN SUPPORT

Many applications require the use of numbers to track invoices, customers, and other objects that get incremented by one whenever a new item is created. In database applications, usually a single column within a table represents a unique identifier for that row and that identifier gets sequentially updated as new records are added. DB2 has two different techniques for updating values in a table. These techniques are discussed in the sections that follow.

Identity Column

DB2 can auto-increment values in a table through the use of identity columns during record insertion. The following example demonstrates a table definition with the EMP_NO column automatically generated:

```
CREATE TABLE EMPLOYEE (
  EMPNO  INT GENERATED ALWAYS AS IDENTITY,
  NAME CHAR(10));

INSERT INTO EMPLOYEE(NAME) VALUES 'Roman','Dirk';

SELECT * FROM EMPLOYEE;

EMPNO        NAME
----------- ----------
          1 Roman
          2 Dirk
```

If the column is defined with GENERATED ALWAYS, then the INSERT statement cannot specify a value for the EMPNO field. By default, the numbering starts at 1 and increments by 1. The range and increment can be specified as part of the column definition, as shown here:

```
CREATE TABLE EMPLOYEE (
  EMPNO  INT GENERATED ALWAYS AS
    IDENTITY(START WITH 100, INCREMENT BY 10)),
  NAME CHAR(10));

INSERT INTO EMPLOYEE(NAME) VALUES 'Roman','Dirk';

SELECT * FROM EMPLOYEE;
```

```
EMPNO          NAME
----------- ----------
        100  Roman
        110  Dirk
```

In addition, the default value can be GENERATED BY DEFAULT, which means that the user has the option of supplying a value for the field. If no value is supplied (indicated by the DEFAULT keyword), DB2 generates the next number in sequence.

By using the IDENTITY clause's CACHE keyword, you can decide how many numbers should be pregenerated by DB2. This can help reduce catalog contention because DB2 caches the specified quantity of numbers in memory rather than go back to the catalog tables to determine which number to generate next.

Identity columns are restricted to numeric values (integer or decimal) and can only be used in one column in the table. The GENERATE keyword can be used for other columns, but they cannot be IDENTITY columns.

The GENERATE keyword can be applied to other columns to generate values automatically. For instance, the EMPLOYEE table could include two columns that are components of the individual's pay, as shown here:

```
CREATE TABLE EMPLOYEE (
   EMPNO   INT GENERATED ALWAYS AS IDENTITY,
   NAME    CHAR(10),
   SALARY  INT,
   BONUS   INT,
   PAY     INT GENERATED ALWAYS AS (SALARY+BONUS)
   );
INSERT INTO EMPLOYEE(NAME, SALARY, BONUS) VALUES
   ('Roman',20000,2000),
   ('Dirk',30000,5000);

SELECT * FROM EMPLOYEE;

EMPNO          NAME          SALARY        BONUS         PAY
----------- ----------- ----------- ----------- ----------
          1  Roman           20000          2000        22000
          2  Dirk            30000          5000        35000
```

EMPNO is generated as an IDENTITY column, and PAY is calculated automatically by DB2. If the SALARY or BONUS columns are modified at a later time, DB2 recalculates the PAY. A GENERATED column has the same options as an IDENTITY column. The value can be either calculated ALWAYS or generated by DEFAULT.

Sequences

The use of the identity column works well for individual tables, but it might not be the most convenient way of generating unique values that need to be used across multiple tables.

The SEQUENCE object in DB2 lets the DBA or developer create a value that gets incremented under programmer control and can be used across many different tables. The following shows a sample sequence number being created for customer numbers using a data type of INTEGER:

```
CREATE SEQUENCE CUSTOMER_NO AS INTEGER
```

By default this sequence number starts at 1, increments by 1 at a time, and is of an INTEGER data type. The application needs to get the next value in the sequence by using the NEXTVAL function. This function generates the next value for the sequence, which can then be used for subsequent SQL statements:

```
VALUES NEXTVAL FOR CUSTOMER_NO
```

Instead of generating the next number with the VALUES function, the programmer could have used this function within an INSERT statement. For instance, if the first column of the customer table contained the customer number, an INSERT statement could be written as follows:

```
INSERT INTO CUSTOMERS VALUE
   (NEXTVAL FOR CUSTOMER_NO, 'Berts House of Moving', ...)
```

If the sequence number needs to be used for inserts into other tables, the PREVVAL function can be used to retrieve the previously generated value. For instance, if the customer number we just created needs to be used for a subsequent invoice record, the SQL would include the PREVVAL function shown here:

```
INSERT INTO INVOICES
   (34,PREVVAL FOR CUSTOMER_NO, 234.44, ...)
```

The PREVVAL function can be used multiple times within the application and it only returns the last value generated by that application. Subsequent transactions might have already incremented the sequence to another value, but the user always sees the last number that they generated.

In addition to being simple to set up and create, the SEQUENCE object has a variety of additional options that allow the user more flexibility in generating the values:

- Use of different data types (SMALLINT, INTEGER, BIGINT, DECIMAL)
- Change starting values (START WITH)
- Change the sequence increment, including specifying increasing or decreasing values (INCREMENT BY)

- Set minimum and maximum values where the sequence would stop (MAXVALUE/ MINVALUE)
- Allow wrapping of values so that sequences can start over again (CYCLE/NO CYCLE)
- Allow caching of sequences to minimize catalog contention (CACHE/NO CACHE)

Even after the sequence has been generated, many of these values can be altered by the user. For instance, the DBA might want to set a different starting value depending on the day of the week.

The one option that a DBA should be aware of is the caching value. This value tells DB2 how many sequence values should be generated by the system before going back to the DB2 catalog to generate another set of sequences. The CACHE value is set to a value of 20 if the user does not specify it at creation time. DB2 automatically generates 20 sequential values in memory (1, 2, ..., 19) when it first starts up the database. Whenever a new sequence number is required, this memory cache of values is used to return the next value to the user. Once this cache of values is used up, DB2 generates the next 20 values (20, 21, ..., 39).

By implementing caching of sequence numbers in this manner, DB2 does not have to continually go to the catalog tables to get the next value. This reduces the overhead associated with retrieving sequence numbers, but it also leads to possible gaps in the sequences if a system failure occurs or if the system is shut down at the end of the day. For instance, if the DBA decided to set the sequence cache to 100, DB2 caches 100 values of these numbers and also sets the system catalog to show that the next sequence of values should begin at 200. In the event that the database is shut down, the next set of sequence numbers begins at 200. The numbers that were generated from 100 to 199 are lost from the set of sequences if they were not used. If gaps in generated values cannot be tolerated in the application, the DBA needs to set the caching value to NO CACHE at the expense of higher system overhead.

This caching problem is compounded in a partitioned DB2 environment. In this case, every database node in the DB2 system requires its own range of identity or sequence values. Only when a set of identity values are exhausted does the database node go back to the catalog node for the next set of values. However, when the database is shut down, the sequences and identities across all of the nodes are lost. This results in a much larger hole of values compared with a nonpartitioned DB2 environment. If the DBA chooses to eliminate caching, the possibility exists for high catalog node contention as each database node attempts to retrieve the next sequence or identity value. DBAs need to balance the need for reducing missing sequence numbers against the performance overhead of retrieving sequence values from the catalog node.

Additional IDENTITY Column Considerations

Although the IDENTITY column can simplify application design, developers should be aware that IDENTITY columns do not guarantee uniqueness of values. Identity values and sequences can run out of values or eventually wrap around and start over again. These starting values can also be changed by a DBA to other values, so the same numbers could get generated again.

For this reason, IDENTITY columns should be defined as primary or unique keys to ensure that duplicate values do not occur.

CALL STATEMENT

A stored procedure serves as an extension to clients and it is run on the database server. They can be invoked from a client application or another routine with a CALL statement. Stored procedures and their calling programs exchange data using parameters defined in the CREATE PROCEDURE statement. Stored procedures can also return result sets to their callers.

There are a variety of benefits of using a stored procedure:

- Enable multiple SQL statements to be issued by a single invocation from the caller, thus minimizing data transfer between the client and the database server. The more SQL statements you include in a stored procedure, the lower the data transfer costs for each individual statement, as compared to issuing the same statements from the client.
- Isolate database logic from application logic.
- Return multiple result sets.
- If invoked from an application, they behave as part of the application.

Once a stored procedure is written and registered with the database, you can invoke it by using the CALL statement. The CALL statement can pass parameters to the stored procedure and receive parameters returned from the stored procedure. Any result sets returned by the stored procedure can be processed once the stored procedure has finished running.

Although the function of the CALL statement did not change in DB2 UDB v8.1, its capabilities have been enhanced.

The CALL statement is now a fully compiled statement. This means that the CALL statement can now be dynamically prepared in CLI, ODBC, embedded SQL, JDBC, and SQLJ. Input arguments to a stored procedure call can be expressions. The syntax of the call statement is shown here:

```
>>-CALL--procedure-name--+--------------------------------+----------->< 
                         |        .-,--------------.       |
                         |        V                |       |
                         '-(----+-expression-+-+---)-'
                                '-NULL-------'
```

An example of calling a stored procedure from a command line interface is shown here:

```
db2 -td%
CREATE PROCEDURE P1(IN nv INT, IN arg1 VARCHAR(10), INOUT arg2 INT,
                    OUT result VARCHAR(40))
BEGIN
  SET result = CHAR(nv) || arg1 || CHAR(arg2);
```

```
  SET arg2 = arg2 + 1;
  RETURN 0;
END%
CALL P1(10, 'John' || ' DOE', 37, ?)%
```

MERGE SQL

One of the most common types of data maintenance applications written today involves the merging of data from a set of new transactions into an existing table. Logic used within these applications follows a set of logic similar to the following:

```
For each record in the transaction table
   Find the corresponding record in the base table
   If the record does not exist in the base table
     Insert this record into the base table (new record)
     Or Issue an error message that the record does not exist
   Else
     Update the existing record with the information from the transaction
   End if
End For
```

Some applications also include logic that would delete records from the existing table that are not found in the transaction table.

Rather than write an application in a conventional programming language, SQL includes the MERGE (or UPSERT) statement that mimics this functionality in a single SQL statement.

A simple example illustrates the power of the MERGE statement. Consider a retail store where a list of products, their description, and quantity are kept in a single table. The definition of this table is shown here:

```
CREATE TABLE PRODUCTS
  (
  PROD_NO      INT          NOT NULL,
  DESCRIPTION  VARCHAR(20),
  QUANTITY     INT          NOT NULL
  );
```

Every morning, stock is delivered to the store and a transaction table is created that includes all of the new merchandise that has been delivered to the store. This transaction table is identical to the PRODUCTS table defined here. SQL has a simple way of creating a table based on an existing table definition:

```
CREATE TABLE PRODUCT_TXS LIKE PRODUCTS;
```

The following MERGE statement takes the contents of the transaction table and updates the existing product table:

```
[1] MERGE INTO PRODUCTS PR
[2]   USING (SELECT PROD_NO, DESCRIPTION, QUANTITY FROM PRODUCT_TXS) TX
[3]         ON (PR.PROD_NO = TX.PROD_NO)
[4]   WHEN MATCHED THEN
[5]       UPDATE SET
[6]             PR.QUANTITY = PR.QUANTITY + TX.QUANTITY
[7]   WHEN NOT MATCHED THEN
[8]       INSERT (PROD_NO, DESCRIPTION, QUANTITY)
[9]             VALUES (TX.PROD_NO, TX.DESCRIPTION, TX.QUANTITY);
```

The original table contains the following rows:

PROD_NO	DESCRIPTION	QUANTITY
1	Pants	10
2	Shorts	5
3	Shirts	20
4	Socks	12
5	Ties	5

In addition, the PRODUCT_TXS (transaction) table contains the following data:

PROD_NO	DESCRIPTION	QUANTITY
1	Pants	15
3	Shirts	30
6	Shoes	5
7	Belts	10

After the MERGE command has run, the PRODUCT table contains the following rows:

PROD_NO	DESCRIPTION	QUANTITY
1	Pants	25
2	Shorts	5
3	Shirts	50
4	Socks	12
5	Ties	5
6	Shoes	5
7	Belts	10

The number of pants and shirts available has increased by the quantity found in the transaction table, and two new entries have been added for shoes and belts.

MERGE Syntax

A closer inspection of the MERGE statement illustrates how it operates against the PRODUCT table. The previous example of the MERGE statement contains nine statements, described in detail here:

1. MERGE INTO PRODUCT PR

   The MERGE INTO statement indicates to DB2 that this is a MERGE statement and it will be modifying the PRODUCT table. The PR after the table name is a label that can be used to refer to this table, rather than using the full name. The MERGE can update either a table or a view, but the view must not identify a catalog table, a system-maintained MQT, a view of a catalog table, or a read-only view.

2. USING (SELECT PROD_NO, DESCRIPTION, QUANTITY FROM PRODUCT_TXS) TX

   The USING clause indicates which table will be used to modify the original table. In this case, the three columns from the PRODUCT_TXS table will be retrieved and used in the MERGE logic. Note that a label is required after this SELECT logic to identify the rows being returned. The portion within the SELECT statement can contain additional logic to restrict the rows being returned from the PRODUCT_TXS table. For instance, the SELECT could contain the following logic to restrict rows containing only products that have an S as their first letter:

   ```
   USING (SELECT PROD_NO, DESCRIPTION, QUANTITY FROM PRODUCT_TXS
                  WHERE DESCRIPTION LIKE 'S%') TX
   ```

3. ON (PR.PROD_NO = TX.PROD_NO)

   The ON clause determines how the base table (PRODUCT) and the transaction table (PRODUCT_TXS) are going to be combined. In the majority of cases, this column should be the primary key of both tables. Trying to run a MERGE command against a table without an index would result in poor performance because the tables would need to be completely scanned to determine the answer set.

4. WHEN MATCHED THEN

   The WHEN MATCHED clause tells DB2 what to do when a row in the transaction table matches a corresponding record in the base table. The WHEN clause can also contain additional logic to determine what happens to the base records. In this example, all transaction records that match base records execute this logic.

5. UPDATE SET

   The UPDATE command is part of the WHEN MATCHED THEN clause. When a transaction record matches a base record, the record can either be updated, deleted, or raise an error condition. In this case, the UPDATE command changes the base record contents.

6. `PR.QUANTITY = PR.QUANTITY + TX.QUANTITY`

The value of the `QUANTITY` field in the `PRODUCT` table is updated to reflect the addition of new stock (`TX.QUANTITY`).

7. `WHEN NOT MATCHED THEN`

The `WHEN NOT MATCHED THEN` clause is executed when the transaction record is not found in the base table. In this situation, only an `INSERT` or raising an error condition is allowed.

8. `INSERT (PROD_NO, DESCRIPTION, QUANTITY)`

The `INSERT` statement is part of the `WHEN NOT MATCHED THEN` clause. These fields are inserted into the base (`PRODUCT`) table.

9. `VALUES (TX.PROD_NO, TX.DESCRIPTION, TX.QUANTITY)`

The values that are being inserted are taken from the transaction (`PRODUCT_TXS`) table. This can include calculations and values from either the base table or the transaction table.

The full syntax of the `MERGE` command is shown here:

```
>>-MERGE INTO--+---table-name--+------------------------------------‡
               '--view-name---'
>----+-------------------------------+----------------------------------‡
       .-AS--.
       '--+------+--correlation-name-'
>--USING-table-reference-ON-search condition--------------------‡
   .----------------------------------------------------------.
   V
>--+--WHEN---matching-condition---THEN--+-modification-operation-+-+‡
                                        '-signal-statement-------'
   .-ELSE IGNORE-------------------.
>--+--------------------------------+----------------------------------><

matching-condition:
|--+--------+--MATCHED--+-------------------------+---------------|
   '--NOT--'            '--AND--search-condition---'

modification-operation:
|--+--UPDATE SET--assignment-clause--------+---------------------|
   +--DELETE-----------------------------+
   '--insert-operation---------------------'
```

```
assignment-clause:
     .-,---------------------------------------------------------.
     V                                                           |
|--+--+--column-name-- = --+--expression--+----------------+--+-------|
     |                     +--DEFAULT-----+                |
     |                     `--NULL--------'                |
     |    .--,----------.                 .--,-------------.    |
     |    V             |                 V                |    |
     `-(-+-column-name-+-)- = -(---+-+-expression-+-+----)-'
                                   +-DEFAULT----+
                                   `-NULL-------'

insert-operation:
|----INSERT---+-------------------------+--------------------------->
             |    .-,--------------.    |
             |    V                |    |
             '-(-----column-name---+---)--'

>-------VALUES--- ---+-+-expression-+----------------+-----------------|
                    | +-DEFAULT----+                |
                    | '-NULL-------'                |
                    |    .-,-----------------.      |
                    |    V                   |      |
                    '-(------+-expression-+--+---)--'
                            +-DEFAULT----+
                            '-NULL-------'
```

Additional WHEN MATCHED Logic

Although the following example can insert new records and update existing ones, it has no ability to delete records from the base table. To allow for this capability in the transaction table, the developer must create an additional column in the transaction table along with some logic to identify which records to delete. A slight modification to the transaction table, shown here, makes this possible:

```
CREATE TABLE PRODUCT_TXS
  (
  TX_TYPE     CHAR(1)     NOT NULL,
  PROD_NO     INT         NOT NULL,
  DESCRIPTION VARCHAR(20),
  QUANTITY    INT
  );
```

This table includes an additional column that determines the transaction type. For simplicity, these codes are I for insert, D for delete, and U for update. A sample set of transactions is shown here:

```
TX_TYPE PROD_NO     DESCRIPTION              QUANTITY
------- ----------- ------------------------ -----------
U             1 -                                   15
D             3 -                                    -
I             6 Shoes                                5
I             7 Belts                               10
```

In this example, Product 1 has 15 additional items, Product 3 is deleted from inventory, and Products 6 and 7 are added to the product line. The MERGE statement that implements the insert, update, and delete logic is shown here:

```
MERGE INTO PRODUCTS PR
   USING (SELECT TX_TYPE, PROD_NO, DESCRIPTION, QUANTITY FROM PRODUCT_TXS) TX
         ON (PR.PROD_NO = TX.PROD_NO)
   WHEN MATCHED AND TX_TYPE = 'U' THEN
       UPDATE SET
              PR.QUANTITY = PR.QUANTITY + TX.QUANTITY
   WHEN MATCHED AND TX_TYPE = 'D' THEN
       DELETE
   WHEN NOT MATCHED AND TX_TYPE = 'I' THEN
       INSERT (PROD_NO, DESCRIPTION, QUANTITY)
           VALUES (TX.PROD_NO, TX.DESCRIPTION, TX.QUANTITY);
```

The WHEN MATCHED clause now contains additional logic to determine when the transaction is applied. For instance, the WHEN MATCHED AND TX_TYPE='D' indicates to DB2 that any base record that matches a transaction record with a transaction type of 'D' should be deleted from the table.

IGNORING Records

What happens when a record does not match any of the criteria in the MERGE statement? In all cases, DB2 ignores the transaction record and continues on to the next one. You can explicitly code this behavior in the MERGE statement by adding the ELSE IGNORE clause. You cannot include any logic with the ELSE clause, so you must use a generic WHEN MATCHED or WHEN NOT MATCHED clause to deal with records that do not match any of the other criteria.

The MERGE statement gets executed sequentially, which means that each WHEN clause of the MERGE statement is executed until one of the conditions is met. Once a condition is met, the logic associated with that statement is executed and processing continues on with the next transaction record. Only one of the WHEN clauses is matched, and the remainder are ignored. This prevents more than one action from occurring against the same record.

Raising Error Conditions

There will be occasions where transaction records are not matched and you need to stop the process of the MERGE statement. To do this, the SIGNAL statement can be used.

The following MERGE statement expands on this example and adds two additional error conditions:

```
MERGE INTO PRODUCTS PR
  USING (SELECT TX_TYPE, PROD_NO, DESCRIPTION, QUANTITY FROM PRODUCT_TXS) TX
        ON (PR.PROD_NO = TX.PROD_NO)
  WHEN MATCHED AND TX_TYPE = 'U' THEN
      UPDATE SET
              PR.QUANTITY = PR.QUANTITY + TX.QUANTITY
  WHEN MATCHED AND TX_TYPE = 'D' THEN
      DELETE
  WHEN MATCHED AND TX_TYPE = 'I' THEN
      SIGNAL SQLSTATE '70001'
        SET MESSAGE_TEXT = 'Record already exists for an INSERT'
  WHEN NOT MATCHED AND TX_TYPE = 'I' THEN
      INSERT (PROD_NO, DESCRIPTION, QUANTITY)
             VALUES (TX.PROD_NO, TX.DESCRIPTION, TX.QUANTITY)
  WHEN NOT MATCHED THEN
      SIGNAL SQLSTATE '70002'
        SET MESSAGE_TEXT = 'Record not found for Update or Delete record'
  ELSE IGNORE;
```

The first error condition is raised when an insert is processed and a record already exists in the transaction table. The SIGNAL statement raises the error code 70001 with the associated error message that the record already exists. For instance, the following transaction record causes the MERGE to fail:

```
TX_TYPE PROD_NO      DESCRIPTION             QUANTITY
------- -----------  --------------------- -----------
D               10 -                               -


MERGE INTO PRODUCT …


SQL0438N  Application raised error with diagnostic text: "Record
already exists for an INSERT".  SQLSTATE=70001
```

When the SIGNAL statement is executed, all processing that has been done up to that point in time will fail. In other words, the entire statement is rolled back.

The syntax of the SIGNAL statement is relatively simple as shown here:

```
                      .-VALUE-.
>>-SIGNAL--+-SQLSTATE--+-------+--sqlstate-string-constant-+---->
           '-condition-name----------------------------------'


>--+-------------------+-------------------------------------->< 
   '-signal-information-'


signal-information:


|--+- SET MESSAGE_TEXT-- = --diagnostic-string-expression-+------|
   '- (--diagnostic-string-expression--)-----------------'
```

Any valid SQLSTATE value can be used in the SIGNAL statement. However, programmers should define new SQLSTATEs based on ranges reserved for applications. This prevents the unintentional use of an SQLSTATE value that might be defined by the database manager in a future release.

- SQLSTATE classes that begin with the characters 7 through 9 or I through Z can be defined. Within these classes, any subclass can be defined.
- SQLSTATE classes that begin with the characters 0 through 6 or A through H are reserved for the database manager. Within these classes, subclasses that begin with the characters 0 through H are reserved for the database manager. Subclasses that begin with the characters I through Z can be defined.

Authorization

The MERGE statement requires that the user have sufficient authority to manipulate the tables or views being used in the statement. The privileges held by the user of the statement must include at least one of the following:

- If an insert operation is specified, INSERT privilege on the table or view; if a delete operation is specified, DELETE privilege on the table or view; and if an update operation is specified, either the UPDATE privilege on the table or view or UPDATE privilege on each column that is to be updated.
- CONTROL privilege on the table.
- SYSADM or DBADM authority.

The privileges held by the user of the statement must also include at least one of the following:

- SELECT privilege on every table or view identified in the table-reference.
- CONTROL privilege on the tables or views identified in the table-reference.
- SYSADM or DBADM authority.

If search-condition, insert-operation, or assignment-clause includes a subquery, the privileges held by the authorization ID of the statement must also include at least one of the following:

- `SELECT` privilege on every table or view identified in the subquery.
- `CONTROL` privilege on the tables or views identified in the subquery.
- `SYSADM` or `DBADM` authority.

SQL Sampling

A database is often used for transactional purposes, but one of the major benefits of the relational model is the ability to perform complex analysis of the data. DB2 has many features and techniques that improve the performance of complex queries including summary tables, dynamic bitmap indexes, MDC, and a variety of SQL optimizations.

DB2 UDB v8.1 introduces another type of SQL optimization in the form of sampling of data during the execution of a statement. Databases are growing so large that it is often impractical to access all of the data relevant to a query. For instance, a query requesting the average sales per month in a large department store might need to read millions of records. In this example, it might be just as valid to sample a portion of the table to come up with an average number. The corresponding savings in execution time might be worth the slight inaccuracy of the result. This is particularly true when someone is trying to analyze trends and exact amounts are not as important as the magnitude of the number.

DB2 implements this type of sampling through the `TABLESAMPLE` clause of the `SELECT` statement. This additional specification is added after the table name in a select statement, as shown here:

```
|--TABLESAMPLE--+-BERNOULLI-+--(--numeric-expression1--)-------->
                '-SYSTEM----'


>--+---------------------------------------+-------------------|
    '-REPEATABLE--(--numeric-expression--)-'
```

The `TABLESAMPLE` clause has two components. The first is the type of sampling that is to occur with the data and the second is the "seed" or randomization number that is to be used to determine which rows get selected. The various parameters and their usage are described in the following sections.

BERNOULLI Sampling

The `TABLESAMPLE` clause is used to obtain a random subset or sample of the rows from the specified table. Of course, this is in addition to any predicates or conditions that are applied to the rows themselves.

Unless the optional REPEATABLE clause is specified, you will get a different result each time the query is executed. In cases where there is a very small table, the results might be the same because DB2 cannot get a large enough sample to generate a random set of records.

The BERNOULLI keyword includes a numeric specification that indicates the approximate percentage of the table that is to be returned. For instance, the following statement only considers 10% of the total number of rows in the table:

```
SELECT COUNT(*) FROM TRANSACTIONS TABLESAMPLE BERNOULLI(10)
```

The number in parentheses must be greater than zero and can be up to 100. Of course, a value of 100 would be equivalent to retrieving the entire table. If a value of zero or less is used, the following error message is returned:

```
SQL20242N The sample size specified in the TABLESAMPLE clause is not
valid.   SQLSTATE=2202H
```

Sampling using the BERNOULLI algorithm considers every row individually. The probability of the row being included in the set is $P/100$ (where P is the percentage used with the BERNOULLI keyword) and excluded with probability $1-P/100$. An SQL count statement executed five times with BERNOULLI(10) sampling retrieves the following values from a table with 10,000 rows:

```
VALUES (1, (SELECT COUNT(*) FROM TRANSACTIONS TABLESAMPLE BERNOULLI(10)))
UNION ALL
VALUES (2, (SELECT COUNT(*) FROM TRANSACTIONS TABLESAMPLE BERNOULLI(10)))
UNION ALL
VALUES (3, (SELECT COUNT(*) FROM TRANSACTIONS TABLESAMPLE BERNOULLI(10)))
UNION ALL
VALUES (4, (SELECT COUNT(*) FROM TRANSACTIONS TABLESAMPLE BERNOULLI(10)))
UNION ALL
VALUES (5,( SELECT COUNT(*) FROM TRANSACTIONS TABLESAMPLE BERNOULLI(10)));


1            2
----------- -----------
          1         988
          2         988
          3         988
          4         988
          5         988

  5 record(s) selected.
```

The result of the SQL statement appears to be exactly the same for each row. One would expect that the results would be random given the definition of the BERNOULLI function. However, the BERNOULLI sampling is done at the beginning of the SQL statement, so any subsequent reference to the same set of rows has the same answer set returned. Each statement in the preceding example is identical, so the results are the same. Using the following SQL logic, the random nature of the BERNOULLI statement can be illustrated as shown here:

```
CREATE TABLE SAMPLES
  (
  RUN     INT,
  CNT     INT
  )$

BEGIN ATOMIC
  DECLARE I INT DEFAULT 0;
  DECLARE ROWS_CNT INT DEFAULT 0;

  SET I = I + 1;
  WHILE I <= 5 DO
    SET ROWS_CNT = (SELECT COUNT(*) FROM TRANSACTIONS TABLESAMPLE
          BERNOULLI(10));
    INSERT INTO SAMPLES VALUES (1,ROWS_CNT);
    SET I = I + 1;
  END WHILE;
END$

SELECT * FROM SAMPLES$

RUN          CNT
----------- -----------
          1         951
          2        1007
          3        1005
          4        1000
          5        1015

  5 record(s) selected.
```

SYSTEM Sampling

SYSTEM sampling permits the database manager to determine the most efficient manner in which to perform the sampling. In most cases, SYSTEM sampling applied to a table means that each page of the table is included in the sample with probability $P/100$, and excluded with probability $1-P/100$. All of the rows found on that page qualify for the sample.

SYSTEM sampling of a table executes much faster than BERNOULLI sampling because fewer data pages need to be retrieved. Using BERNOULLI sampling requires that all pages be read to determine which rows are part of the set. The following SQL query was run against a 100,000-row table using BERNOULLI sampling:

```
SELECT TX_ITEM, AVG(TX_QUANTITY) FROM STORE_TXS TABLESAMPLE BERNOULLI(10)
GROUP BY TX_ITEM
```

The corresponding visual explain statement for this SQL is shown in Figure 17.3.

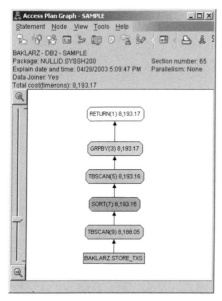

Figure 17.3
EXPLAIN statement for BERNOULLI sampling.

The cost for this SQL statement is 8,193 units. Converting this statement to use SYSTEM sampling results in the visual EXPLAIN shown in Figure 17.4.

Using SYSTEM sampling, we are able to bring the cost down to 870 units, or a tenfold reduction in work. This improved performance does come at the cost of having more variable results.

The two sets of SQL statements were executed 25 times and compared against the exact answers that would be produced without sampling. The results were plotted as a ratio against the correct result. For example, an exact result would score 100. Answers higher or lower than 100 would have slightly incorrect answers because of the sampling that was done. The two SQL statements are compared in Figure 17.5.

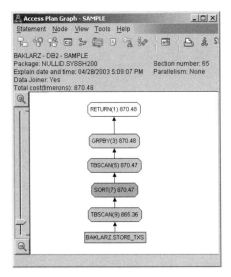

Figure 17.4
EXPLAIN statement for SYSTEM sampling.

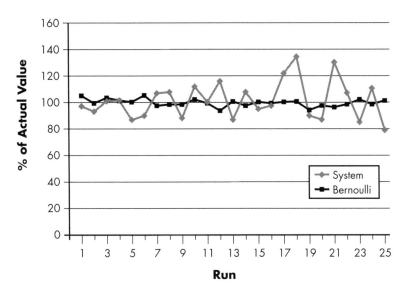

Figure 17.5
Comparison of SYSTEM versus BERNOULLI accuracy.

With a 10% sampling of rows, the BERNOULLI sampling is less variable than the SYSTEM sampling. However, during the execution of this query, the SYSTEM example took .221 seconds to execute, whereas the BERNOULLI example took 1.281 seconds. The user must choose between fast execution speeds and a higher variability in results.

REPEATABLE Sampling

During query testing or debugging, it might be useful to have exactly the same results returned during sampling. This can be accomplished by specifying the REPEATABLE clause after the sampling specification. Every time the query is executed, the same sample is returned, unless the data has been changed or updated. This first example shows the results of two average calculations without the REPEATABLE clause:

```
SELECT AVG(TX_QUANTITY) FROM STORE_TXS TABLESAMPLE SYSTEM(10)
  WHERE TX_ITEM='A40';

1
-----------
        49

 1 record(s) selected.

SELECT AVG(TX_QUANTITY) FROM STORE_TXS TABLESAMPLE SYSTEM(10)
  WHERE TX_ITEM='A40';

1
-----------
        48

 1 record(s) selected.
```

Issuing the same SELECT statements with a REPEATABLE clause produces identical results:

```
SELECT AVG(TX_QUANTITY) FROM STORE_TXS TABLESAMPLE SYSTEM(10)
REPEATABLE(12345)
  WHERE TX_ITEM='A40';

1
-----------
        49

 1 record(s) selected.

SELECT AVG(TX_QUANTITY) FROM STORE_TXS TABLESAMPLE SYSTEM(10)
REPEATABLE(12345)
  WHERE TX_ITEM='A40';

1
-----------
        49

 1 record(s) selected.
```

If the results are supposed to be consistent throughout a large set of SQL statements, a global temporary table should be used. Create the temporary table and populate it with a SELECT statement that uses the TABLESAMPLE clause to generate a subset to the data. The remainder of the SQL can then refer to the temporary table. When the SQL goes into production, the TABLESAMPLE clause can be eliminated or the SQL modified to point to the original table.

Any numeric value can be used in the REPEATABLE clause. This value is used to seed the random number generator that is used to select the rows. To obtain the same sampling, the number must be used in every TABLESAMPLE clause for that table. Otherwise, different results will be produced.

Additional Considerations

There are a few additional considerations when taking advantage of the TABLESAMPLE clause:

1. Sampling can only occur on base tables and MQTs.
2. Sampling occurs before any predicates are applied (the WHERE clause). Multiple tables can be sampled in the same SQL statement to test join conditions and other complex SQL without using entire tables.
3. Any calculations done in the SELECT list must account for the percentage of sampling done. For instance, the average calculation (AVG) should not be any different when working with 10% of the table or 50% of the table. However, a SUM or COUNT calculation must be scaled by multiplying the result by 100 and dividing by the sampling percentage to get the proper result. For instance, the following SQL scales SUM by 5 (100/20) to get the proper results because only 20% of the data was sampled:

   ```
   SELECT SUM(TX_QUANTITY) * 5 FROM STORE_TXS TABLESAMPLE
   SYSTEM(20)
     WHERE TX_ITEM='A40';
   ```

4. SYSTEM sampling is almost always faster than BERNOULLI sampling, but the results are often less accurate. This might be sufficient for testing and for quick reporting, but the results should be used with the appropriate caveats.

In general, the TABLESAMPLE clause can be extremely useful in prototyping SQL against large tables, and for getting quick answers to "what if" questions.

SUMMARY

This chapter has covered some of the SQL enhancements that have been introduced in DB2 UDB v8.1. These enhancements include the following:

- New functions for monitoring the operational state and health of a database, XML publishing, and date conversions

- The MERGE command to combine a transaction table with a base table
- New techniques for sampling data within a SELECT statement
- Improvements to the UNION ALL command to allow inserts, updates, and deletes across all of the tables in a view
- An INSTEAD OF trigger for complex view processing
- IDENTITY and SEQUENCE value support in a partitioned environment
- ORDER BY and FETCH FIRST enhancements to reduce the amount of data being retrieved during a sort
- A dynamic CALL statement that makes it more flexible to use

All of these features add to the already rich set of SQL support found within DB2 UDB. For more information on these and other SQL features, see the *DB2 UDB Version 8.1 SQL Reference* manuals.

C H A P T E R **18**

Application Development Enhancements

D B2 UDB v8.1 introduces a number of new development features to help in the creation and distribution of applications. This chapter deals with features that are of interest to all developers, whether they are working with Java, C++, or SQL PL. An additional chapter focuses on the Microsoft interfaces available in this release, including the new .NET drivers.

DEVELOPMENT CENTER

In DB2 UDB v8.1, the Development Center replaces the Stored Procedure Builder. The Development Center provides an easy-to-use interface for developing routines such as stored procedures and UDFs.

The Development Center provides a single development environment that supports the entire DB2 family ranging from the workstation to z/OS. You can launch the Development Center as a stand-alone application from the DB2 Universal Database program group or from a DB2 Universal Database center, such as the Control Center, the Command Center, or the Task Center.

With the Development Center, you can do the following:

- Create, build, and deploy Java and SQL stored procedures
- Create, build, and deploy UDFs:
  - SQL table and scalar UDFs
  - UDFs that read MQSeries messages
  - UDFs that access OLE DB data sources
  - UDFs that extract data from XML documents
- Debug SQL stored procedures using the integrated debugger

- See the contents of the server for each database connection in your project or that you have explicitly added to the server view. You can also view and work with other database objects such as tables, triggers, and views.
- Export and import routines and project information

The Development Center also provides a DB2 development add-in for each of the following development environments:

- Microsoft Visual C++
- Microsoft Visual Basic
- Microsoft Visual InterDev

With the add-ins, you can access the features of the Development Center and other DB2 centers from the Microsoft development environment, making it easy to develop and incorporate stored procedures and UDFs.

A sample Development Center screen is shown in Figure 18.1.

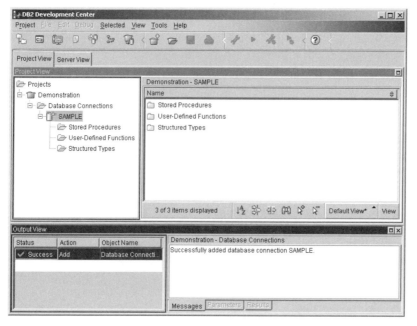

Figure 18.1
Development Center.

Starting the Development Center

The Development Center can be launched from the DB2 program group or from the integrated development environments such as WebSphere Studio or Microsoft Visual Studio.

The DB2 program group includes a folder called Development Tools that contains the Development Center shortcut (Figure 18.2).

Figure 18.2
Starting the Development Center.

From the Control Center, the Development Center can be started by clicking the Development Center icon (Figure 18.3).

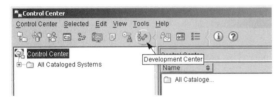

Figure 18.3
Starting the Development Center from the Control Center.

Finally, the Development Center can also be accessed from a Visual Studio or Visual Basic environment by selecting add-ins from the main menu and selecting the IBM DB2 Development add-in (Figure 18.4).

Figure 18.4
Starting the Development Center from Visual Basic.

Project View

The Development Center Launch Pad (Project View) is displayed when starting the Development Center for the first time (Figure 18.5).

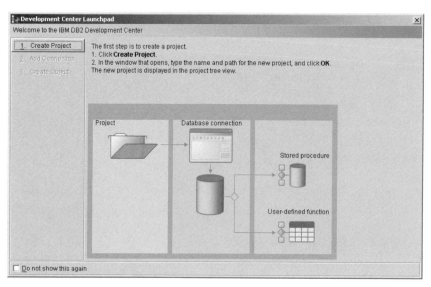

Figure 18.5
Development Center Launch pad.

This panel is used to define the project that you are going to develop. If you do not want the project view to be displayed during Development Center startup, you can select the Do Not Show This Again option.

The first step in developing a project is defining the project name and file locations (Figure 18.6).

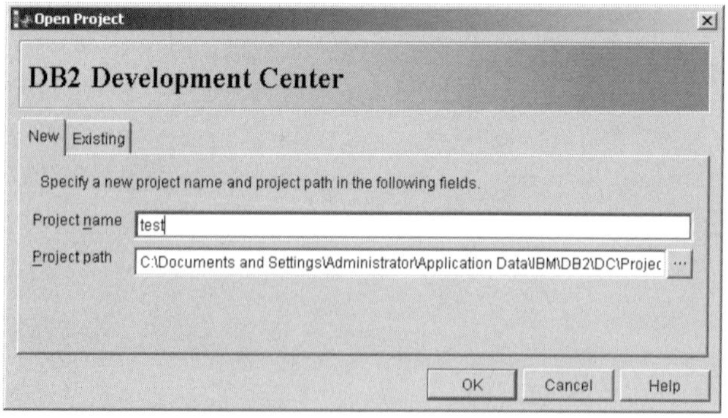

Figure 18.6
Project name and location.

You can also select an existing project to continue to work on it. After defining the project name, the database connection needs to be created. You can continue to define your project without a connection, but the Development Center requests a connection when it is required to complete a task (Figure 18.7).

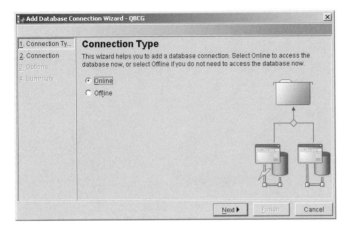

Figure 18.7
Database connection screen.

There are a variety of options associated with a database connection. The first panel after deciding on offline/online connections is the actual database name (Figure 18.8).

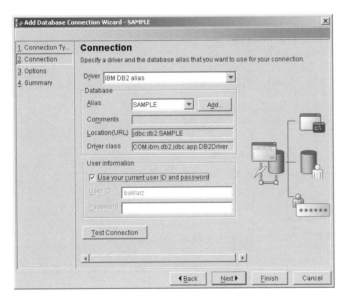

Figure 18.8
Database connection screen.

The Database panel must be completed with the database name that you want to access as part of your project. The user information must also be completed to allow the connection. For convenience, your current user ID and password can be used for the connection, but you can supply other user IDs and passwords on this panel. The Test Connection button gives you the ability to check the connection before continuing onto the next step (Figure 18.9).

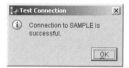

Figure 18.9
Testing the database connection.

There are two additional panels that allow you to add SQL schema and default authorization IDs to your project. Once you have completed this information you can look at the summary page to see a list of all specified options, or continue on to the next step by clicking Finish.

The final step in the project definition is to create the objects (Figure 18.10).

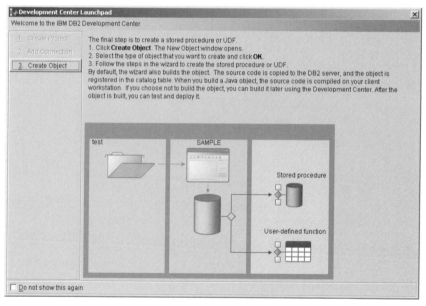

Figure 18.10
Create objects.

Clicking Create Object displays the Object Creation panel, where the user can create either stored procedures or UDFs (Figure 18.11).

Figure 18.11
Create Object list.

From this panel, the user can create the following:

- Stored procedures
  - Java with either JDBC or SQLJ
  - SQL Procedural Language
- UDFs
  - SQL scalar UDFs for UNIX and Windows
  - SQL table UDFs for UNIX and Windows
  - UDFs that read MQSeries queues
  - UDFs that access OLE DB data providers
  - UDFs that work with XML data

Each one of these stored procedure or function types would have a panel specific to it. An example of creating a UDF or stored procedure is shown in a separate section.

Once the stored procedure or UDF has been defined, the user is returned to the Create Object screen. This way, multiple stored procedures or UDFs can be created for a project. Once all of the objects have been created, the user can close the Development Center launch pad and work directly in the Development Center (Figure 18.12).

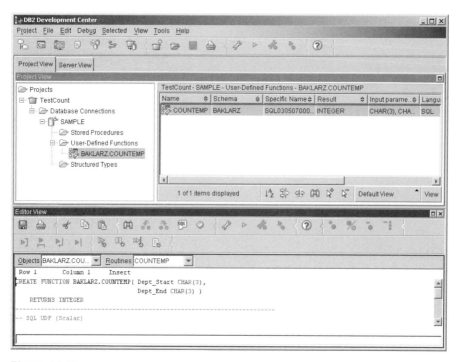

Figure 18.12
Development Center.

Creating a UDF

The initial screen for creating a UDF lets the user decide which type of function he or she will generate. There are four types of UDFs, including SQL procedure language, MQSeries, XML, and OLE DB functions. Depending on which type of UDF is chosen, the options change (Figure 18.13).

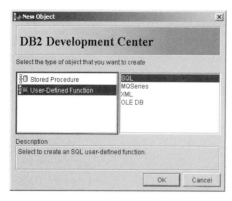

Figure 18.13
Types of UDFs.

The following example is based on the SQL procedure language. Once the user selects OK, the initial UDF creation panel is displayed (Figure 18.14).

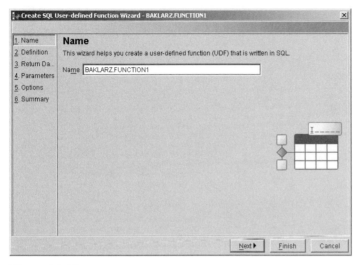

Figure 18.14
UDF name.

There are six panels associated with UDF creation:

- Function Name—The function name and location are defined in the Name panel.
- Definition—The definition panel allows the user to define the SQL statement, the output type, header and pre-return fragments, variables, and exception handlers that are associated with the function.
- Return Value—This defines the type of return value the function will return.
- Parameters—This panel defines the parameters that will be used as input to the function.
- Options—Any additional options associated with the type of function are found in this panel.
- Summary—The Summary screen gives the developer a quick review of the function being created, along with a button that lets him or her view the SQL statement that will generate the function definition.

Function Name

The initial function definition screen asks for the schema and name of the function. By default, the schema name is that of your current connection. The name of the function must adhere to normal SQL naming rules so it cannot be longer than 18 characters and should not have the same name as any of the existing functions in the database.

Figure 18.14 shows an example of the function name definition.

Definition

The definition screen is used to create the body of the function. There are six portions of the function that can be defined on this screen (Figure 18.15).

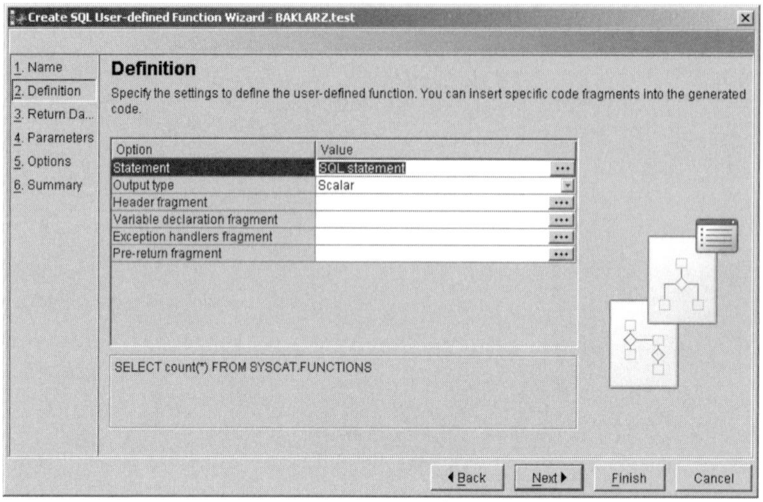

Figure 18.15
UDF definition.

The first line lets the developer define the SQL statement that will be contained in the body of the function. The [...] button beside the value field links users to a panel that lets them define the value. In the case of the Statement field, this is a panel that allows the user to enter the SQL to be run (Figure 18.16).

Figure 18.16
SQL statement for UDF.

The user can create an SQL statement or an expression. If the developer requires help in defining the SQL, the SQL Assist function can be used. This tool is described in the section on SQL Assist.

The output type defines the type of data that is going to be returned by the function. The type of data can be either a single scalar value or a table. User-defined table functions are used in conjunction with the FROM clause in a SELECT statement. Instead of returning a single value to the SQL, a table UDF returns rows. The SQL that you developed in the previous step is dependent on which type of output you specified in this line.

The remainder of the lines define code fragments, including these:

- Header fragment
- Variable declaration fragment
- Exception handlers fragment
- Prereturn fragment

These fragments are included as files from within the local development environment (Figure 18.17).

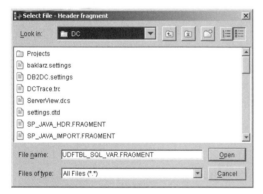

Figure 18.17
Defining a header fragment.

The header fragment refers to code that you might want at the beginning of your code. For instance, you might have standard header fragments that include copyright information and any comments associated with a project.

The variable fragment contains variables that are commonly used in function definitions. Note that not all of these fragments need to be defined for a function. You can choose to use only one fragment to define all headers, variables, and exception information. However, the prereturn fragment would typically be defined separately from the rest.

The exception handlers fragment contains SQL that defines the common error conditions and how the code will handle them. Because this is a common activity for most functions and stored procedures, creating one common exception handler fragment could save a lot of development time.

The prereturn fragment defines any code that needs to be executed before the function returns its information.

Return Value

The Return Value panel lets the developer describe the format of the data being returned by the function (Figure 18.18).

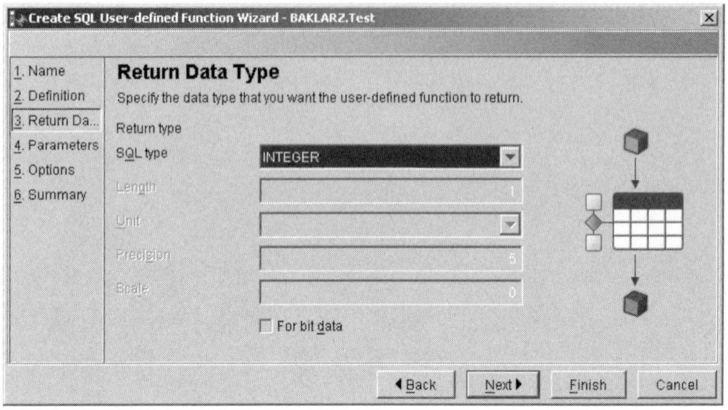

Figure 18.18
Format of returned value.

This panel shows the format of the data being returned from a scalar function. In this case only one value is being returned. If this was defined as a table function, the user would need to define the columns being returned as part of the table.

Parameters

The Parameters panel defines the parameters that will be passed to the function (Figure 18.19).

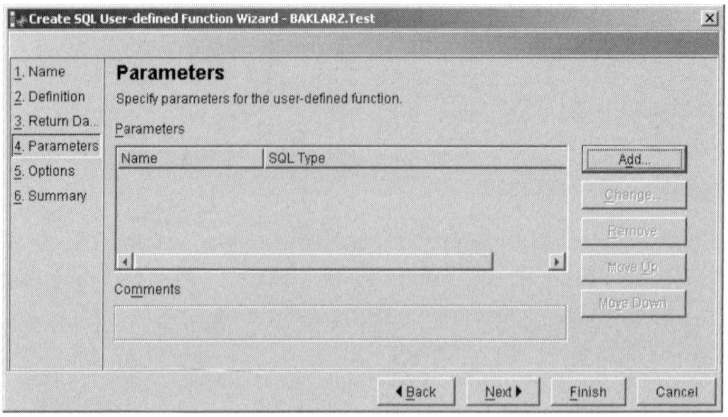

Figure 18.19
Parameter definition.

Each input parameter needs to be separately defined by clicking Add until they are all done. Every time Add is clicked, the variable definition screen is displayed (Figure 18.20).

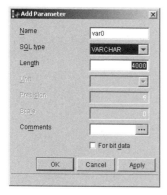

Figure 18.20
Adding an additional parameter.

Any variables that were used in the definition stage of the SQL would automatically be added to this list. This reduces the possibility of using incorrect variable names.

Options

The Options panel lets the user add a specific name to the function definition and request that the function be built when Finish is clicked (Figure 18.21).

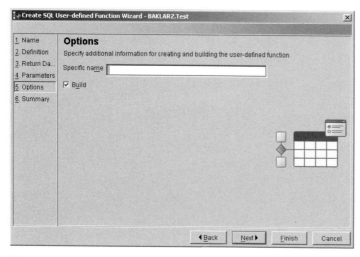

Figure 18.21
Options for function creation.

The specific name provides a unique name for the instance of the function that is being defined. This specific name can be used when sourcing on this function, dropping the function, or commenting on the function. It can never be used to invoke the function.

Summary

The Summary panel lists all of the major options for the function you have defined (Figure 18.22).

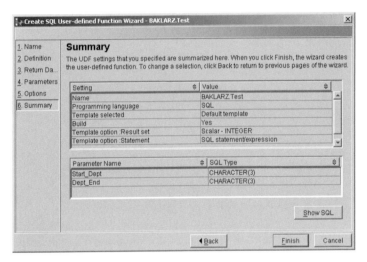

Figure 18.22
Summary of function definition.

The Show SQL button can be used to view the SQL command that will be used to define the function, but it does not show the function logic.

Once the function definition is complete, the user can add more functions to the project or continue work within the Development Center. When the function is successfully created, the Development Center is updated to reflect this (Figure 18.23).

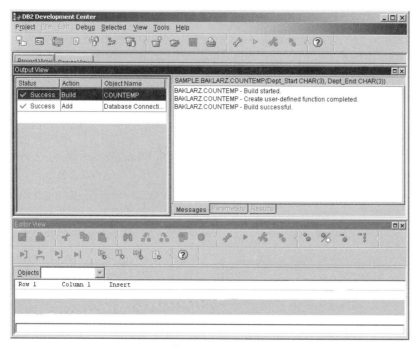

Figure 18.23
Successful creation of a function.

Creating a Stored Procedure

Creating a stored procedure is very similar to creating a UDF. With the Development Center we can create stored procedures that use either the SQL procedure language (SQL PL) or Java in their logic (Figure 18.24).

Figure 18.24
Stored procedure types.

There are five steps involved in creating a stored procedure:

- Procedure Name—The procedure name and location are defined in the Name panel.
- Definition—The Definition panel allows the user to define the SQL statements, result sets, error handling, header and prereturn fragments, variables, and exception handlers associated with the routine.
- Parameters—This panel defines the parameters that will be used as input and output to the function.
- Options—Any additional options associated with the type of function are found on this panel.
- Summary—The Summary screen gives the developer a quick review of the procedure being created, along with a button that lets him or her view the SQL statement that will generate the procedure definition.

All of the steps involved in stored procedure creation are identical to those for creating a UDF, except for the procedure definition. The procedure definition has a few additional fields that need to be filled in (Figure 18.25).

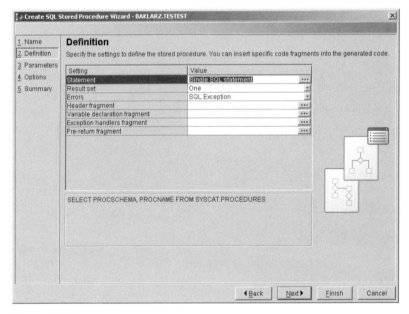

Figure 18.25
Stored procedure definition.

A stored procedure can contain more than one SQL statement, and can execute INSERT, UPDATE, and DELETE commands in addition to SELECT. The Statement section of this panel allows the user to define more than one SQL statement as part of the procedure body. If this was a UDF definition, only one SQL statement would be allowed.

Stored procedures can also return result sets. These are cursors that are opened by the stored procedure for the calling program to manipulate. The stored procedure does the work in selecting the appropriate records, but does not do any processing of the individual records. This is left to the calling application, which takes control of the answer set (cursor) and processes the records. This parameter defines how many answer sets the stored procedure returns.

The Error field defines what type of error gets returned from a stored procedure. A stored procedure communicates with the calling program through the use of parameters and result sets. The actual return code from a stored procedure is used by the calling application to determine the success or failure of what the procedure did. In the case of a stored procedure, it can be designed to return the highest SQLSTATE, SQLCODE, both values, or generate an SQL exception. How errors are returned is determined by the setting of this option (Fig. 18.26).

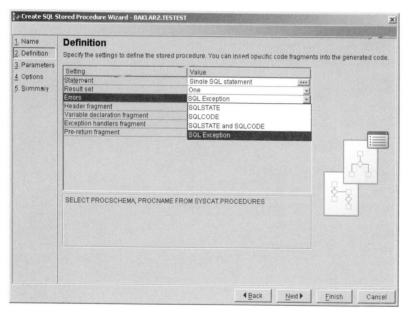

Figure 18.26
Error definition.

The remainder of the options deal with fragments. As with the fragments defined in UDFs, these fragments are included as files from within the local development environment.

The fragments are the following:

- Header fragment—The header fragment refers to code that you might want at the beginning of your code.

- Variable fragment—The variable fragment contains variables that are commonly used in procedure definitions.

- Exception handlers fragment—The exception handlers fragment contains SQL that defines the common error conditions and how the code handles them.

- Prereturn fragment—The prereturn fragment defines any code that needs to be executed before the procedure returns its information.

Development Center

After all of the functions and stored procedures have been defined for a project, the user is shown the Development Center view. This panel contains information on all of the objects associated with a project or a particular system (Figure 18.27).

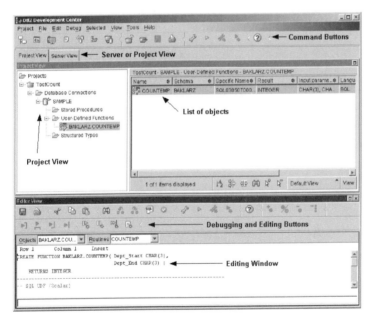

Figure 18.27
Development Center.

The Development Center can be broken up into three major areas. The left side of the screen contains a view of either the project or the system. The objects included in the view are stored procedures, UDFs, and structured types.

The right side of the screen shows the objects within a certain view. Clicking Stored Procedures would result in this side being refreshed with the names of all stored procedures created under the current schema.

The bottom panel is used to edit, debug, and test the stored procedures and UDFs that have been written. This area of the screen can change depending on the function that someone is performing.

Existing objects within a view can be selected and modified by either using the command buttons at the top of the screen or clicking on the object (Figure 18.28).

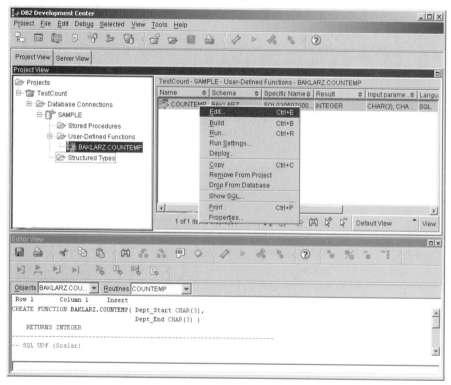

Figure 18.28
Editing an object.

A variety of options are displayed for what can be done with the object. This list changes depending on the type of object you are dealing with.

To create a new object in that view, the user must click on the view name and select which type of object he or she wishes to create (Figure 18.29).

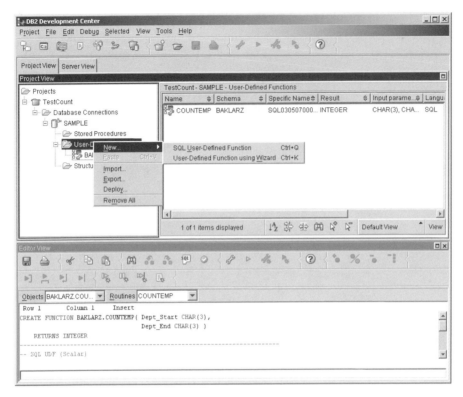

Figure 18.29
Creating a new object.

When selecting a new object, users can use the wizard to prompt them through the steps again, or they can define it directly. Many experienced developers skip the prompting step when they become more familiar with the structure of UDFs and procedures.

In addition to creating objects through prompting and wizards, the user also has the option of importing (or exporting) a command that would generate the object. Some developers and DBAs prefer to keep their object definitions in separate files for recovery purposes. This way, the import utility can be used to import the function and stored procedure definitions.

Finally, a function or stored procedure can be deployed to another system for production. The Deploy Wizard takes the user through the steps of moving a stored procedure or function to another system.

Debugging and Testing

One of the major features of the Development Center is the ability for a user to debug a function or stored procedure directly from this interface. The user has the ability to single-step code, set breakpoints, modify variables, and examine call stacks, all from within the Development Center.

The debugging can be done locally or on the remote server that contains the database. This feature greatly simplifies the development environment.

Details about the debugging capability for SQL PL and Java routines are found in the later section "Debugging Java and SQL PL."

To test a function or stored procedure, select the object and click Run. Alternatively, the menu includes an option for running the program. Figure 18.30 shows the execution of a function.

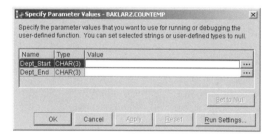

Figure 18.30
Running a function.

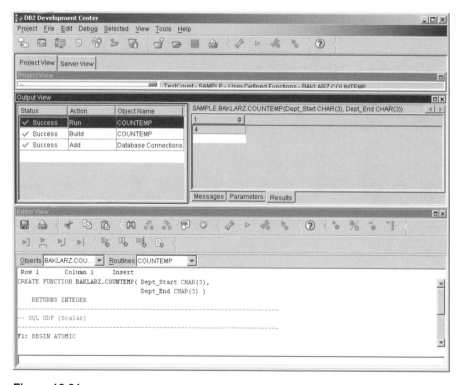

Figure 18.31
Results window.

Because the function requires two parameters, the Development Center requests input for them. The parameter types have already been checked, so the user can tell what is required. When the appropriate values have been included, the program or function executes and the results are displayed (Figure 18.31).

If the user wants to test the execution of a stored procedure one step at a time, he or she can run the program in debug mode. This option is available during the creation of the stored procedure. Without this, it is not possible to debug the application.

Once the stored procedure is compiled using the debug option, the program can be run in debug mode (Figure 18.32).

Users can set breakpoints, watch variables, single-step through the code, and perform other debugging steps as they watch the execution of the program. This flexibility makes the Development Center a key tool in the creation and testing of stored procedures.

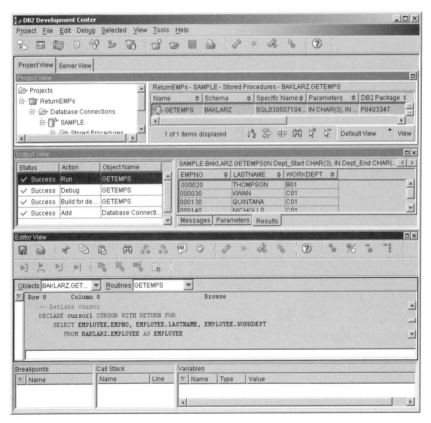

Figure 18.32
Debug window.

DEBUGGING JAVA AND SQL PL

The Development Center allows a user to develop, test, and deploy Java and SQL PL stored procedures. The Development Center includes integrated debuggers that can help a user debug problems with stored procedures that run either locally or remotely.

SQL PL Debugger

The Development Center debugger can be used to debug SQL stored procedures as they run on a DB2 server. By stepping through the code in debug mode and viewing the results, you can discover problems with your stored procedure and make the necessary changes.

The debugger allows you to do the following:

- Step through your code one statement at a time
- Set line or variable breakpoints
- View and change variable values
- View call stack information for nested procedures
- Switch between different stored procedures on the call stack

The debugger supports debugging of fenced and unfenced stored procedures.

To debug SQL stored procedures that run on DB2 for z/OS or OS/390, you need the IBM Distributed Debugger and the IBM Debug Tool for z/OS.

To debug an SQL stored procedure, perform the following steps:

- Build the stored procedure for debugging
- Run the stored procedure in debug mode
- Optional: Set line and variable breakpoints
- Optional: Modify variable breakpoint values
- Optional: Use the toolbar buttons to step over, step into, step return, or step to cursor
- Continue running in debug mode until the stored procedure returns the desired results

Debugging Java Stored Procedures

With the Development Center, you can create and build Java stored procedures that are prepared for debugging, but the debugging occurs outside of the Development Center. You need to use the IBM Distributed Debugger to perform the debug actions.

To debug Java stored procedures that run on z/OS or OS/390, you need the IBM Distributed Debugger on the client and the IBM Debug Tool for z/OS on the server.

To debug Java stored procedures that run on UNIX or Windows servers, you need the IBM Distributed Debugger installed on both the client and server.

To debug Java stored procedures, perform these steps:

- Set up the client for debugging by installing the IBM Distributed Debugger:
  - Choose all available options.
  - The Distributed Debugger is available with VisualAge for Java, and on the DB2 Universal Database v8.1 Distributed Debugger for Java Stored Procedures CD.
- Set up the server for debugging:
  - For DB2 Universal Database for UNIX and Windows, install the IBM Distributed Debugger, choosing all available options.
  - For DB2 for OS/390 and z/OS, install the IBM Debug Tool.
- Configure the IBM Distributed Debugger:
  - For UNIX and Windows only, enable the DB2 server to use the IBM Distributed Debugger to debug Java stored procedures. On the DB2 server, enter the following command:

      db2set DB2ROUTINE_DEBUG=ON

- Disconnect all DB2 applications from the DB2 server and then restart the server.

In the Development Center, run a Java stored procedure in debug mode. The IBM Distributed Debugger then opens and allows you to debug the stored procedure.

SQL Assist

With SQL Assist and some knowledge of SQL, you can create SELECT, INSERT, UPDATE, and DELETE statements. SQL Assist is a tool that uses outline and details panels to help you organize the information that you need to create an SQL statement.

DB2 UDB v8.1 enhancements include the following:

- A redesigned user interface for easy inspection and modification of SQL statement elements
- Assistance for creating table joins
- SQL syntax checking
- The option to copy and paste an existing SQL statement into SQL Assist, then use the SQL Assist interface to make modifications

Starting SQL Assist

The SQL Assist tool is available from within a number of the DB2 tools. The Development Center, SQL PL builder, and Command Center give the user access to SQL Assist. In most cases, any code that requires SQL script has the SQL Assist button beside the SQL input box, as shown in Figure 18.33.

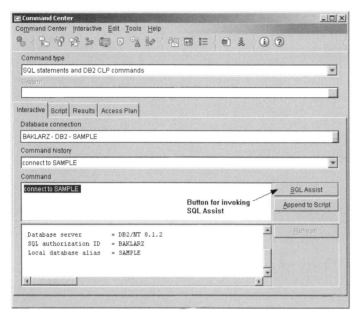

Figure 18.33
Command Center invoking SQL Assist.

The initial SQL Assist screen asks the user which type of SQL statement he or she wants to create. This can be a `SELECT`, `INSERT`, `UPDATE`, or `DELETE` statement. Once the appropriate statement is selected, the user would click OK to continue on to the next step.

SQL Assist Structure

The SQL Assist panel is divided into a number of sections that a user needs to be aware of. The general structure of the SQL Assist panel is shown in Figure 18.34.

The three major sections of the panel are as follows:

- Outline view—The Outline view contains a high-level representation of the current SQL statement. With the Outline view, you can visually examine an outline of the SQL statement and navigate through the steps of building the SQL statement.
- Details area—Use the Details area to add elements to the SQL statement. The Details area changes based on what node you select in the Outline view. When you select a node in the Outline view and make changes in the Details area, the SQL code is generated in the SQL Code view.
- SQL Code view—The SQL Code view contains the SQL code that is generated based on the contents of the Outline view and changes that you made in the Details area. The code is syntax-highlighted. In some environments, you can edit the SQL code in this view.

Outline View   Details View   Selected objects

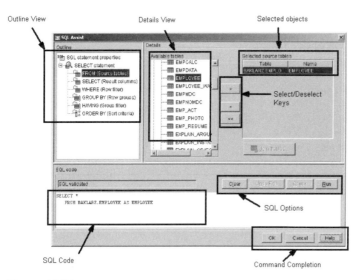

Figure 18.34
SQL Assist structure.

Outline View

Each SQL command has a different set of nodes. Depending on which command you choose, a different panel is displayed with the corresponding nodes available. The SELECT command generates the nodes shown in Figure 18.35.

Figure 18.35
SELECT options.

When the user selects any one of the nodes in the list, the Details panel is updated to contain the names of objects associated with that node. For instance, selecting the FROM node generates a list of tables in the current database (Figure 18.36).

Figure 18.36
Table list.

The types of commands that are available and their associated nodes are as follows:

- SELECT
  - FROM—Source tables to select from
  - SELECT—Columns to display from the selected tables
  - WHERE—Filtering of the rows through the use of the WHERE clause
  - GROUP BY—How the rows will be grouped together to produce aggregated results
  - HAVING—Filtering of results of the GROUP BY clause
  - ORDER BY—Sort criteria of the final result
- INSERT
  - INSERT INTO—Table to insert into
  - VALUES—Row values being inserted into the table
- UPDATE
  - UPDATE—Target table to update
  - SET—The columns to update and their new value
  - WHERE—Which rows to update
- DELETE
  - DELETE FROM—Which table to delete rows from
  - WHERE—Which rows to delete

Details Area

Once the user has selected the appropriate node, a list of objects associated with that node is displayed in the Object Selection panel. Selecting the FROM node in the outline view produces a list of schemas currently associated with the current connection to the database (Figure 18.37).

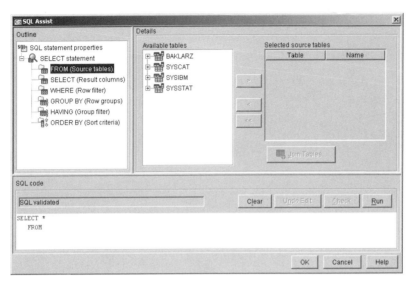

Figure 18.37
Available schemas.

The types of objects that are displayed are based on the node type. Because a FROM statement needs to be connected to an individual table, the list of schemas must be expanded so one table can be selected. Figure 18.38 contains a list of tables found under the BAKLARZ schema.

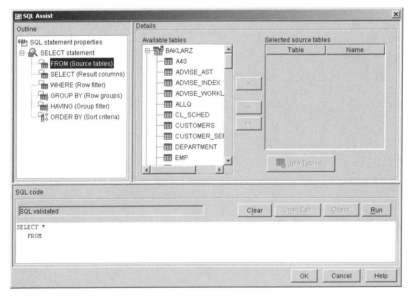

Figure 18.38
Expanded BAKLARZ schema.

At this point, the user can select the individual table and place it into the selected object window. There are two methods for doing so. The user can either double-click the object in the available object list, or highlight the object with a single click and use the select/deselect buttons.

The [>] button places an object into the selected object window, and the [>>] button places all objects into the selected object window. The [>>] might not be visible for all object types.

Similarly, the [<] button removes an object from the selected object window, and the [<<] button removes all of the objects.

Figure 18.39 displays the state of the Details area after the EMPLOYEE table has been selected from the available tables list.

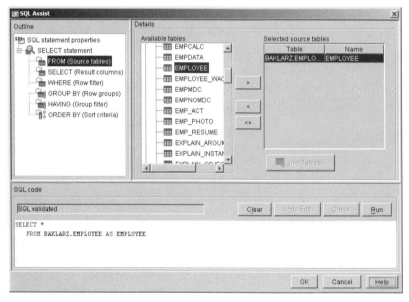

Figure 18.39
EMPLOYEE table added to selected list.

UPDATE, INSERT, and DELETE commands only allow one table to be selected. Because a SELECT statement can reference many tables, the user can continue to add tables to the selected object list. Placing a table into the selected object list does not necessarily mean that you have to use it. However, any table that you plan to reference in your SQL statement must be placed into the selected object list.

SQL Code

The SQL Code window displays the current SQL that has been generated based on the selections that the user has made. Four buttons are associated with the SQL Code window to allow the user to clear the current SQL, undo any editing changes made, check the SQL syntax, and execute the final SQL statement:

- Clear—Use the Clear button to reset an SQL statement and all of its associate elements. The contents of the Outline view and the SQL code view are replaced with an empty template.
- Undo Edit—You can insert, delete, and edit code that is found within the SQL Code window without having to change any of the previous settings in the SQL Assist panels. If you want to restore the SQL to what the SQL Assist tool had generated, click Undo Edit. SQL Assist prompts you to confirm that you want your current SQL to be overwritten.
- Check—Once you have modified the SQL manually, the SQL Assist tool can be used to check the SQL to make sure the syntax is correct and whether or not it can be generated by the SQL Assist tool. If the SQL that you have created is too complex, the SQL Assist tool cannot generate it.
- Run—When the SQL has been successfully generated, the Run button can be used to view the results of the statement, or to execute the INSERT, DELETE, or UPDATE command.

Panel Buttons

There are three additional buttons found at the bottom of the SQL Assist tool:

- OK—Once you have completed editing your SQL statement, clicking OK returns you to the tool that invoked the SQL Assist tool. Any of the SQL that was generated by the SQL Assist tool is placed into the SQL text portion of the calling tool. For instance, the SQL Procedure Builder Wizard places the generated SQL into the current SQL PL code.
- Cancel—Clicking Cancel cancels any of the SQL creation or editing that has been done and returns the user directly to the calling application.
- Help—To get additional help with the SQL Assist tool or editing help, the user can click Help.

Sample SQL Assist Session

The following set of panels illustrates the operation of the SQL Assist tool. The first step in generating an SQL statement is to select the type of SQL being created (Figure 18.40).

In this example, the SELECT statement is used. Once the SELECT statement has been chosen, the Details panel is populated with the schemas that are available to select tables from (Figure 18.41).

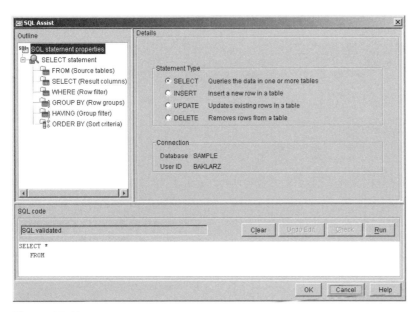

Figure 18.40
Selecting type of SQL statement.

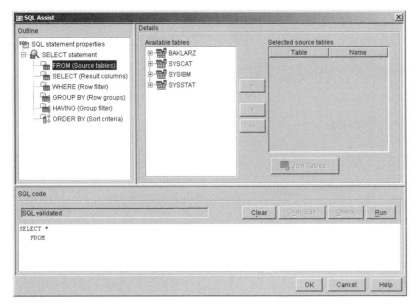

Figure 18.41
Schemas available for SELECT statements.

Expanding the BAKLARZ schema results in a list of tables that the user can select from (Figure 18.42).

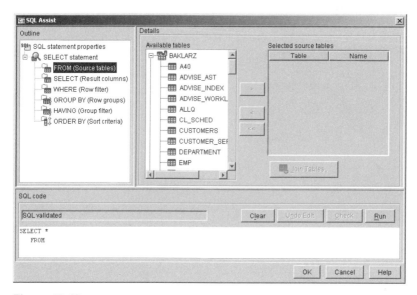

Figure 18.42
Available tables in the BAKLARZ schema.

To select the EMPLOYEE table, the user must either double-click the EMPLOYEE table name or select it and use the [>] button. The EMPLOYEE table is then placed into the selected source table list (Figure 18.43).

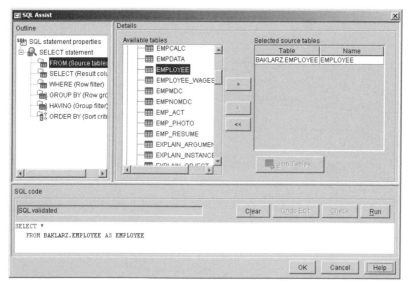

Figure 18.43
EMPLOYEE table added to selected list.

The next step in generating the SQL statement would be to determine which columns are to be included in the answer set. The user must click the SELECT node to get the list of available columns (Figure 18.44).

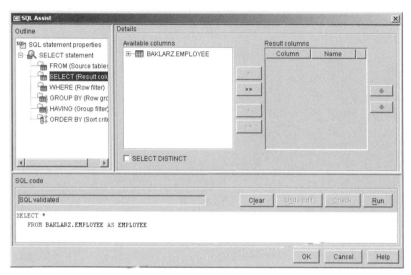

Figure 18.44
Available tables for the SELECT list.

The initial screen shows the only tables that have been selected, and not the column names. The user must expand the table name to display the list of columns (Figure 18.45).

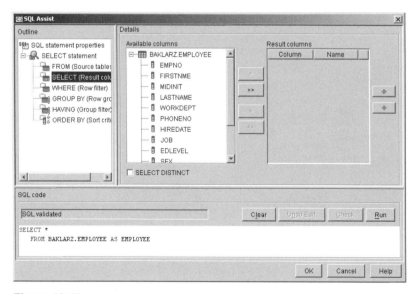

Figure 18.45
EMPLOYEE table columns.

Note that the user must always add the column to the selected object list before continuing on to the next step. In this case, two columns are selected from the EMPLOYEE table; the department number (WORKDEPT) and the employee number (EMPNO). The final SQL counts the number of employees found in the range of departments between C01 and E01. The panel with the two selected columns is shown in Figure 18.46.

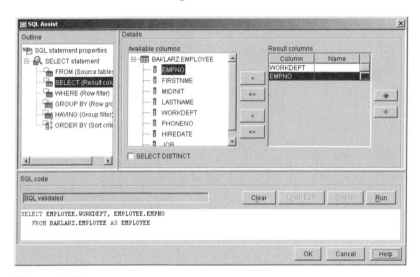

Figure 18.46
WORKDEPT and EMPNO added as columns to the select list.

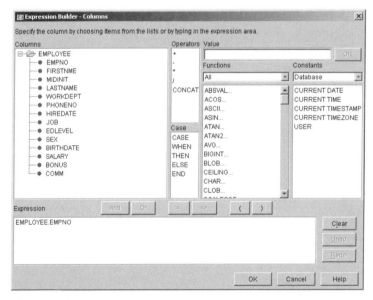

Figure 18.47
Expression Builder screen.

Because the final query needs to find a COUNT of employees, the EMPNO column must be modified. To do this, the […] button beside the EMPNO field is clicked to display the Expression Builder screen (Figure 18.47).

To create a COUNT function, the user would select COUNT from the functions list. This generates an additional panel that needs to be filled in (Figure 18.48).

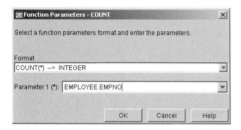

Figure 18.48
COUNT function builder.

The EMPNO column is selected as the parameter for the count function. When you click OK, the COUNT function is returned to the expression window in the Expression Builder panel (Figure 18.49).

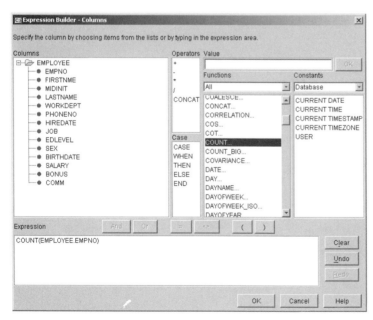

Figure 18.49
Generated COUNT expression.

When OK is clicked in the Expression Builder panel, the function is returned back to the main SQL Assist panel and this value replaces the EMPNO field in the selection list (Figure 18.50).

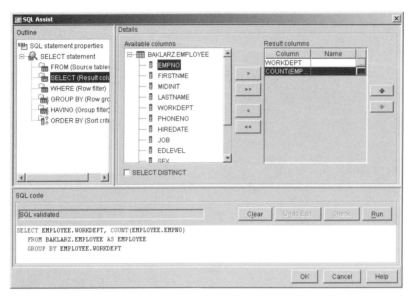

Figure 18.50
Modified select list.

The next step in building the SQL statement would be to add the WHERE logic that selects which rows should be included in the calculations. Pressing the WHERE node generates the panel shown in Figure 18.51.

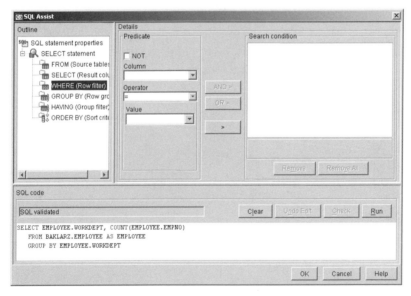

Figure 18.51
WHERE clause construction.

Multiple search conditions can be added to a WHERE clause. Each expression needs to be built separately using the supplied input fields and buttons.

The WHERE clause requires a column name, an operator, and a value or column to compare against.

The first field that needs to be filled in is the column that is going to be tested against a condition. This is a drop-down field. When the user clicks on the down arrow, the system displays a list of fields that are available for testing (Figure 18.52).

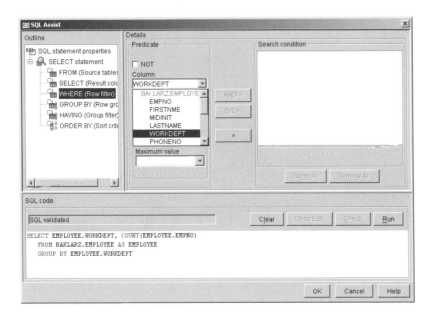

Figure 18.52
Columns available for testing.

One of the fields would be selected (WORKDEPT) from this list.

The additional fields also have drop-down values. The comparison field contains any of the normal algebraic comparison operators, including some specific to SQL. In some cases the choice of comparison operator might change the number of value fields. This is the case with the SQL BETWEEN operator. The BETWEEN operator always requires two values to check between a range of numbers.

The final field contains the value or column the comparison would occur against. In this example, the BETWEEN operator is selected so a minimum and maximum value must be entered. The user can enter an expression, a list of values, or a host variable. A host variable is only relevant when you are developing SQL within the procedure or function builder (Figure 18.53).

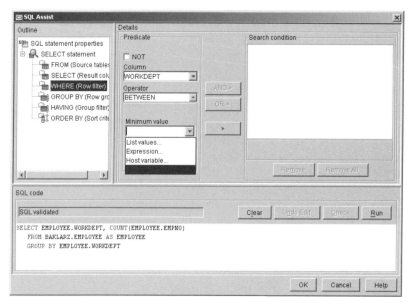

Figure 18.53
Selecting values for a comparison operator.

Selecting List Values… generates a list of values that are found in the WORKDEPT column. The user can then select a department number from this list to include in the value field (Figure 18.54).

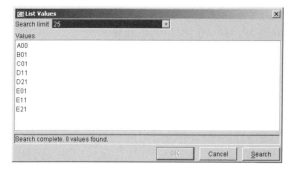

Figure 18.54
List of WORKDEPT values.

Once the minimum and maximum values for the BETWEEN comparison operator have been entered, the user must remember to add the logic to the list by clicking [>] (Figure 18.55).

Note that as changes are made in the SQL Assist tool, the SQL is updated to reflect the changes. The SQL can be verified at any time by running the statement and viewing the results.

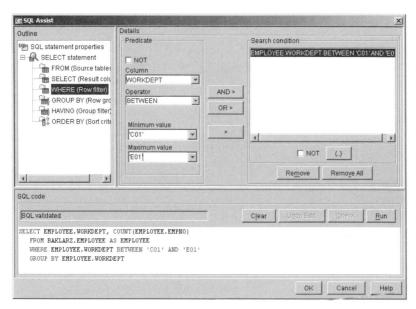

Figure 18.55
Logic added to the SELECT clause.

Because the SQL is counting the number of employees per department, a GROUP BY clause must be generated. The tool is aware of this requirement and has already generated the appropriate SQL (Figure 18.56).

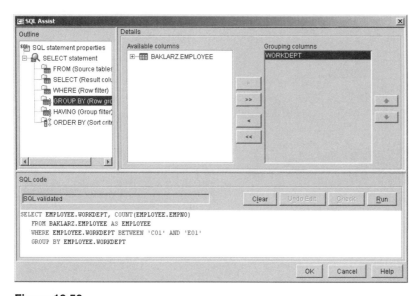

Figure 18.56
Generated GROUP BY clause.

The next node in the select statement is the HAVING clause. This clause limits the rows returned by the GROUP BY clause. The WHERE clause restricts the rows returned based on their contents, and the HAVING clause restricts the rows returned by the GROUP BY clause. In this example, the HAVING clause statement needs to be modified to return GROUP BY values that have a value of 2. In other words, it will only return the list of departments that have at least two employees (Figure 18.57).

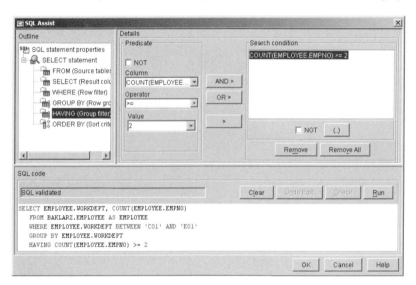

Figure 18.57
HAVING clause.

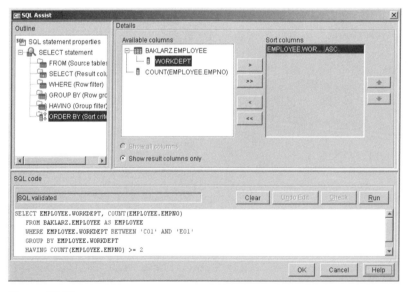

Figure 18.58
Sort results by department number.

The last step in generating the SQL is to decide in which order the rows should be sorted. In this example, the rows are sorted by department number (Figure 18.58).

Now that the SQL statement has been completed, the user can click OK to return the SQL to the calling application, or click Run to view the results. Running the SQL before placing it into an application helps in verifying the results before placing it into production (Figure 18.59).

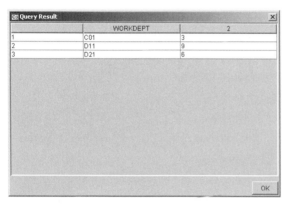

Figure 18.59
Results from SQL statement.

Summary

The SQL Assist tool is extremely helpful in developing SQL for the end user. The tool can create INSERT, DELETE, UPDATE, and SELECT statements by prompting the user for appropriate input. The tool can also be used for prototyping SQL for applications and checking the results.

JAVA ENHANCEMENTS

Many new features and enhancements have been made to the JDBC drivers in DB2 UDB v8.1. The biggest change is a new JDBC driver architecture known as the IBM DB2 JDBC Universal Driver.

The JDBC Universal driver is a new driver for DB2 UDB v8.1. This is not a follow-up release of existing JDBC or CLI drivers, nor does it have any dependency on CLI (ODBC). This driver is designed to replace the Type 3 driver and users should migrate applets to the Type 4 driver in preparation for the end of Type 3 driver support.

The Universal Driver is a JDBC driver for distributed and local DB2 access. It is independent of any particular JDBC driver-type connectivity or target operating system and it supports both all-Java connectivity (Type 4) and JNI-based connectivity (Type 2) to DB2 in a single-driver instance.

A single JDBC Universal Driver instance is loaded by the driver manager for both Type 4 and Type 2 implementations. This characteristic minimizes behavioral differences between the various driver types.

The Type 4 connectivity provided by the JDBC Universal Driver is all-Java remote connectivity, which is based on the Distributed Relational Database Architecture (DRDA) for cross-platform access to DB2. The Type 2 connectivity is based on shared memory using local DRDA application server buffers.

Type 4 Driver Platform Support

For DB2 UDB v8.1, the universal JDBC driver supports Type 4 connectivity with the UNIX, Windows, and OS/390 DRDA application servers.

Because the JDBC Universal Driver Type 4 implementation is pure Java, it is an ideal JDBC driver for Java applet and servlet deployments. The universal JDBC driver supports Type 4 connectivity to the following:

- DB2 UDB, v8.1, for Windows (2000, ME, Windows NT, and XP 32-bit), Windows 2003 32-bit and 64-bit, AIX 32-bit and 64-bit, Solaris Operating Environment 32-bit and 64-bit, Linux IA-32 and z31-bit, and HP 32-bit and 64-bit
- The JDBC Universal Driver does not provide support for Type 4 connectivity to previous versions of DB2 UDB on UNIX and Windows platforms
- DB2 UDB for z/OS(TM) and OS/390 versions 6, 7, and 8
- Cloudscape Network Server 5.1

Type 2 Platform Support

The JDBC Universal Driver supports Type 2 connectivity to DB2 UDB, v8.1, for Windows (2000, ME, Windows NT, and XP 32-bit), Windows 2003 32-bit and 64-bit, AIX 32-bit and 64-bit, Solaris Operating Environment 32-bit and 64-bit, Linux IA-32 and z31-bit, and HP 32-bit and 64-bit.

Additional Features

Additional features of the new JDBC drivers include the following:

- A new SQLJ profile customizer that uses the Type 4 JDBC driver.
- 64-bit platform support.
- Compatible with Java 2 JRE 11.3.1 clients.
- Better memory management improves the stability and performance of the drivers.
- The new SQLJ translator supports the java.sql.Blob and java.sql.Clob types of JDBC 2.0, as well as host variable expressions.

PACKAGE VERSION IDENTIFIERS

DB2 has the ability to support multiple versions of the same package in a single system using the new version option for packages. This option allows a developer to introduce and test a new version of a package on the system without affecting users of the existing version of the package. The support of the version option allows ongoing package maintenance to occur without interruption of end-user access to the system.

Package Overview

DB2 allows a developer to use a variety of programming languages and APIs to access a database. Programs written in a high-level programming language such as C, C++, COBOL, or FORTRAN, can contain embedded SQL statements rather than calls to a function library. This simplifies development of database applications, but to make these applications work against a database, they must be precompiled. The precompilation step converts the embedded SQL into native language calls and also generates a package.

A package is a database object that contains optimized SQL statements. A package corresponds to a single-source programming module and sections correspond to the SQL statements contained in the source program module.

The package can be stored directly in the database or the data needed to create a package can be stored in a bind file. Creating a bind file and binding it in a separate step is known as *deferred binding*.

The bind process needs to be performed following each successful precompile of the application source modules. When the bind file is created, a timestamp is stored in the package. The timestamp is sometimes referred to as a *consistency token*. This same timestamp is also stored in the database when the bind is completed and is used to ensure that the resulting application executes the proper SQL statement.

The modified source module (output from the precompile) attempts to execute the SQL statements by package name and section number. If the required package and section are not found, an error message is generated. If the required package and section exist in the database system catalogs, the timestamp is then checked. If the timestamp in the application executable does not match the timestamp stored in the system catalog tables in the database, the following message is returned:

```
SQL0818N A timestamp conflict occurred. SQLSTATE=51003
```

To avoid this problem, you can use the VERSION option during the precompilation step. The VERSION option allows multiple packages that share both the schema and package ID to coexist in the system catalogs. The PREP, BIND, REBIND, and DROP PACKAGE facilities have also been enhanced to support package versioning.

VERSION Example

A sample application called PAYROLL is compiled from PAYROLL.SQC. This application would be precompiled and the package PAYROLL bound to the database and the application delivered to the users. The users could then run the application in production.

If the application required modification (even without SQL changes), the process of recompiling, binding, and sending the application to the users must be repeated. If the VERSION option was not specified for this second precompilation of PAYROLL, the first package is replaced by the second package. Any user who attempts to run the old version of the application receives the SQLCODE -818 error, indicating a mismatched timestamp error.

The use of the VERSION option avoids the mismatched timestamp error and allows both versions of the application to run at the same time. When the first version of PAYROLL was created, the VERSION option should be used during the precompiler step.

As an example, when you build the first version of PAYROLL, precompile it using the VERSION option, as follows:

```
DB2 PREP PAYROLL.SQC VERSION V1.1
```

This first version of the program can now be run in production. When a change is made to the application, the precompile command should use a different version number, as shown here:

```
DB2 PREP PAYROLL.SQC VERSION V1.2
```

At this point this new version of the application will also run, even if there still are instances of the first application executing. Because the package version for the first package is V1.1 and the package version for the second is V1.2, no naming conflict exists: Both packages can exist in the database and both versions of the application can be used.

In addition to the VERSION option, the ACTION option of the PRECOMPILE or BIND commands can also be used to control the way in which different versions of packages can be added or replaced.

Package Privileges

A GRANT or REVOKE of a package privilege applies to all versions of a package that share the name and creator. Therefore, if package privileges on package PAYROLL were granted to a user or a group after V1.1 was created, when V1.2 is distributed, the user or group has the same privileges on V1.2. Normally this behavior makes sense because the same users and groups will want to use this package. If you do not want the same package privileges to apply to all versions of an application, you should not use the PRECOMPILE VERSION option to accomplish package versioning. Instead, you should use different package names and grant user access to them.

FLUSH PACKAGE CACHE

This function introduces the ability to remove cached dynamic SQL statements from the package cache using a new SQL statement, FLUSH PACKAGE CACHE. This statement allows you to remove cached dynamic SQL statements from the package cache by invalidating them.

Although most normal activities that affect the validity of cached dynamic SQL statements are already handled by DB2, certain activities, such as the new online update of database and database manager configuration parameters, are not. This statement allows you to manually invalidate cached dynamic SQL statements for those scenarios not automatically handled by DB2.

The FLUSH PACKAGE CACHE statement removes all cached dynamic SQL statements currently in the package cache. This statement causes the logical invalidation of any cached dynamic SQL statement and forces the next request for the same SQL statement to be implicitly compiled by DB2.

This is the syntax for the command:

```
>>-FLUSH PACKAGE CACHE--DYNAMIC-------------------------------.-------><
```

This statement affects all cached dynamic SQL entries in the package cache on all active database partitions.

Any cached dynamic SQL statement currently in use is allowed to continue to exist in the package cache until it is no longer needed by the current user; the next new user of the same statement forces an implicit prepare of the statement by DB2, and the new user executes the new version of the cached dynamic SQL statement.

SUMMARY

DB2 UDB v8.1 introduces a number of new and enhanced functions for the application developer.

The Development Center and SQL Assist tool both aid the developer in producing functions, stored procedures, and SQL statements. Included with the Development Center are new object creation and debugging tools that give the user improved capability over the old Stored Procedure Builder.

Java support has been enhanced in DB2 UDB with the introduction of a new driver architecture and a native Type 4 driver.

Finally, versioned package support and the ability to flush dynamic statements from memory round out the application development enhancements found in this release.

CHAPTER **19**

DB2 in the Microsoft Environment

DB2 UDB has supported the Windows environment for many years. Enhancements to DB2 have included support for the operating system, application development environment, database APIs, subsystem support, and Windows certification. A small sample of this support includes the following:

- Operating system support, such as Windows NT, Windows 2000, and Windows 2003
- Windows API support—ODBC and OLE-DB
- Operating system exploitation—NTFS, kernel threads, and security integration
- Windows certification—BackOffice certification, Windows 2000 Datacenter Server certification
- Subsystem support—Distributed Transaction Services (COM+/DTS), Microsoft Cluster Server (MSCS)
- Application development—Visual Studio and Visual Basic integration

DB2 UDB v8.1 continues to enhance support for the Microsoft environment. Improvements in DB2 include support for the following:

- Windows 2003 family of servers
- OLE DB and .NET driver support enhancements
- COM+/DTS improvements
- Windows Management Interface support
- Visual Studio .NET integration

One of the key features from a development perspective is the support for the .NET Framework. These features include the following:

- A native DB2 for .NET Data Provider that is developed and supported by IBM. No third-party drivers or bridge solutions are needed.
- A collection of add-ins for the Visual Studio .NET IDE that simplify creation of the applications that use the ADO.NET API. These add-ins also extend the power of Visual Studio .NET to developing DB2 server-side objects such as stored procedures and UDFs.
- Cross-platform support with access to a tremendous volume of data stored in thousands of DB2 databases. Applications that are developed on Windows can access DB2 servers on Windows, UNIX, Linux, and mainframes.

These features, along with additional Windows enhancements, are described in this chapter.

WINDOWS 2003 SUPPORT

The Windows version of DB2 UDB v8.1 provides more than just a platform port. DB2 for Windows exploits key capabilities of the Windows operating system. Earlier versions of DB2 included integration with the Windows security model, Active Directory, and key administrative tools. DB2 UDB v8.1 builds on this foundation and adds support for the Windows 2003 Server platform including the 64-bit architecture.

DB2 UDB v8.1 supports the following versions of Windows 2003:

- Server Edition
  - Up to 4-way SMP support
  - 4 GB of RAM
- Enterprise Server Edition
  - Up to 8-way SMP support
  - 32 GB of memory on 32-bit version, 64 GB of memory on 64-bit version
  - Support for eight-node clustering
- Datacenter Server Edition
  - Up to 32-way SMP support (8-way minimum), 64 GB of memory on 32-bit version
  - Up to 64-way SMP support, 512 GB of memory on 64-bit version
  - Support for eight-node clustering

In addition, DB2 UDB v8.1 supports the Windows XP Professional product for both 32-bit and 64-bit versions. However, the DB2 Enterprise Server Edition can only be used for testing purposes on this platform. Either the Windows 2000 or Windows 2003 servers must be used for production.

The DB2 products that support the 32-bit Windows 2003 environment include the following:

- DB2 UDB Servers
  - Personal Edition
  - Workgroup Server Edition
  - Workgroup Server Unlimited Edition
  - Enterprise Server Edition (including partitioning)
  - DB2 UDB Express Edition

- Developer Kits
  - Personal Developer's Edition
  - Universal Developer's Edition
- DB2 Connect
  - Personal Edition
  - Connect Enterprise Edition
  - Connect Unlimited Edition
  - Application Server Edition
- DB2 Extenders
  - Net Search Extender
  - Spatial Extender
- Additional products
  - DB2 Warehouse Manager Standard Edition
  - DB2 UDB Data Warehouse Standard Edition
  - DB2 UDB Data Warehouse Enterprise Edition
  - DB2 Intelligent Miner Modeling
  - DB2 Intelligent Miner Scoring
  - DB2 Intelligent Miner Visualization
  - DB2 Cube Views

For the 64-bit environment, the following products run in native 64-bit mode:

- DB2 UDB Servers
  - Personal Edition
  - Enterprise Server Edition (including partitioning)
- Developer Kits
  - Personal Developer's Edition
  - Universal Developer's Edition
- DB2 Connect
  - Personal Edition
  - Connect Enterprise Edition
  - Connect Unlimited Edition
  - Application Server Edition
- DB2 Extenders
  - Net Search Extender
  - Spatial Extender

DB2 DEVELOPMENT ADD-INS FOR VISUAL STUDIO .NET

Microsoft Visual Studio .NET is a key integrated software development environment on the Windows platform. The DB2 Development Add-Ins for Visual Studio .NET provide a set of tightly integrated application development and administration tools specifically designed for DB2 Universal Database that integrate into this environment.

With the DB2 Development Add-Ins for Visual Studio .NET, you can do the following:

- Add DB2 database projects to your applications that use the DB2 managed provider.
- Create DB2 scripts for creating and managing stored procedures, UDFs, tables, views, indexes, triggers, and any other database elements.
- Use predefined code templates or script generation wizards.
- Explore the catalog information of the DB2 family of servers and view properties, source code, and data of tables, views, and routines.
- Drag and drop your server objects onto your Visual Basic and C# Windows forms to automatically generate the required DB2 managed provider ADO.NET code.
- Configure your DB2DataAdapter, DB2Connection, and DB2Command managed provider toolbox controls.
- Launch various DB2 development and administration centers.

Product Availability

The Visual Studio .NET add-ins require the DB2 UDB v8.1 development client for code development, and an environment that supports development in the .NET Framework. For Visual Studio .NET this can include Windows NT, Windows 2000, Windows XP, and Windows 2003. Developers should consider migrating from Windows NT because a number of Visual Studio .NET features are not supported in this environment.

The database server can be local on the development machine, or remote on any one of these servers:

- DB2 UDB v8.1 on Windows NT, Windows 2000, Windows XP, and Windows 2003
- DB2 UDB v8.1 on Linux
- DB2 UDB v8.1 on HP, AIX, and Solaris Operating Environment
- DB2 for z/OS and OS/390 version 7 or greater

Registering the Visual Studio .NET Add-Ins

The DB2 Development Add-Ins are installed as part of DB2 Application Development Client installation. DB2 UDB must be installed at the v8, FixPak 2 level to get this support.

If Visual Studio .NET was installed before you installed DB2, the DB2 Development Add-Ins are registered automatically. The initial Visual Studio .NET startup screen displays the DB2 Project Tools icon as a visual confirmation that this support is installed (Figure 19.1).

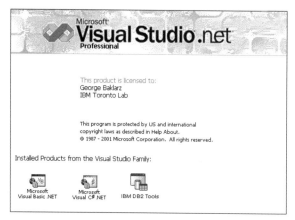

Figure 19.1
Visual Studio .NET startup.

If Visual Studio .NET was installed after DB2 or modified after DB2 installation, the add-ins must be manually registered. Registration can be accomplished through the DB2 setup tools or with a command. The setup tool is found within the DB2 folder on the desktop (Figure 19.2).

Figure 19.2
Registering DB2 project add-ins.

Alternatively, the DB2VSRGX.BAT command can be run before Visual Studio .NET is started. The DB2VSURGX.BAT command is used to unregister DB2 from the Visual Studio .NET environment.

Development Overview

The key integrated development features of the DB2 Development Add-Ins for Visual Studio .NET includes the following:

- Solution explorer—Enables database developers to build DB2 server-side objects, including routines, triggers, tables, and views using script files.
- Server explorer—Gives application developers access to DB2 server-side objects from any tier of their application, including Win/Web forms in the presentation layer, and class assemblies/Web services in the business and data access layers.

- SQL editor—Enables application developers to use the Visual Studio .NET editor to edit and view DB2 scripts.
- Dynamic help—Provides application developers with fast access to DB2 Development Add-Ins help topics.
- Output views—Provides a medium for showing the results of compiling or testing the various DB2 script files and server objects.
- Managed provider—Enables application developers to code to the DB2 server-side objects using ADO.NET programming model.

In addition, database developers can launch development and administration tools from a toolbar.

Solution Explorer

The Visual Studio .NET solution explorer provides you with an organized view of your projects and their files as well as ready access to the commands that pertain to them (Figure 19.3).

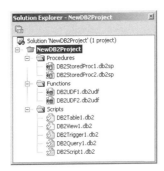

Figure 19.3
Visual Studio Solution Explorer—DB2 database project.

You can add a variety of project types to each Visual Studio .NET solution including C#, Visual Basic, and database projects. Each project can contain one or more folders and subfolders for grouping project items. For a typical database project, these project items include queries, procedures, functions, tables, and views.

The DB2 Development Add-In extends the Visual Studio .NET project templates to include an IBM Projects folder with a specific DB2 database project that can be created and managed in the Solution Explorer.

DB2 Database Project

The DB2 database project lets you use script-based development of server-side objects. Each script file can contain DB2 DDL and data manipulation language (DML) SQL statements. Using these scripts, you can create SQL stored procedures, SQL UDFs, tables, views, indexes, triggers, and user-defined types.

With a DB2 database project, you can do the following:

- Add new or existing SQL stored procedure scripts
- Add new or existing SQL UDF scripts
- Add new or existing scripts based on generic templates that contain supported DB2 DDL and DML
- Specify project dependencies and project build order in the solution
- Specify build configuration options including script files build order
- Check your script files into any configured source control management system such as Microsoft Visual Source Safe

Script Template Files

The DB2 database project provides you with an initial set of predefined script templates. These script files serve as an initial starting point for developing DB2 scripts:

- Stored Procedure script—A script to drop and then create a sample SQL stored procedure. You can modify the script to include additional supporting SQL such as granting access for the procedure and altering the procedure.
- SQL Scalar UDF script—A script to drop and then create a sample SQL scalar UDF. You can modify the script to create SQL table functions or to include additional SQL for managing or testing the table function.
- Sample table creation script—A script to drop and then create a sample table. You can expand the script to include advanced table properties, such as table spaces, indexes, constraints, and referential integrity rules.
- Sample view creation script—A script to drop and then create a sample table view.
- Sample trigger script—A script to drop and then create a sample trigger. Multiple triggers can be defined in the same script file.
- Query script—A script to query data from database tables. Multiple queries can be defined, including other SQL statements like INSERT, UPDATE, and DELETE.
- Blank generic script—Any valid DB2 SQL can be defined in this script. One way to use this type of script would be to write test scripts that are not part of the project build, but can be executed as required to test some server-side objects.

With Visual Studio .NET customization options, you can also add your own set of DB2 script templates that apply to your project requirements.

Script Wizards

The DB2 database project also provides a set of script generation wizards that allows for the customization of the generated script files.

- SQL Stored Procedure Wizard—The DB2 SQL Stored Procedure Wizard guides you through the steps required to customize an SQL procedure script, including adding one or more SQL statements, specifying parameters, and inserting code and script fragments from flat text files.

- SQL User-Defined Function Wizard—The DB2 SQL User-Defined Function Wizard guides you through the steps required to customize an SQL function script similar to the procedure script customization with the additional support for generating scalar or table functions.

Server Explorer

The DB2 Development Add-In extends the Visual Studio .NET environment by adding a new tool window called IBM Explorer. The IBM Explorer provides Visual Studio .NET users with access to IBM database connections using the Data Connections folder. The Data Connections folder in IBM Explorer is similar to the Data Connections folder in the Server Explorer, but it is specifically designed for DB2 managed provider connections (Figure 19.4).

Figure 19.4
DB2 Data Connections folder.

The Data Connections folder in the IBM Explorer enables you to do the following:

- Work with multiple named DB2 connections supporting connect-on-demand technology
- Specify database catalog filters and local caching for higher performance and scalability
- View properties of server objects including tables, views, and routines
- Retrieve data from tables and views
- Execute test runs for routines
- View source code for SQL stored procedures and UDFs
- Generate ADO .NET code using drag and drop

Working with Connections

Using the Add Connection menu entry off the Data Connections folder, you can add any number of DB2 managed provider connections (Figure 19.5).

- Multiple `DB2Parameter` objects based on the parameters information for the procedure or function.

The `DB2Connection` and corresponding `DB2Command` objects are visible in the component tray. The command parameters are invisible.

SQL Editor

The DB2 Development Add-In extends the native Visual Studio .NET editor with a specialized DB2 SQL editor. With the editor you can view and modify your DB2 SQL code and script files as shown in Figure 19.6.

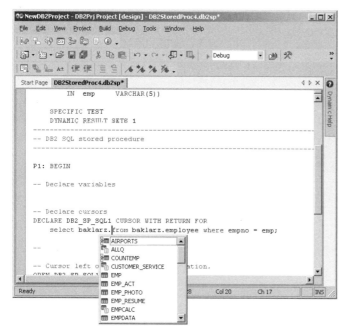

Figure 19.6
DB2 SQL editor.

The DB2 SQL editor includes the following features:

- Colorized SQL text for increased readability based on DB2 SQL syntax.
- Integration with the Microsoft Visual Studio .NET IntelliSense feature, which allows for intelligent autocompletion while typing DB2 scripts. This includes object names for a given schema, column names for tables or views, and parameters for procedures and functions.
- An editor menu that lets you insert frequently used SQL code fragments.

Dynamic Help

The DB2 Development Add-In Help feature integrates tightly with the Visual Studio .NET help facility. You can access the content-based help for a specific topic, or you can view the dynamic help based on the development context you are in (Figure 19.7).

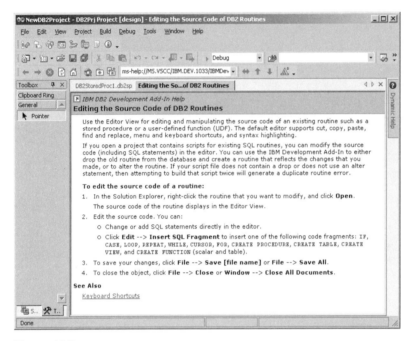

Figure 19.7
DB2 Development Add-In Help.

Output Views

The DB2 Development Add-In for Visual Studio .NET makes use of the standard views to show results of various actions. The example given in Figure 19.8 shows the results of a SELECT statement being returned into a standard DataGrid and messages in Output window.

A read-only DB2 output data grid is shown whenever you execute a development task that results in a data set. This includes the following:

- Issuing a test run on any language stored procedure or UDFs.
- Retrieving data from tables or views.
- Executing DB2 scripts that call stored procedures or UDFs.
- Executing DB2 scripts that insert, delete, update, or select data from DB2 tables or views.

The standard output pane is used to display compiled results for project script items. More detailed information pertaining to executing development tasks against DB2 servers is displayed

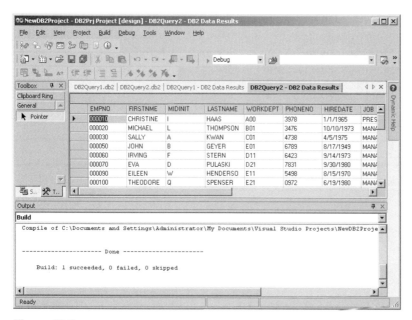

Figure 19.8
SELECT statement results

in the DB2 Message pane. This includes messages resulting from executing DB2 scripts or catalog access queries.

Customizing the DB2 Development Tools

You can customize the DB2 Development Add-In for Visual Studio .NET by setting various tool
options using the standard Visual Studio .NET Options dialog box. The Options dialog box can
be launched using the Tools ➤ Options… menu entry. Select the IBM DB2 Tools Options folder
(Figure 19.9).

Figure 19.9
DB2 Development settings.

Not all of the options are included in the Options dialog box. You can manually modify all of the supported options shown in Figure 19.9 by editing the *userOptions.xml* file in the %APP-DATA%\IBM\vsnet folder. Make sure to exit Visual Studio .NET before modifying this file. To revert back to the default settings, simply delete this file.

The options and their default settings are found in Table 19.1.

Table 19.1 Development Options

Name	Default	Description
StatementSeparator	@	Character to be used as the DB2 script file statement delimiter.
MaxRows	100	Maximum number of rows to retrieve for tables and views.
Timeout	30	Database command execution timeout in seconds.
PrefetchCache	True	Prefetch filtered database catalog data cache on first retrieval.
HideExtensions	True	Hide file name extensions.
PromptConnOnNew	true	Show connection selection dialog box when a new project is created.
UsePrimaryKeys	False	Optimize SQL WHERE clause code generation for UPDATE and DELETE using primary keys.
FontName	Arial	Font name for dialog boxes, wizards, and other windows.
FontSize	8	Font size for dialog boxes, wizards, and other windows.

Edit the *userOptions.xml* file for a complete list of options with their descriptions.

Launching DB2 Development and Administration Tools

You can launch DB2 development and administration tools from the Visual Studio.NET IDE, including the following:

- Development Center—Use the Development Center to develop routines such as SQL and Java (JDBC or SQLJ) routines. Using the Development Center, you can do the following:

  - Create routines and structured types
  - Build routines and structured types on local and remote DB2 servers
  - Modify and rebuild existing routines
  - Run routines for testing and debugging
  - Deploy routines from a development project or database to a production server

  The Development Center provides a single development environment that supports the entire DB2 family ranging from the workstation to z/OS. For more information on the Development Center, refer to Chapter 18.

- Command Center—The Command Center is used to execute DB2 commands and SQL statements, execute z/OS or OS/390 host system console commands, work with command scripts, and view a graphical representation of the access plan for explained SQL statements.
- Control Center—The Control Center is used to manage systems, DB2 UDB instances, DB2 UDB for OS/390 and z/OS subsystems, databases, and database objects such as tables and views. In the Control Center, you can display all of your systems, databases, and database objects and perform administration tasks for those objects.
- Task Center—The Task Center is used to organize task flow, schedule tasks, and distribute notifications about the status of completed tasks. You can create tasks using a script that contains DB2, operating system, or MVS JCL commands.
- Health Center—The Health Center is the tool that identifies key performance and resource allocation problems within DB2, through notifications such as alarms or warnings. It also provides recommended actions that can help to resolve the problems.
- Journal Center—The Journal displays historical information about tasks, database actions and operations, Control Center actions, messages, and alerts.
- Replication Center—The Replication Center administers relational data between DB2 servers or databases. From the Replication Center, you can define replication environments, copy designated changes from one location to another, and synchronize the data in both locations.
- Information Center—The Information Center contains information on commands, instructions, messages, and other information about DB2 UDB.

You can launch these tools either from the DB2 Tools toolbar (Figure 19.10) or by Tools ➤ IBM DB2 Tools (Figure 19.11).

Figure 19.10
DB2 Tools toolbar.

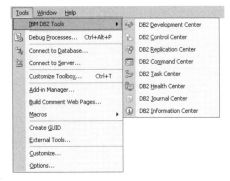

Figure 19.11
DB2 Tools menu.

Summary

The DB2 Development Add-In for Microsoft Visual Studio .NET provides you with a set of seamlessly integrated application development tools for developing applications specifically designed for DB2 UDB servers.

With the DB2 Development Add-In, you can now use your Visual Studio .NET IDE to develop applications that leverage the power and rich functionality of the DB2 UDB for z/OS, Windows, Linux, and UNIX servers.

NATIVE MANAGED .NET PROVIDERS

DB2 UDB v8.1 (FP2) ships with a .NET managed provider, IBM.Data.DB2, which is specifically designed to work with DB2 servers. This native managed provider can give you significant performance improvement over the OLE DB and ODBC bridges, and it also provides the ability to exploit the specific features of DB2 servers.

DB2 Managed Provider ADO.NET Objects

The DB2 managed provider classes are similar to Microsoft SQL Server (System.Data.SqlClient) classes. They include the following:

- IBM.Data.DB2.DB2Connection—This object establishes a connection to a DB2 data source.
- IBM.Data.DB2.DB2Command—This object executes an SQL statement or stored procedure call against a DB2 data source.
- IBM.Data.DB2.DB2CommandBuilder—This object automatically generates commands to reconcile changes made to a DataSet with the associated DB2 data source.
- IBM.Data.DB2.DB2DataAdapter—This object defines a set of data commands and database connection that are used to fill a DataSet and update the DB2 data source.

DB2 Objects in the Visual Studio .NET Data Toolbox

When the DB2 managed provider is installed, a set of DB2 ADO.NET objects are added to the Data tab of the Visual Studio .NET toolbox. These objects include the DB2DataAdapter, DB2Connection, and DB2Command (Figure 19.12).

You can drag and drop these controls and drop them on a form, which adds the appropriate DB2 managed provider objects to your form's design-time component tray. Appropriate ADO.NET code is generated to initialize these objects.

Figure 19.12
Managed provider in toolbox.

Sample DB2 ADO.NET Code

The following example illustrates sample DB2 ADO.NET code that creates a data adapter and binds it to a data grid:

```
// Create a connection string and make the connection to a database
string connectionString = "Database=Sample";
DB2Connection myDB2Connection = new DB2Connection();
myDB2Connection.ConnectionString = connectionString;

// Now create a DB2Command to present a SELECT statement
DB2Command db2SelectCommand = new DB2Command();
db2SelectCommand.CommandText = "Select * from Customers";
db2SelectCommand.Connection = myDB2Connection;

// Create a DataAdapter for executing the Select statement
DB2DataAdapter da = new DB2DataAdapter();
DB2DataAdapter.SelectCommand = db2SelectCommand;

// Create DataSet object and fill it with data
DataSet ds = new DataSet();
da.Fill(ds, "Customers");

// Attach this dataset to a data-bound visual control (DataGrid).
DataGrid dataGrid1 = new DataGrid();
dataGrid1.DataSource = ds.DefaultViewManager;
```

Managed Provider Tools

The DB2 Development Add-Ins for Visual Studio .NET provides integrated user interfaces to surface some of the features of the DB2 managed provider.

DB2 Data Connection Editor

The Data Connection editor lets you choose a DB2 managed provider data connection from the list of connections in IBM Explorer. You also have the option of adding a new connection. When a connection is chosen, the DB2 managed provider connection string is automatically generated for the DB2 ADO .NET connection object (Figure 19.13).

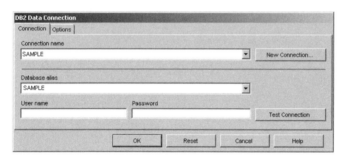

Figure 19.13
DB2 Data Connection editor.

The Data Connection editor dialog box is displayed when clicking the ellipses (…) for the connection string property of the DB2 ADO.NET connection object shown in the design-time component tray of a form.

DB2 Data Adapter Configuration Wizard

Use the DB2 Data Adapter Configuration Wizard to set or modify the various properties of a DB2 ADO.NET Data Adapter object. These properties include the data connection string and the SELECT, INSERT, UPDATE, and DELETE statements and parameters.

The Data Adapter Configuration Wizard is automatically launched when you drop a data adapter control from the toolbox onto a form. You can launch it any time to reconfigure an existing data adapter in the form's design-time component tray.

The DB2 Data Adapter Configuration Wizard takes you through the following steps:

1. Select a data connection from the drop-down list. This list includes the data connections that are currently in IBM Explorer. If you want to add a new connection, click New Connection. The DB2 Data Adapter uses the specified database connection information to load and update data.

2. Specify statement options. If your DB2 data adapter is used to update the data source, the wizard can generate the INSERT, UPDATE, and DELETE statements. The wizard also steps you through the generated statements for further modification and optimization. The DB2 Data Adapter uses the SQL INSERT, UPDATE, and DELETE statements to update the data source.

3. Specify the SQL SELECT statement and its parameters. The DB2 Data Adapter uses the specified SELECT statement to load the data into the data set and to generate the INSERT, UPDATE, and DELETE statements.

4. Specify the optional SQL INSERT statement and its parameters. The INSERT statement is used to add new data to the data source. You can either generate or type the statement.

5. Specify the optional SQL UPDATE statement and its parameters. The UPDATE statement is used to update the data source. You can either generate or type the statement.

6. Specify the optional SQL DELETE statement and its parameters. The DELETE statement is used to delete data from the data source. You can either generate or type the statement.

DB2 Command Text Editor

The DB2 Command text custom editor allows for entering the appropriate SQL SELECT, INSERT, UPDATE, or DELETE statements, as well as the list of command parameters for a DB2 ADO.NET command object (Figure 19.14 and 19.15).

The DB2 Command text editor appears when you click the ellipses (...) for the command text property of the DB2 ADO.NET command object shown in the design-time component tray of a form. It can also be launched when clicking the ellipses (...) for the command text property of the DB2 ADO.NET command object that is part of a DB2 Data Adapter object.

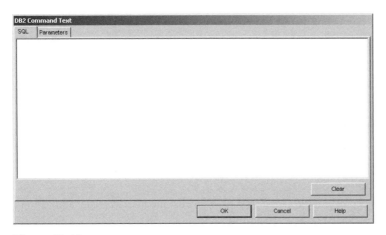

Figure 19.14
DB2 Command text editor—SQL statement tab.

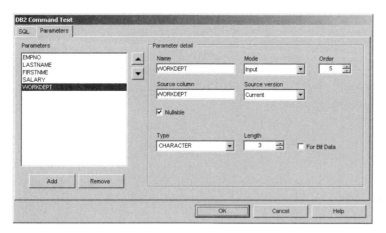

Figure 19.15
DB2 Command text editor—SQL statement Parameters tab.

The SQL tab of the Command text editor lets you specify the actual SQL statement; the Parameters tab lets you define and configure the list of command parameters. Any parameter markers specified using the question mark (?) or a colon (:) followed by the parameter name (:ParameterName) are automatically added as parameters to the command in the Parameters tab.

DB2 Database Project for Visual Studio .NET

The DB2 Database Project template for Visual Studio.NET lets you use scripts for developing server-side objects, including stored procedures, UDFs, tables, views, indexes, and additional objects. These DB2 scripts can contain DB2 DDL and DML SQL statements.

With a DB2 database project, you can do the following:

- Add new or existing SQL stored procedure scripts
- Add new or existing SQL UDF scripts
- Add new or existing scripts based on generic templates that contain supported DB2 DDL and DML
- Specify project dependencies and project build order in the solution
- Specify build configuration options including script files build order
- Check your script files into any configured source control management system such as Microsoft Visual Source Safe

Many of the wizards and scripts that are found in this section are also available in a simplified form in the Development Center. See the Development Center section in Chapter 18 to see some of the additional screens that are associated with the stored procedure and UDF wizards.

Adding a DB2 Database Project

You can add a DB2-specific database project to your Visual Studio solution using the Add New Project dialog box. The DB2 Development Add-Ins for Visual Studio.NET provide you with a new DB2 database project under the IBM Projects folder (Figure 19.16).

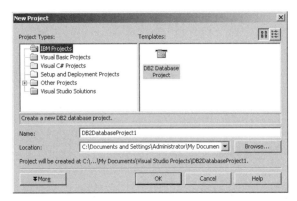

Figure 19.16
Add a new DB2 project.

All of the files related to this DB2 project are saved in the directory that is specified on this panel.

Choosing a DB2 Database Reference for Projects

When you build a DB2 database project, the project script files are compiled. Compiling a script file means executing the DDL and DML script against a DB2 database reference that is defined for your project. You can elect to choose a different database reference in each project build configuration.

After you specify the name of your project, the system prompts you for a data connection (Figure 19.17).

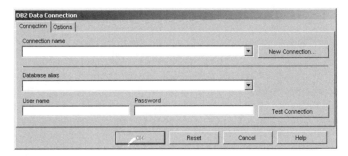

Figure 19.17
DB2 data connection.

If a data connection has already been defined, you can select it from the list. If not, the New Connection button lets you create a new database connection (Figure 19.18).

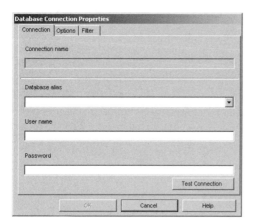

Figure 19.18
Add new DB2 database.

The database alias list contains a list of databases currently catalogued on the system. The user would select one of the databases and fill in any additional details or options that are required for this connection. The panel also includes a test button that can be used to verify that the connection works correctly. Once the database connection has been defined, the user is returned to the DB2 data connection screen with this new database in the list (Figure 19.19).

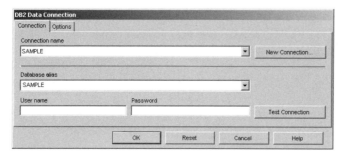

Figure 19.19
SAMPLE database in connection list.

Alternatively, you could choose a database reference by specifying the DB2 data connection name in the Data Connection project property. Clicking on the [...] property button launches the Data Connection dialog box, which allows you to select an existing IBM Explorer connection or add a new one.

DB2 Project Scripts

For any Visual Studio project, you can add new or existing items to a project. New items can be added directly under the project folder or any of the project subfolders.

All of the items in the DB2 project folders are DDL or DML script files. Although DB2 supports stored procedures and UDF in Java and other languages, only SQL language routines are shown. This restriction only applies to scripts for creating such routines—you can still view and use these routines using the IBM Explorer.

There are three default folders in the DB2 database project: procedures, functions, and scripts. Additional folders can be added to the project. These folders serve to organize your project items, which are DB2 scripts. Entries under each of the project folders are DB2 script file names and do not necessarily map to any actual object names that might be created by the script file.

The DB2 database project items are in two categories:

- Script template file entries that require no user input apart from the script file name to generate a default script file. These items include procedures, scalar and table functions, triggers, tables, table views, queries, and other generic DB2 scripts.
- Script wizard entries that launch an interactive wizard for customizing and generating the script file. These include wizards for creating SQL stored procedures and UDFs.

You can also add your own item templates using the Add New Items dialog box.

Procedure Scripts

The Procedures folder of your DB2 database project can contain any script files that are used to create and manage DB2 SQL stored procedures. These script files typically contain DROP and CREATE statements, as well as GRANT permission statements.

The stored procedure script files have been separated from generic script files to allow you to specify additional stored procedure build options including z/OS and OS/390 advanced build and execution options such as the WLM environment option (Figure 19.20).

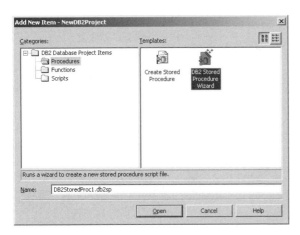

Figure 19.20
Adding a DB2 stored procedure to a DB2 database project.

Procedure Script Template

If you choose the Create Stored Procedure project item template shown in Figure 19.20, a default DB2 stored procedure script file is added to your project and shown in the editor. You can modify the script to include additional supporting DDL such as granting access for the procedure, altering the procedure, and so on, as shown here:

```
-- <ScriptOptions errors="off" platform390="off"/>
@
-- Drop the stored procedure if one already exists
DROP SPECIFIC PROCEDURE MySpecificSP
@
COMMIT
@
-- <ScriptOptions errors="on"/>
@
-- Create stored procedure
CREATE PROCEDURE MyProcedure (  )
  SPECIFIC MySpecificSP
  LANGUAGE SQL
  DYNAMIC RESULT SETS 1
------------------------------------------------------------
-- SQL Stored Procedure
------------------------------------------------------------
P1: BEGIN
-- Declare cursors
DECLARE DB2_SP_SQL1 CURSOR WITH RETURN FOR
  Select ROUTINENAME, ROUTINESCHEMA, LANGUAGE from
SYSIBM.SYSROUTINES;
-- Cursor left open for client application.
  OPEN DB2_SP_SQL1;
END P1
@
-- Grant access privileges to stored procedure
GRANT EXECUTE ON SPECIFIC PROCEDURE MySpecificSP TO PUBLIC
@
```

All of the other script wizards produce similar script files. The initial part of the script contains SQL that drops the existing object, followed by the SQL required to re-create it. In most cases, it also contains commands that modify the behavior of a script. These commands are discussed in the section on Advanced Script Options.

Procedure Script Wizard

If you choose the Create Stored Procedure Wizard project item template, the DB2 SQL Stored Procedure Wizard guides you through the steps required to customize the stored procedure body and script file according to your project requirements (Figure 19.21).

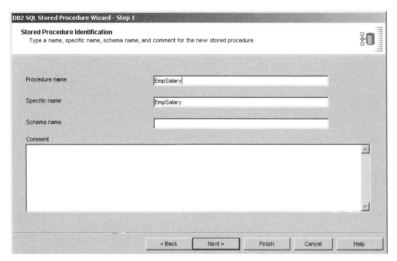

Figure 19.21
DB2 SQL Stored Procedure Wizard.

The Stored Procedure Wizard takes you through these steps:

1. Identification—Specify the procedure name, schema, specific name, and comment.
2. SQL statements—Create one or more SQL statements for the stored procedure.
3. Parameters—Specify parameters for the stored procedure.
4. Code options—Specify the files that contain code fragments that you want to insert in the generated stored procedure code. Also, specify the SQL error-handling code that you want to include in the stored procedure.
5. Script options—Specify files that contain script fragments that you want to insert in the generated stored procedure script. Also, specify additional SQL statements that you want to generate.
6. Summary and show code—Displays a summary of your options and the script file that will be generated.

Function Scripts

The Functions folder of your DB2 database project can contain any script files that are used to create and manage DB2 SQL UDFs. These script files typically contain DROP and CREATE statements, as well as GRANT permission statements (Figure 19.22).

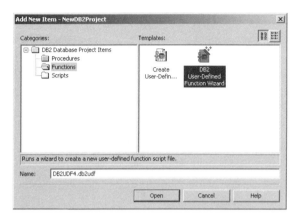

Figure 19.22
Adding a UDF to a DB2 database project.

If you choose the Create User-Defined Function project item template, a default DB2 script file
is added to your project and shown in the editor. If you choose the Create User-Defined Function
Wizard project item template, the wizard guides you through the steps required to customize the
UDF body and script file according to your project requirements (Figure 19.23).

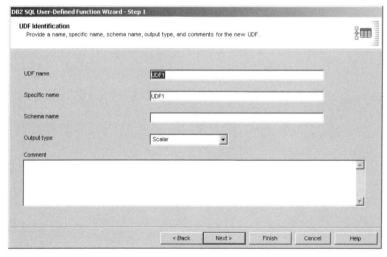

Figure 19.23
Using a wizard to create an SQL UDF.

The UDF wizard takes you through these steps:

    1. Identification—Specify the function name, schema, specific name, output type (table or
    scalar), and comment.

2. SQL statements—Create the scalar or tabular SQL query.

3. UDF return data type—Select the scalar type or the set of table column names and types.

4. Parameters—Specify input parameters for the UDF.

5. Code options—Specify the files that contain code fragments that you want to insert in the generated UDF code. Also, specify the SQL error-handling code that you want to include in the UDF.

6. Script options step—Specify files that contain script fragments that you want to insert in the generated UDF script. Also, specify additional SQL statements that you want to generate.

7. Summary and show code step—Displays a summary of your options and shows you the DB2 script file that will be generated.

Generic Scripts

Apart from supporting stored procedure and UDF scripts, the Add New Item Wizard lets you create generic DB2 script files that can contain any valid SQL statements. There are default templates for creating tables, views, triggers, and queries. These script files are added to your project and shown in the editor. You need to modify the script file according to your project requirements (Figure 19.24).

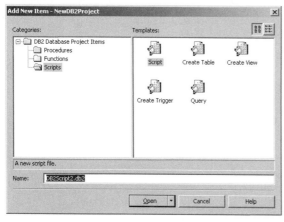

Figure 19.24
Adding a script for a DB2 database project.

Using the DB2 database project, you can create any number of DB2 tables and table indexes in a generic script file. If you choose the Create Table script file template, a default script file is added to your project and shown in the editor. You can modify the script to include advanced table properties, such as table spaces, indexes, constraints, and referential integrity rules.

When a script file is compiled, the old version of the table is dropped first and then the new one is created. Execution results are displayed in the output pane, but the new table does not appear automatically in IBM Explorer. You need to refresh the appropriate folder first.

In addition to tables, you can generate scripts for views, triggers, and queries. All of these scripts create a template with SQL related to the task.

In addition to these templates, a generic script template also exists. The generic script template is a blank script file. You can code any supported SQL statements in these script files. This is useful for developing applications. For example, you might have a project in which tables are created and data loaded as well. You can achieve this by coding the SQL load statement in a generic script, with the data being loaded from a text item that was added to the project in a generic project folder.

Advanced Scripting and Script Options

The DB2 Development Add-Ins for Visual Studio .NET provide a functionally rich scripting engine that goes above and beyond the creation of database server-side objects. You can also create custom scripts that use advanced scripting options to better meet project requirements.

Test Scripts

Using the generic script template, you can create a script file that tests the various database elements created by your DB2 project. For example, you could create a test script that creates a temporary table, populates it with test data, invokes a project stored procedure that operates on this table, passes in any required input parameters, and then cleans up and rolls back the transaction. This script can thus be used to test the functionality of the stored procedure.

Do not include these scripts in the project build; they typically reside in their own test DB2 database project.

Scripts and Database Transactions

By default, each script is executed as one unit of work. A new transaction is created at the start of a script file compilation. The transaction is committed at the end of the script file compilation if no errors were encountered. When an error is encountered during the compilation, the script execution ends and the transaction rolls back.

You can also embed your own set of `COMMIT` or `ROLLBACK` statements in the script file if you need to control transactions at a more granular level than a script file.

Advanced Script Options

The DB2 database project script files support a special XML tag that allows you to define script execution options. The special XML tag is preceded by the standard DB2 comment delimiter, namely, a double dash (`--`). The XML tag for this script option is `<ScriptOptions>`.

Ignoring Errors Option

When an error is encountered when a script file executes, the compilation step is halted. This might not be desirable in certain cases where the error is really a warning, allowing for the script execution to continue. One example would be a DROP SPECIFIC PROCEDURE statement before a CREATE PROCEDURE statement. The drop is there to ensure that the script can be built multiple times and that the older version of the procedure is deleted. This drop will fail the first time the script is executed because the procedure has not yet been created.

To treat errors as warnings, set the value of the *errors* script options property to Off. To revert back to the default behavior of treating errors as failures, set the property value to On, as shown here:

```
-- <ScriptOptions errors="off"/>
@
-- Drop the stored procedure if one already exists
DROP SPECIFIC PROCEDURE MySchema.MySpecificSP
@
-- <ScriptOptions errors="on"/>
@
```

Data Grid Output Option

For any database operation performed during a script file execution that results in a data set, the data set is displayed in an output data grid as well as in the DB2 Development Add-In output view.

Although this might be very desirable, especially for viewing results from executing test scripts, it is not always required. One example would be to avoid displaying results from an SQL INSERT statement, when displaying the resulting number of rows inserted in the output pane is sufficient.

To disable displaying data sets resulting from script execution in a data grid, set the value of the displayGrid script options property to Off. To revert back to the default behavior, set the property value to On, as shown here:

```
-- <ScriptOptions displayGrid="off"/>
@
-- Insert one record into the table
INSERT INTO MySchema.MyTable VALUES (1,'Kreg', 15, 'Mgr', '1990-01-01'
,
40000.00, 1000.00)
@
-- <ScriptOptions displayGrid="on"/>
@
```

Statement Separator Option

In most cases, your database project scripts contain more than one SQL statement. These statements must be separated by a character delimiter. The default character delimiter is the @ character. This default can be modified by directly accessing the *userOptions.xml* file or by using Tools ➤ Options ➤ IBM DB2 Tools.

When the separator is specified, it should remain the same. To ensure this, the `statementSeparator` option is used to specify this value, as shown here:

```
-- <ScriptOptions statementSeparator="@"/>
@
```

Platform Restriction Option

Although most of the DDL and DML in your scripts should abide by the DB2 family compatibility rules, there are situations in which it would make sense to have platform-specific SQL statements. These statements should only be executed on specific DB2 platforms. One such example is the use of the `PRIMARY KEY` clause in the `CREATE TABLE` statement. On Linux, UNIX, and Windows, DB2 automatically creates the required table index to enforce the key uniqueness. For z/OS, you must manually create the index. The platform restriction option allows you to accomplish this using the same script file.

To disable executing statements on the Linux, UNIX, and Windows platforms, set the `platformLUW` script options property to Off. To revert back to the default behavior, set the property value to On, as shown here. For z/OS and OS/390, use the platform390 script option property.

```
-- <ScriptOptions platformLUW="off"/>
@
-- Create primary key table index for z/OS
CREATE UNIQUE INDEX MySchema.MyTableIndex ON MySchema.MyTable(ID)
@
-- <ScriptOptions platformLUW="on"/>
@
```

Project Configurations and Properties

Although the standard Visual Studio database project does not support configurations, the DB2 database project does. Every project in Visual Studio can support multiple build configurations. This feature is driven at a solution or project level. The list of solution configurations for a given solution is managed by the Solution Configurations dialog box.

The ability to have multiple build configurations for a DB2 database project lets you choose different project database references, different SQL build options that are specific to a target database platform, different sets of script files that are to be compiled (executed) against that database connection, and so on.

The standard Visual Studio .NET properties grid with custom property value editors is used for managing project and project item properties.

Project Properties

Each DB2 project has a set of configuration-independent (common) properties, as well as configuration-specific properties. Project properties include such things as default database reference (for script execution), database user name and password, and so on (Figure 19.25).

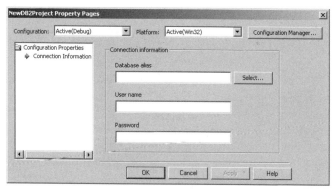

Figure 19.25
Visual Studio .NET project configurations dialog box for a DB2 database project.

Note that configuration-specific properties take precedence over common project properties; hence the ability to specify a different database connection per configuration (Figure 19.26).

Figure 19.26
Visual Studio .NET project properties for a DB2 database project.

Item Properties

Each DB2 project item has a set of configuration-specific properties, as well as configuration-independent properties.

Configuration-specific properties take precedence over common properties; hence the ability to specify different database build options per configuration (Figure 19.27).

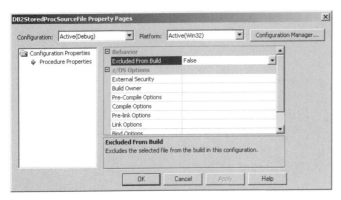

Figure 19.27
DB2 stored procedure properties.

Configuration-independent properties are divided into two groups: source-based and designer-based (see Figure 19.28). Source-based properties are parsed from the actual script file for the object (such as procedure name and schema). Parsing occurs when a file is opened or saved. Designer-based properties are not defined in the source (e.g., the z/OS build options).

Figure 19.28
Configuration-independent properties.

Persisting Properties

For DB2 projects, a project's common and configuration-specific properties are persisted in an XML project file. For DB2 project items, configuration-specific properties are persisted in the project file, but common properties (script-based and designer-based) are persisted in an XML file that is associated with each of the project items. This implementation has the advantage of always associating a project item with its properties, including the ability to check in these files into source code management systems or importing them into other projects as existing items.

To illustrate this, consider the project item procedure1. This item has a *procedure1.db2sp* script file and a *procedure1.db2spx* properties file (XML-based). Both *procedure1.db2sp* and *procedure1.db2spx* are treated as one item and are checked into and out of the source code management system together.

File Extensions

Table 19.2 includes the set of file extensions supported by DB2 projects.

Table 19.2 DB2 Project Items File Extensions

Item Type	Script Extension	Metadata Extension
Stored procedures	db2sp	db2spx
UDFs	db2udf	db2udfx
Scripts	db2	db2x
Miscellaneous	Any extension	None

Project Dependencies and Build Order

Like most other Visual Studio .NET projects, DB2 database projects participate in the solution project dependencies and build order.

Project Dependencies

Using the Dependencies folder of the Project Dependencies dialog box, you can specify cross-project dependencies (Figure 19.29).

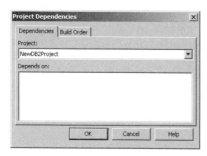

Figure 19.29
Cross-product dependencies.

This is a very useful and powerful feature. You can envision a situation where a DB2 functional test project would depend on another DB2 project that actually creates the set of DB2 objects to be tested by the test project. Taking this further, it is possible for a Web services C# project to have a dependency on a DB2 project that creates a set of SQL stored procedures that needs to be surfaced as Web services.

Project Build Order

The Build Order tab of the Project Dependencies dialog box shows you the resulting project build order based on the set of project dependencies specified in the Dependencies dialog box. When you execute a solution build command, the projects in the solution are built in the order shown (Figure 19.30).

Figure 19.30
Build order.

Project Items Build Order

Within a DB2 database project, you can specify the build order for project script items. By default, all script files are built in the order in which they appear in the project.

You can choose a different build order using the Item Build Order dialog box (Figure 19.31). This powerful feature lets you resolve cross-script dependencies in which one script file, ScriptX, can reference objects created in another script file, ScriptY, indicating that ScriptY must be compiled first.

Summary

The DB2 database project feature of the DB2 Development Add-Ins for Visual Studio .NET is a set of tightly integrated set of tools that extends the Visual Studio .NET IDE to allow for rapid server-side development of DB2 objects. Some of the advantages of using a DB2 database project over a Visual Studio .NET generic database project include the following:

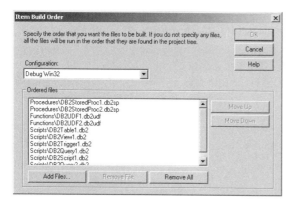

Figure 19.31
Specifying the file build order.

- Support for DB2 managed provider data connections from IBM Explorer
- Full-featured scripting wizards for generating DB2-specific DDL and DML scripts
- Predefined SQL code fragment insertion in the editor
- Advanced scripting options that provide support for error handling, display, and transaction management
- Specialized output pane for tracking detailed script execution results
- Support for multiple configuration options allowing for possibly different data connection and script build options
- Definition of the build order of script items within a project
- Content and dynamic help support

LOOSELY COUPLED TRANSACTION SUPPORT

The X/Open XA Interface is an open standard for coordinating changes to multiple resources, while ensuring the integrity of these changes. Software products known as transaction processing monitors typically use the XA interface. DB2 supports this interface so one or more DB2 databases can be concurrently accessed as resources in such an environment.

The XA interface provides two means by which application threads of control (TOC) can participate in a single XA global transaction. From a DB2 perspective, the TOC is the actual logical connection or application. All work performed in these TOC is atomically completed. This means that the transaction completes successfully or it does not.

Within a single global transaction the relationship between any pair of participating connections is either tightly coupled or loosely coupled:

- Tightly coupled—A tightly coupled relationship is one in which a pair of TOC is designed to share resources. An RM's isolation policies treat the pair as a single entity.

For a pair of tightly coupled TOC, the RM must guarantee that resource lock timeout or deadlock will not occur between the transactions.

- Loosely Coupled—A loosely coupled relationship provides no guarantee that resource lock timeout or deadlock will not occur. An RM's isolation policies treat the pair as if they were in separate global transactions even though the work will be automatically completed.

Prior to DB2 UDB v8.1, DB2 implemented tightly coupled transactions by guaranteeing that only a single TOC can be active at any one time, therefore eliminating all locking issues associated with the global transaction.

For loosely coupled transactions, each TOC was treated as a completely separate global transaction. There was no consideration that these TOC might have been part of a larger unit of work or global transaction.

This transaction behavior resulted in frequent lock timeout and deadlock situations when running applications in the Microsoft COM+/DTC environment. The COM+/DTC environment relies on loosely coupled support for distributed objects that perform work on behalf of the same global transaction. From a customer perspective, transactional COM+ applications would cause more lock timeouts and deadlocks than necessary when accessing DB2.

In DB2 UDB v8.1, loosely coupled transactions are now identified as belonging to the same global transaction. This change results in the reduction of lock timeouts and prevents deadlocks from occurring between transactions that are part of the same global transaction.

WINDOWS MANAGEMENT INSTRUMENTATION (WMI)

Web-Based Enterprise Management (WBEM) is an industry initiative that establishes management infrastructure standards and provides a way to combine information from hardware and software management systems. WBEM is based on the Common Information Model (CIM) schema, which is an industry standard driven by the Desktop Management Task Force (DMTF).

Microsoft WMI is an implementation of the WBEM initiative for supported Windows platforms. WMI is useful in a Windows enterprise network, where it reduces the maintenance and cost of managing enterprise network components. WMI provides the following:

- A consistent model of Windows operation, configuration, and status
- A COM API to allow access to management information
- The ability to operate with other Windows management services
- A flexible and extensible architecture allowing vendors a means of writing other WMI providers to support new devices, applications, and other enhancements
- The WMI Query Language (WQL) to create detailed queries of the information
- An API for management application developers to write Visual Basic or Windows Scripting Host (WSH) scripts

The WMI architecture has two parts:

- A management infrastructure that includes the CIM Object Manager (CIMOM) and a central storage area for management data called the CIMOM object repository. CIMOM allows applications to have a uniform way to access management data.
- WMI providers. WMI providers are the intermediaries between CIMOM and managed objects. Using WMI APIs, WMI providers supply CIMOM with data from managed objects, handle requests on behalf of management applications, and generate event notifications.

Figure 19.32 illustrates the various components in a WMI environment.

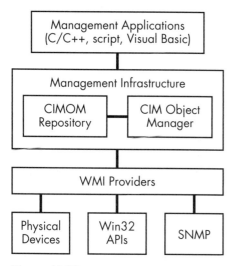

Figure 19.32
WMI environment.

WMI providers are standard COM or DCOM servers that function as mediators between managed objects and the CIMOM. If the CIMOM receives a request from a management application for data that is not available from the CIMOM object repository, or for events, the CIMOM forwards the request to the WMI providers. WMI providers supply data and event notifications for managed objects that are specific to their particular domain.

The snapshot monitors can be accessed by WMI by means of the DB2 performance counters using the built-in PerfMon provider.

The DB2 profile registry variables can be accessed by WMI by using the built-in registry provider.

The WMI Software Development Kit (WMI SDK) includes several built-in providers:

- PerfMon provider
- Registry event provider
- Registry provider
- Windows NT event log provider
- Win32 provider
- WDM provider

The DB2 errors that are in the event logs can be accessed by WMI by using the built-in Windows NT/2000 event log provider.

DB2 UDB has a DB2 WMI Administration provider and sample WMI script files to access the following managed objects:

1. Instances of the database server, including those instances that are partitioned. The following operations can be done:
   - Enumerate instances
   - Configure database manager parameters
   - Start, stop, and query the status of the DB2 server service
   - Set up or establish communication
2. Databases. The following operations can be done:
   - Enumerate databases
   - Configure database parameters
   - Create and drop databases
   - Backup, restore, and roll forward databases

You need to register the DB2 WMI provider with the system before running WMI applications by entering the following commands:

```
mofcomp %DB2PATH%\bin\db2wmi.mof
```

This command loads the definition of the DB2 WMI schema into the system.

```
regsvr %DB2PATH%\bin\db2wmi.dll
```

This command registers the DB2 WMI provider COM DLL with Windows.

In both commands, `%DB2PATH%` is the path where DB2 is installed. The *DB2WMI.MOF* file contains the DB2 WMI schema definition.

There are several benefits to integrating with the WMI infrastructure:

1. You are able to easily write scripts to manage DB2 servers in a Windows-based environment using the WMI provided tool. Sample Visual Basic scripts are provided to carry out simple tasks such as listing instances, creating and dropping databases, and

updating configuration parameters. The sample scripts are included in the DB2 Application Development for Windows product.

2. You can create powerful management applications that perform many tasks using WMI. The tasks could include the following:

   ○ Displaying system information
   ○ Monitoring DB2 performance
   ○ Monitoring DB2 system resource consumption

   By monitoring both system events and DB2 events through this type of management application, you can manage the database better.

3. You can use existing COM and Visual Basic programming knowledge and skills. By providing a COM or Visual Basic interface, programmers can save time when developing enterprise management applications.

OLE DB PROVIDER

The IBM OLE DB Provider for DB2 allows DB2 to act as a resource manager for the OLE DB provider. This support gives OLE DB-based applications the ability to extract or query DB2 data using the OLE interface.

The IBM OLE DB Provider for DB2 offers the following features:

- Supports Level 0 of the Microsoft OLE DB 2.5 provider specification, including some additional Level 1 interfaces
- A free threaded provider implementation, which enables the application to create components in one thread and use those components in any other thread
- An error lookup service that returns DB2 error messages

If DB2 Connect is installed, OLE DB users can also access data on host database management systems such as DB2 for MVS, DB2 for VSE & VM, and SQL/400.

With the IBM OLE DB Provider for DB2, you can create the following types of applications:

- ADO applications, including:
  ○ Microsoft Visual Studio C++ applications
  ○ Microsoft Visual Basic applications
- C/C++ applications that access IBMDADB2 directly using the OLE DB interfaces, including ATL applications with Data Access Consumer Objects that were generated by the ATL COM AppWizard.

Enhancements

The DB2 UDB v8.1 OLE DB driver included the following enhancements over prior versions of the driver:

- MTS and large object (LOB) support

- Server-side scrollable cursors (IRowsetChange)
- Support for loosely coupled transactions in server-side scrollable cursors:
  - Ability for a distributed COM object to participate in a transaction coordinated by MTS
  - Includes UPDATE WHERE CURRENT OF for server-side scrollable cursors
- Data Link Connection Properties dialog box
- Enumerator (servers, databases)
- Event notification:
  - IConnectionPoint, IconnectionPointContainer
  - ItransactionOutcomeEvents
- ADO Parameters.Refresh for binding stored procedure parameters:
  - ICommandWithParameters::GetParameterInfo describes a CALL statement to v8 and 390 servers
- Multiple parameter sets
- IpersistFile—saving info to file to prevent multiple logons
- ADO error object
- IcolumnsRowset

Restrictions

The following are the restrictions for the IBM OLE DB provider:

- IBMDADB2 supports autocommit and user-controlled transaction scope with the ITransactionLocal interface. Autocommit transaction scope is the default scope. Nested transactions are not supported.
- ISQLErrorInfo is not supported. The IErrorLookUp, IErrorInfo, and IErrorRecords interfaces are supported.
- RestartPosition is not supported when the command text contains parameters.
- IBMDADB2 does not quote table names passed through the DBID parameters, which are parameters used by the IOpenRowset interface. Instead, the OLE DB consumer must add quotes to the table names when quotes are required.
- Only a single set of parameters is supported. Multiple parameter sets are not yet supported.
- Named parameters are not supported. When ICommandWithParameters::MapParameterNames is called, DB_S_ERRORSOCCURRED is always returned. Parameter names are ignored in ICommandWithParameters::GetParameterInfo and ICommand-WithParameters::SetParameterInfo, because only ordinals are used.

SUMMARY

DB2 UDB v8.1 continues to enhance the support for the Windows development environment by delivering a number of new features including these:

- Visual Studio .NET integration
- Windows Server 2003 support
- OLE DB enhancements
- WMI
- Enhanced Microsoft DTS support

The Visual Studio .NET integration is of particular benefit to developers who can now easily embed DB2 objects into their database projects. This, along with numerous other enhancements, makes DB2 UDB v8.1 a key release for software developers.

Information Integration

- Federated Systems
- Web Services
- Replication Enhancements

C H A P T E R **20**

Federated Systems

This chapter discusses a variety of features new to DB2 UDB v8.1 that involve federated data sources. Together, these enhancements serve to improve the access to data outside of DB2 UDB for Linux, UNIX, and Windows.

DB2 INFORMATION INTEGRATOR

The DB2 Information Integrator is designed to provide users with uniform access to all their business information. Integrated, real-time access is provided regardless of whether the information is distributed across a wide variety of servers or if it exists in disparate formats. In short, users can see and manipulate all their information as if it resides in a single data source.

At the heart of the DB2 Information Integrator offering is the Federated Data Server, which provides an ever-expanding set of wrappers for a wide variety of data sources. DB2 Information Integrator version 8.1 features wrappers for major relational database management systems, life sciences data sources, WebSphere MQ message queues, Web services, flat files, spreadsheets, and numerous other data sources. For exact details on which wrappers are provided in DB2 Information Integrator version 8.1, see the upcoming section "Data Sources Available in DB2 Information Integrator."

The Federated Data Server enables you to easily consolidate your data from various sources and provides optimized access to it. Even while you are using the Federated Data Server, you do not need to reconfigure your existing databases and other data sources.

The Replication Server is able to use the access to diverse data sources provided by the Federated Data Server to enable replication between mixed relational databases.

DB2 UDB v8.1 has some limited integration capabilities. Its supported data sources include all the DB2 family databases, Informix, OLE DB, and WebSphere MQ message queues. The DB2 Information Integrator complements DB2 UDB by making many more data sources available.

Even for environments that feature disparate data sources, but do not run DB2 UDB, DB2 Information Integrator would be of tremendous use in managing the data.

FEDERATED SYSTEMS ENHANCEMENTS

Manipulating Data on Data Sources

In DB2 UDB v8.1, you are able to write data to a federated data source. As a result, you can now issue INSERT, UPDATE, and DELETE statements on nicknames. This also enables you to replicate data from federated data sources.

> **NOTE**
> For the data sources accessible to DB2 UDB v8.1, INSERT, UPDATE, or DELETE statements against nicknames cannot involve LOB values.

To INSERT, UPDATE, or DELETE data using a nickname, the privileges held by the authorization ID of the statement must include the following:

- The appropriate privilege on the nickname (for the federated database to accept the request)
- The appropriate privilege on the underlying table object (for the data source to accept the request)

Manipulating Tables on Data Sources

You can create and then modify tables in relational data sources without using PASSTHRU sessions. This capability is known as *transparent DDL*. This is beneficial for DB2 DBAs as they can use a DB2 interface (the DB2 CLP or the DB2 Control Center) and the DB2 CREATE TABLE, ALTER TABLE, and DELETE TABLE statements to manipulate tables on data sources.

> **NOTE**
> You cannot alter or drop tables that were created at the data source.

Creating Tables on Data Sources

Before you can create a table on a data source, you must configure the federated server to access the data source. This involves creating the following database objects:

- A wrapper for the appropriate data source type

- A server definition for the server where the remote table is to be located
- User mappings between DB2 and the data source server

To manipulate tables on a data source, the authorization ID must have at least one of the following privileges:

- SYSADM or DBADM authority.
- CREATETAB authority on the database and USE privilege on the table space. If the implicit or explicit schema name of the table does not exist, you must also have IMPLICIT_SCHEMA authority on the database. If the schema name of the table refers to an existing schema, you must also have CREATEIN privilege on the schema.

A transparent DDL CREATE TABLE statement creates a remote table at the data source and a nickname for that table at the federated server all in the same transaction. It maps the DB2 data types you specify to the remote data types using the default reverse type mappings provided in the wrappers.

You can create a table on a data source in nearly the same manner as on a DB2 database. The most significant difference is that you must specify a remote server name and, optionally, a remote schema and an unqualified name for the remote table that is to be created. There are also some limitations on what can be included in the CREATE TABLE statement:

- Only columns and a primary key can be created on the remote table.
- MQTs cannot be created on the remote data source.
- The remote data source must support the column data types and the primary key option in the CREATE TABLE statement.

The following is an example of a transparent DDL CREATE TABLE statement:

```
CREATE TABLE INVENTORY_I
    SKU_NUM SMALLINT NOT NULL,
    NAME VARCHAR(9),
    ACQ_DATE DATE,
    WORTH DECIMAL(7,2),
    PRIMARY KEY (INSURANCE_NUM)
    OPTIONS (REMOTE_SERVER 'ISERIESBOX',
    REMOTE_TABNAME 'INVENTORY', REMOTE_SCHEMA 'SANDRA')
```

The previous CREATE TABLE statement resulted in the creation of a table named SANDRA .INVENTORY on a remote server identified by the SERVER database object named ISERIESBOX.

Altering Tables on Data Sources

You can alter tables on data sources (this only applies to tables not created at the data source) by using either the DB2 Control Center or the ALTER TABLE statement. The extent to which you can modify remote tables is limited to the creation of additional columns and modification of the primary key. You cannot drop a column or rearrange any columns in a remote table.

The following is an example of a transparent DDL ALTER TABLE statement:

```
ALTER TABLE INVENTORY_I
   ADD COLUMN DEPRECIATION DECIMAL(7,2)
```

Dropping Tables on Data Sources

You can drop tables on data sources (this only applies to tables not created at the data source) by using either the DB2 Control Center or the DROP TABLE statement. Dropping a remote table that was created using transparent DDL also drops the corresponding nickname for that table.

The following is an example of a transparent DDL DROP TABLE statement:

```
DROP TABLE INVENTORY_I
```

Transparent DDL Transaction Restriction

COMMIT or ROLLBACK statements need to be issued immediately before and after transparent DDL transactions. Transparent DDL creates a table on a remote data source and creates a nickname in the local federated database for the remote table. Because transparent DDL is updating both local and remote objects at the same time, each transparent DDL statement must be the only update within the transaction.

MQTs for Data Sources

An MQT contains summary data that is created from the result set of a query. Unlike a view, an MQT stores the actual data from the result set. The primary reason DBAs use MQTs is for performance, especially for complex queries that are to be issued against large tables. You can realize these same performance benefits for data source tables by creating an MQT on a nickname. You can also create MQTs in DB2 UDB v8.1 databases that reference a combination of nicknames and local tables. These MQTs can only be cataloged with the REFRESH DEFERRED option.

DB2 Control Center Administration of Federated Objects

Besides administering federated systems from the CLP, you can use the DB2 Control Center. From a database's Federated Database Objects folder in the DB2 Control Center (see Figure 20.1), you can quickly and easily create wrappers, supply server definitions, identify user mappings, and create nicknames for data source objects.

You can also use the Control Center to show all of the remote tables on a data source. From this view, you can create a remote table on a data source using transparent DDL, and add columns to a remote table that was created using transparent DDL.

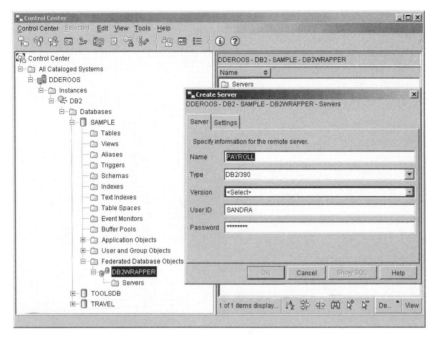

Figure 20.1
Control Center administration of federated database objects.

More Supported Federated Server Platforms

Before DB2 UDB v8.1, only AIX and Windows NT servers could be federated servers. Platform support has expanded considerably with the enablement of federated server functionality on the following operating systems:

- Windows 2000
- Linux
- Solaris Operating Environment
- HP-UX

Data Sources Available in DB2 Information Integrator

For extended federated systems functionality, use DB2 Information Integrator. It greatly expands on a number of federated systems features in DB2 UDB v8.1, most significantly the numerous supported data sources. DB2 UDB v8.1 supports only DB2 family, Informix, and OLE DB data sources. The following list identifies all the relational and nonrelational data sources supported by the DB2 Information Integrator:

- DB2 Universal Database for Linux, UNIX, and Windows
- DB2 Universal Database for iSeries

- DB2 Server for VM and VSE
- DB2 Universal Database for z/OS and OS/390
- Informix
- Microsoft SQL Server
- ODBC
- OLE DB
- Oracle
- Sybase
- Teradata
- BLAST search algorithms
- Documentum data files
- Entrez
- IBM Lotus Extended Search
- HMMER
- Microsoft Excel spreadsheets
- Table-structured files
- XML files

WEBSPHERE MQ INTEGRATION ENHANCEMENTS

WebSphere MQ provides the ability for message operations and database operations to be combined. A set of WebSphere MQ functions and utilities are provided with DB2 to enable SQL statements to include messaging operations. In DB2 UDB v8.1, integration with WebSphere MQ is further improved with enhancements in data integrity, flexibility, and performance.

Asynchronous MQ Listener

In DB2 UDB v8.1.2, an asynchronous MQ listener utility is available. The asynchronous MQ listener is a configurable service that accepts messages from WebSphere MQ queues and promptly calls custom stored procedures as messages arrive.

The MQ listener runs as a single multithreaded process. Each thread or task establishes a connection to its configured message queue for input and a connection to a DB2 database. The listener waits for a message to arrive on the queue. When a message arrives, the listener starts the transaction. The listener reads the message from the queue and removes the message from the queue. Then, it invokes a DB2 stored procedure, passing the message to the stored procedure. The listener sends a resulting reply to the reply-to queue, if one is available. The reply-to queue is specified by the incoming message, not the MQ listener configuration. When DB2 completes the transaction, the listener commits or rolls back the transaction. The listener reports any errors to the reply-to queue.

You can invoke the MQ listener from the command line with the `db2mqlsn` command. Its options are as follows:

- run—Starts the listener with a set of configurations.
- add—Adds tasks to the configuration to run.
- remove—Removes tasks from the configuration.
- show—Displays configuration information.
- admin—Sends an administration command to the running listener. The options are either shutdown or restart. Shutdown exits a running listener when it finishes processing the current message. Restart performs a shutdown, then rereads the configuration and restarts.
- help—Supplies detailed information about a particular command.

The following command demonstrates the addition of a stored procedure task to the configuration:

```
db2mqlsn add -configDB sampleDB
             -config nightlyruns
             -inputQueue queue3
             -procSchema mqproc -procName proc3
             -dbName messageDB
             -dbUser sandra -dbPwd my2cats
```

The stored procedure for the MQ listener accepts a parameter for the request message and returns another parameter for the reply message. The following is an example of this stored procedure format:

```
schema.proc(in inMsg inMsgType, out outMsg outMsgType)
```

Transactional Support for Websphere MQ Message Queues

Versions of DB2 UDB prior to v8.1.2 did not provide full transactional support for WebSphere MQ message queues. In DB2 UDB v8.1.2, you have the option of creating one-phase commit transactional MQ functions to avoid this potential for data loss.

When you define the MQ functions, you can choose if the functions will be transactional or non-transactional. This is controlled by the enable_MQFunctions command's -v parameter. The parameter value can be either all, 0pc, or 1pc. When you specify 0pc, the enablement creates the MQ functions in the DB2MQ schema. If you specify 1pc, then the enablement creates the MQ functions in the DB2MQ1C schema. If you specify all, then the enablement creates the MQ UDFs in both schemas (DB2MQ and DB2MQ1C). The schema the MQ functions are defined in determine if they are transactional (DB2MQ1C) or nontransactional (DB2MQ).

Single-Phase Commit Transactional MQ Functions

If you want to use transactional MQ UDFs, make sure that the database is configured for federated operations. Do this with the following command:

```
update dbm cfg using federated yes
```

On UNIX, ensure that the user account associated with UDF execution is a member of the mqm group.

The following command presents the syntax for creating single-phase commit transactional MQ functions:

```
enable_MQFunctions -n <dbname> -u <user> -p <passwd> -v 1pc
```

If your application uses one-phase commit over your data sources and a transaction is rolled back, the application might discard the message or produce an error. This can result in an inconsistent state.

The restrictions for one-phase commit with SYNCPOINT=ONEPHASE are as follows:

- Updates are allowed only for one data source.
- Messaging functions cannot be combined with other updates.

Nontransactional MQ Functions

The following command presents the syntax for creating single-phase commit transactional MQ functions:

```
enable_MQFunctions -n <dbname> -u <user> -p <passwd> -v 0pc
```

If your application uses nontransactional UDFs, any DB2 COMMIT or ROLLBACK operations are independent of the WebSphere MQ operations. If you roll back a transaction, the MQ functions do not discard the messages that you sent to a queue within the current unit of work.

In this environment, WebSphere MQ controls its own queue operations. A DB2 COMMIT or ROLLBACK does not affect when your application adds or deletes messages to or from a WebSphere MQ queue.

Web Services

Web services represent a new approach for applications to communicate with one another. Using the open standards of UDDI, Web Service Definition Language (WSDL), Simple Object Access Protocol (SOAP), and XML over an Internet protocol (e.g., HTTP), your applications can access Web service applications regardless of platform, language, or any other implementation details.

Specifically, a Web service is an application that can be invoked over the Internet (or an intranet) by another application. There are numerous publicly available Web services your applications can access, such as, a currency exchange rate service, a Major League Baseball statistics service, and online dictionaries.

With DB2 UDB v8.1.2, you can make use of Web services technology to better leverage your data and to increase the ease with which applications can access your database.

DB2 AS A WEB SERVICES CONSUMER

DB2 UDB v8.1.2 enables you to integrate Web services data into your database tables and database applications. This ability to be a *Web services consumer* is provided by the SOAP UDFs. The SOAP UDFs enable all the SQL statements that DB2 executes, including stored procedures, to become SOAP clients and request Web services from SOAP servers.

All Web services are described by their own WSDL file, which identifies details relevant to a Web service's communications and capabilities. To communicate with a Web service, your SQL application must send the service a SOAP request and process the SOAP response. The request and the response must map to the WSDL of the Web service being accessed. Based on the information you provide, the SOAP UDFs handle all communications with Web services. Specifically, the SOAP UDFs perform the following tasks:

- Generate a SOAP request
- Post the SOAP request to the Web service
- Receive the SOAP response
- Process the SOAP response and return the SOAP body

This insulates you and your applications from a layer of complexity in accessing Web services.

Installing the SOAP UDFs

DB2 UDB v8.1.2 includes an XML parser and XML extender, that are used in the installation and use of the SOAP UDFs.

Before you use the SOAP UDFs, you must enable XML extender for the database where you will be cataloging the SOAP UDFs. For example:

```
dxxadm enable_db <database-name>
```

To install the SOAP UDFs, run the following utility:

```
db2enable_soap_udf -n <database-name> -u <userID> -p <password> [-force]
```

The -force option causes existing SOAP UDFs to be dropped and then re-created.

You can uninstall the SOAP UDFs with the following utility:

```
db2disable_soap_udf -n <database-name> -u <userID> -p <password>
```

Signatures of the SOAP UDFs

There are five SOAP UDFs, all of which belong to the DB2XML schema. They differ only in the data type of the return value and the soap_body input parameter. Their signatures are as follows:

```
db2xml.soaphttpv (endpoint_url VARCHAR(256), soap_action VARCHAR(256),
soap_body VARCHAR(3072)) RETURNS VARCHAR(3072)
db2xml.soaphttpv ( endpoint_url VARCHAR(256), soapaction VARCHAR(256),
soap_body CLOB(1M)) RETURNS VARCHAR(3072)
db2xml.soaphttpc ( endpoint_url VARCHAR(256), soapaction VARCHAR(256),
soap_body CLOB(1M)) RETURNS CLOB(1M)
db2xml.soaphttpc ( endpoint_url VARCHAR(256), soapaction VARCHAR(256),
soap_body VARCHAR(3072)) RETURNS CLOB(1M)
db2xml.soaphttpcl ( endpoint_url VARCHAR(256), soapaction VARCHAR(256),
soap_body VARCHAR(3072)) RETURNS CLOB(1M) AS LOCATOR
```

Your choice of which SOAP UDF to use depends on the size of the SOAP request body and the size of the SOAP response you expect.

SOAP UDF Parameters

- endpoint_url—Contains the URL of the desired web service.

- `soap_action`—Indicates the intent of the Web service request. This is an optional field, typically left blank or filled in with *http://tempuri.org/*. This field can be used by Web servers to filter SOAP requests.
- `soap_body`—The XML content of the SOAP request body, which includes the name of an operation with requested namespace URI, an encoding style, and input arguments.

Using the SOAP UDFs

To illustrate the usage of a SOAP UDF, the following statement sends a request to a currency conversion Web service for the U.S. dollar's conversion rate into Canadian dollars:

```
VALUES SUBSTR(
      DB2XML.SOAPHTTPV ('http://services.xmethods.net:80/soap', '',
   XML2CLOB( XMLELEMENT(NAME "ns:getRate",
      XMLATTRIBUTES ('urn:xmethods-CurrencyExchange' AS "xmlns:ns"),
         XMLELEMENT(NAME "country1", 'united states'),
         XMLELEMENT(NAME "country2", 'canada')))), 1, 160)
```

The XML functions XMLELEMENT, XMLATTRIBUTES, and XML2CLOB provide an easy means of generating the content required for the `soap_body` parameter.

The following is the SOAP request envelope constructed by DB2 for the previous query:

```
** Send 631 bytes
POST /soap HTTP/1.0
Host: services.xmethods.net
Connection: Keep-Alive
User-Agent: DB2SOAP/1.0
Content-Type: text/xml; charset="UTF-8"
SOAPAction: ""
Content-Length: 452

<?xml version='1.0' encoding='UTF-8'?>
<SOAP-ENV:Envelope
   xmlns:SOAP-ENV=http://schemas.xmlsoap.org/soap/envelope/
   xmlns:SOAP-ENC=http://schemas.xmlsoap.org/soap/encoding/
   xmlns:xsi=http://www.w3.org/2001/XMLSchema-instance
   xmlns:xsd="http://www.w3.org/2001/XMLSchema">
   <SOAP-ENV:Body>
      <ns:getRate xmlns:ns="urn:xmethods-CurrencyExchange">
         <country1>united states</country1>
         <country2>canada</country2>
      </ns:getRate>
```

```
    </SOAP-ENV:Body>
  </SOAP-ENV:Envelope>
```

The following is the SOAP response envelope received by DB2 for the previous request:

```
HTTP/1.1 200 OK
Date: Wed, 28 May 2003 06:40:24 GMT
Server: Electric/1.0
Content-Type: text/xml
Content-Length: 492
X-Cache: MISS from www.xmethods.net
Keep-Alive: timeout=15, max=100
Connection: Keep-Alive

<?xml version='1.0' encoding='UTF-8'?>
<soap:Envelope
    xmlns:soap='http://schemas.xmlsoap.org/soap/envelope/'
    xmlns:xsi='http://www.w3.org/2001/XMLSchema-instance'
    xmlns:xsd='http://www.w3.org/2001/XMLSchema'
    xmlns:soapenc='http://schemas.xmlsoap.org/soap/encoding/'
    soap:encodingStyle='http://schemas.xmlsoap.org/soap/encoding/'>
    <soap:Body>
        <n:getRateResponse xmlns:n='urn:xmethods-CurrencyExchange'>
            <Result xsi:type='xsd:float'>1.3737</Result>
        </n:getRateResponse>
    </soap:Body>
</soap:Envelope>
```

The application that called the SOAP UDF with the currency exchange rate request would receive the following output:

```
<n:getRateResponse xmlns:n="urn:xmethods-CurrencyExchange">
    <Result xsi:type="xsd:float">1.3756</Result>
</n:getRateResponse>
```

Web Service Consumer Sample UDFs

To provide suggested usages of the SOAP UDFs, some samples are provided in DB2 UDB v8.1.2. They are located in sqllib/samples/soap, in the file *soapsample.sql*. One of the samples is a UDF called GetRate that accepts the names of two countries and returns their current currency exchange rate. This is the GetRate function's signature:

```
GetRate (from VARCHAR(32), to VARCHAR(32)) RETURNS VARCHAR(40)
```

Encapsulating the call to a Web service in a UDF provides a powerful means for you to integrate Web services content in your database and database applications. To illustrate this, we will select some records from the EMPLOYEE table in the sample database and present the salaries converted from U.S. to Canadian funds.

```
SELECT empno, salary AS salary_US,
    DECIMAL(DOUBLE(getRate('us', 'canada')) * salary, 10, 2)
        AS salary_CDN
    FROM employee WHERE empno < '000060'
```

This query produces the following result:

```
EMPNO    SALARY_US     SALARY_CDN
------   -----------   -----------
000010     52750.00      72752.80
000020     41250.00      56892.00
000030     38250.00      52754.40
000050     40175.00      55409.36
```

DB2 AS A WEB SERVICE PROVIDER

In addition to accessing Web services, you can configure your DB2 UDB v8.1.2 database server to host Web services. For example, you can expose a number of stored procedures as Web services to provide simple and flexible access to your database. By using Web services, you can greatly simplify application implementation and deployment. Web-service-enabled client applications do not need to use SQL to call stored procedures, and the computers running the client applications do not require the presence of a DB2 Run-Time Client.

You can leverage much of your existing application logic using Web services by incorporating them into DB2 Web services.

DB2 Web Services Architecture

This capability to be a *Web services provider* is provided by the Web Object Runtime Framework (WORF), an extension to Apache SOAP 2.2. WORF creates the WSDL interfaces to the DB2 Web services, thus providing a point of access for Web service requestors. The WORF also provides run-time support for invoking the DB2 Web services. Specifically, the WORF performs the following tasks:

- Analyze the Web service SOAP request
- Connect to the database
- Execute the SQL request
- Encode the output message from the SQL results
- Return a SOAP message back to the Web service requestor

The WORF deploys DB2 Web services as resources in the form of Document Access Definition Extension (DADX) files. A DADX file, which specifies a DB2 Web service, is to be located in the directory of your Web application. When a request for this Web service comes in, the WORF loads the DADX file and provides the Web service.

The Web services provided by WORF will run on a servlet engine supported by J2EE-compliant and SOAP 2.2-compatible Web application servers (e.g., WebSphere Application Server and Apache Jakarta Tomcat).

DADX Files

DADX files are XML documents (based on IBM's DADX schema) that WORF uses to provide DB2 Web services. In a DADX file, you define a Web service by specifying SQL statements, a list of parameters, and optionally, Document Access Definition (DAD) file references that define a set of operations. (DAD is an XML document format used by DB2 XML Extender to define the mapping between XML and relational data.) You can define two kinds of operations in your DADX files: SQL operations or XML collection operations.

SQL Operations

The SQL operations enable you to query and update the database and call stored procedures. The operations (where applicable) return result sets to the Web service requestor with default tagging. Your application returns the data by using a simple mapping of SQL data types, using column names as elements. The SQL operation elements are:

- <query>—Queries the database.
- <update>—Inserts into a database, deletes from a database, or updates a database.
- <call>—Calls stored procedures that can return zero or more result sets.

The following are the contents of a DADX file that defines a DB2 Web service with a single SQL operation:

```
<?xml version="1.0" encoding="UTF-8"?>
<DADX xmlns="http://schemas.ibm.com/db2/dxx/dadx">
    <operation name="showSales">
        <query>
        <SQL_query>SELECT * FROM SALES</SQL_query>
        </query>
    </operation>
</DADX>
```

This Web service issues a simple query against the SALES table of the SAMPLE database and returns the results to the Web service requestor.

XML Operations

The XML operations enable you to map XML document structures to DB2 tables. You can either generate XML documents from existing DB2 data or store XML documents into DB2 data.

The two elements that make up the XML collection operation type are:

- `<retrieveXML>`—Generates XML documents.
- `<storeXML>`—Stores XML documents.

The DAD file provides close control over the mapping of XML documents to a DB2 database for both storage and retrieval.

The XML operations require the activation of the XML Extender on the database that your Web service runs on. For example:

```
dxxadm enable_db sample
```

The following are the contents of a DADX file that defines a DB2 Web service with a single XML operation:

```
<?xml version="1.0" encoding="UTF-8"?>
<DADX xmlns="http://schemas.ibm.com/db2/dxx/dadx"
      xmlns:xsd="http://www.w3.org/2001/XMLSchema"
      xmlns:xhtml="http://www.w3.org/1999/xhtml">
    <operation name="findAll">
            <retrieveXML>
            <DAD_ref>getstart_xcollection.dad</DAD_ref>
            <no_override/>
            </retrieveXML>
    </operation>
</DADX>
```

> **NOTE**
> The *getstart_xcollection.dad* file can be found in the sqllib/samples/db2xml/dad directory.

This Web service contains a single operation, called findAll. It retrieves the result set from the query defined in the *getstart_xcollection.dad*, and returns the result set in XML, according to the SQL mapping defined in this DAD file. You can override default queries by using the `<SQL_override>` element. When overriding queries, you must ensure that the result set is compatible with the SQL mapping defined in the DAD file.

Additional Information on DADX

For detailed documentation on DADX syntax, SQL and XML operations, and SQL to XML data-type mappings, please refer to the *IBM DB2 Information Integrator Developer's Guide, Version 8.*

Installing and Configuring WORF

All of the WORF files are located in the *dxxworf.zip* archive in the following directory:

```
sqllib\samples\java\Websphere\
```

Once you expand this archive, you need to configure your Web application server to use the WORF utilities and classes.

For detailed documentation on how to configure WORF with WebSphere Application Server, or with Apache Jakarta Tomcat, please refer to the *IBM DB2 Information Integrator Developer's Guide, Version 8.*

To provide Web services from your database server, you need a Web application server that is J2EE compliant and SOAP 2.2 compatible (e.g., the Web application servers mentioned earlier).

DB2 WEB TOOLS AND THE APPLICATION SERVER FOR DB2

In DB2 UDB v8.1.2, the DB2 Web Tools enable you to remotely administer DB2 without an Administration client. The DB2 Web Tools consist of the Web Command Center and the Web Health Center. Both of these tools run as applications on a Web application server to provide access to DB2 servers through Web browsers.

You can serve the DB2 Web Tools using an existing Web application server or the server that ships with DB2.

The DB2 Web Tools and the Web application server can be installed from the *Java Application Development and Web Administration Tools Supplement for DB2* CD-ROM.

> **N O T E**
> Due to license restrictions, this Web application server cannot be used for providing Web services you develop for your database server.

XML ENHANCEMENTS

With XML Extender, DB2 UDB is an XML-enabled DBMS. As such, you can use DB2 to perform the following tasks:

- Store and access XML documents
- Generate XML documents from data in tables
- Insert data from XML documents into tables

To facilitate these functions, XML Extender provides data types, functions, and stored procedures.

The XML enhancements in DB2 UDB v8.1.2 increase the flexibility with which you can handle XML documents.

Before using any XML Extender functionality, ensure that XML Extender is enabled with your database by executing the following command:

```
dxxadm enable_db <database-name>
```

Migrating XML-Enabled Databases to v8

After upgrading your DB2 UDB instance to v8.1, you need to migrate your databases with the MIGRATE DATABASE command. For the databases that are XML-enabled, the MIGRATE DATABASE command also re-enables them to use the new XML functions, data types, and stored procedures.

Automatically Validating XML Documents against Schemas

In DB2 UDB v8.1, you can automatically validate XML documents that use schemas. In prior releases, automatic validation was only possible for XML documents based on DTDs.

To validate the composed XML document against an XML schema, add information to the DAD file to identify the applicable schema and indicate that validation is desired. First, insert the schema tags that associate the DAD file with the schema file. For example:

```
<schemabindings>
<nonamespacelocation location="path/schema_name.xsd"/>
</schemabindings>
```

Use the validation tag to indicate whether DB2 XML Extender will validate the XML document:

```
<validation>YES</validation>
```

Manually Validating XML Documents

You can validate your schema-based and DTD-based XML documents manually by passing them to a validation UDF.

The DVALIDATE function validates an XML document against a specified DTD, and the SVALIDATE function validates an XML document against a specified schema. The XML document, the DTD, and the schema can exist as CLOBs in a DB2 table or as files outside the database. You can name the DTD or schema in the UDF call, or the UDF can use the DTD or schema named in the XML document.

If the document is valid, SVALIDATE returns 1. If the document is invalid, SVALIDATE returns 0 and writes an error message in the XML Extender trace file (if the trace is enabled). To collect trace data, enable the trace before calling the DVALIDATE or SVALIDATE functions as follows:

```
dxxtrc on <trace-directory>
```

The following statement validates an XML document using a specified schema. Both the document and schema are stored in a table called SALES.

```
SELECT DB2XML.SVALIDATE(s_doc, s_schema) FROM sales WHERE id=1
```

New XML UDFs

In DB2 UDB v8.1 and v8.1.2, new XML UDFs were made available to present efficient ways of generating XML data from relational data in DB2. The following sections introduce the new XML UDFs.

XMLCONCAT

XMLCONCAT returns the concatenation of a variable number of XML arguments. The arguments must be expressions of data type XML. The result has the same internal XML data type as the arguments.

The following example demonstrates the use of XMLCONCAT by returning the first and last name for each applicable employee in the EMPLOYEE table.

```
SELECT e.empno, XML2CLOB(XMLCONCAT(XMLELEMENT(NAME "firstname", e.firstnme),
     XMLELEMENT(NAME "lastname", e.lastname)))
   AS "Result" FROM employee e
   WHERE e.edlevel = 12
```

This query produces the following result:

```
EMPNO   RESULT
------  ---------------------------------------------------------------------
000290  <FIRSTNAME>JOHN</FIRSTNAME><LASTNAME>PARKER</LASTNAME>
000310  <FIRSTNAME>MAUDE</FIRSTNAME><LASTNAME>SETRIGHT</LASTNAME>
```

XMLFOREST

XMLFOREST constructs a sequence (forest) of XML elements from its arguments. The result has the same internal XML data type as the arguments.

The following example demonstrates the use of XMLFOREST by producing an element for each employee in the EMPLOYEE table, which contains subelements for the full name and the hire date.

```
SELECT empno, (XML2CLOB(XMLELEMENT(NAME "Emp",
  (XMLFOREST(e.firstname  || ' ' || e.lastname AS "Name" , hiredate))))
  AS "Result" FROM employee e WHERE edlevel = 12
```

This query produces the following result:

```
EMPNO  Result
------ -------------------------------------------------------------------
000290 <Emp><Name>JOHN PARKER</Name><HIREDATE>1980-05-30</HIREDATE></Emp>
000310 <Emp><Name>MAUDE SETRIGHT</Name><HIREDATE>1964-09-12</HIREDATE></
Emp>
```

REC2XML

REC2XML returns a string formatted with XML tags and containing column names and column data. The REC2XML UDF is demonstrated in Chapter 17, "SQL Enhancements."

Normalization of Timestamp Data

XML Extender normalizes timestamps for DB2 automatically, if needed. Timestamps are normalized to the *yyyy-mm-dd-hh.mm.ss.nnnnnn* format or the *yyyy-mm-dd-hh mm.ss.nnnnnn* format.

For example:

```
1998-1-11-11.12.13
```

is normalized to:

```
1998-01-11-11.12.13.000000
```

XML Extender Functionality in Partitioned Database Environments

In a partitioned database environment, data is split across multiple physical database partitions in an unpredictable manner. When using XML Extender functionality in a partitioned database environment, ensure the following:

- Use the XMLVARCHAR or XMLCLOB data types instead of XMLFile in your UDFs.
- Store your XML files on a file server, and mount or map that server to each machine so that the file has the same path regardless of what machine accesses it.
- Create a response file when you install DB2 on the instance owning computer. Use this response file for the rest of your installations. This ensures that the same components are installed and configured the same way on each machine.
- Specify the root id in the enable_column command with the -r option so that a consistent partitioning key is used for all the table data.

> **N O T E**
> The XSLT functions (XSLTransformToCLOB and XSLTransform-ToFile) are not supported in partitioned database environments.

New XML MQ UDFs and Stored Procedures

XML Extender provides a series of WebSphere MQ UDFs and stored procedures that pass XML messages between DB2 and WebSphere MQ message queues. Specifically, the WebSphere MQ XML UDFs and stored procedures enable you to retrieve an XML document from a message queue, decompose it into untagged data, and store the data in DB2 tables. You can also compose an XML document from DB2 table data and send the document to a message queue.

To enable these UDFs and stored procedures, you must properly enable your database. You can do this with the following commands:

```
dxxadm enable_db <database-name>
enable_MQXML -n <database-name> -u <userID > -p <password>
```

WebSphere MQ XML UDFs

Table 21.1 presents all of the WebSphere MQ XML UDFs. These UDFs have a DB2XML database schema. They are not under MQ UDF transactional control.

Table 21.1   WebSphere MQ XML UDFs

WebSphere MQ XML Function Name	Description
MQPublishXML	Publish XMLVARCHAR and XMLCLOB data to a publication service.
MQReadXML	A nondestructive read of matching XML messages from the queue.
MQReadAllXML	A nondestructive read of all XML messages from the queue.
MQReadXMLCLOB	A nondestructive read of matching XML CLOB messages from the queue.
MQReadAllXMLCLOB	A nondestructive read of all XML CLOB messages from the queue.
MQReceiveXML	A destructive read of matching XML messages from the queue.
MQReceiveAllXML	A destructive read of all XML messages from the queue.
MQRcvAllXMLCLOB	A destructive read of matching XML CLOB message(s) from the queue.
MQReceiveXMLCLOB	A destructive read of all XML CLOB messages from the queue.
MQSendXML	Send an XML message to the queue.
MQSendXMLFILE	Send an XML message from an XML file to the queue.
MQSendXMLFILECLOB	Send an XML message from an XML file to the queue as XMLCLOB data.

WebSphere MQ XML Stored Procedures

Table 21.2 presents all of the WebSphere MQ XML stored procedures. These stored procedures have a DB2XML database schema.

Table 21.2 WebSphere MQ XML Stored Procedures

WebSphere MQ XML Stored Procedure Name	Description
dxxmqGen	Compose XML documents, using a DAD file as an input parameter. The document type is XMLVARCHAR(4000).
dxxmqGenCLOB	Compose XML documents, using a DAD file as an input parameter. The document type is XMLCLOB(1M).
dxxmqRetrieve	Compose XML documents, using a collection name as an input parameter. The document type is XMLVARCHAR(4000).
dxxmqRetrieveCLOB	Compose XML documents, using a collection name as an input parameter. The document type is XMLCLOB(1M).
dxxmqShred	Decompose an XML document using a DAD file as an input parameter. The document type is XMLVARCHAR(4000).
dxxmqShredCLOB	Decompose an XML document using a DAD file as an input parameter. The document type is XMLCLOB(1M).
dxxmqShredAll	Decompose multiple XML documents using a DAD file as an input parameter. The document type is XMLVARCHAR(4000).
dxxmqShredAllCLOB	Decompose multiple XML documents using a DAD file as an input parameter. The document type is XMLCLOB(1M).
dxxmqInsert	Decompose an XML document using a collection name as an input parameter. The document type is XMLVARCHAR(4000).
dxxmqInsertCLOB	Decompose an XML document using a collection name as an input parameter. The document type is XMLCLOB(1M).
dxxmqInsertAll	Decompose multiple XML documents using a collection name as an input parameter. The document type is XMLVARCHAR(4000).
dxxmqInsertAllCLOB	Decompose multiple XML documents using a collection name as an input parameter. The document type is XMLCLOB(1M).

Replication Enhancements

The DB2 UDB replication tools provide a powerful means of copying table data from one place to another. With the release of DB2 UDB v8.1, the replication tools are made more powerful with significant enhancements in flexibility, usability, and performance.

REPLICATION CENTER

The Replication Center is a new graphical interface you can use to set up, administer, and maintain your replication environment. It supports DB2-to-DB2 replication environments and replication between DB2 and non-DB2 relational databases. The Replication Center is part of the DB2 Control Center set of tools and shares the look and feel of the other DB2 centers.

You can use the Replication Center to complete the following replication tasks:

- Create profiles where you can define default settings for creating control tables, source objects, and target objects
- Create replication control tables
- Register replication sources
- Create subscription sets and add subscription set members to subscription sets
- Operate the Capture program
- Operate the Apply program
- Monitor the replication process
- Perform basic troubleshooting for replication

Starting the Replication Center

You can start the Replication Center in any of the following ways:

- Select Replication Center from the Tools menu of another DB2 center.
- Enter the `db2rc` command from a DB2 command line.
- On Windows systems, click the Start button and select Programs ➤ IBM DB2 ➤ General Administration Tools ➤ Replication Center.
- Click the replication icon (Figure 22.1) from the toolbar of another DB2 center.

Figure 22.1
Replication Center icon.

Replication Center Launchpad

Included in the Replication Center is a launchpad that guides you through the basic tasks needed to set up a DB2 replication environment. As shown in Figure 22.2, the launchpad shows you graphically how the different replication steps are related to one another.

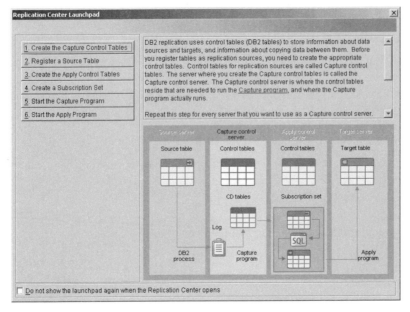

Figure 22.2
Replication Center launchpad.

Replication Definitions Folder

The Replication Definitions folder (see Figure 22.3) contains all the objects associated with replication. From this folder, you can create and modify the properties of replication objects. In Figure 22.3, you can see all the possible actions that can be performed with a replication source table.

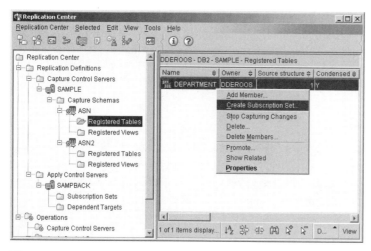

Figure 22.3
Replication Definitions folder.

Operations Folder

The Operations folder (see Figure 22.4) shows the three replication servers: the Capture, Apply, and Monitor Control servers. From each of these servers, you can administer their respective replication program instances. In Figure 22.4, you can see all the Capture program-related tasks.

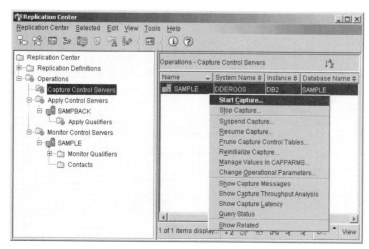

Figure 22.4
Replication Operations folder.

REPLICATION MONITORING

The capability to monitor replication activities has greatly increased with the release of DB2 UDB v8.1. You can now define alert conditions. When triggered, these alert a user via pager or e-mail. You can thus monitor the current status of running replication programs, and you can analyze historical data about the replication programs.

Replication Alert Monitor

The Replication Alert Monitor runs continuously and monitors the Capture and Apply programs based on the criteria you provide. You define alert conditions for criteria that you want to monitor and specify people who should be contacted automatically when the alert conditions are met or exceeded. You can also set up the monitor so that it sends a pager signal or an e-mail when an operational error occurs.

You can start the Replication Alert Monitor from either the Replication Center or the `asnmon` command. If you are using the DB2 command line, you can configure the Replication Alert Monitor with the `asnmcmd` command.

To monitor your replication environment with the Replication Alert Monitor, you must first create Monitor control tables on a server. The server on which you create these tables is called a *monitor control server.*

You can run a monitor control server on each server where you have replication programs running, or you can define a centralized monitor control server. There are costs and benefits for each approach. Centralized monitor control servers have consolidated data and a simple overall configuration, whereas having a monitor control server on every server running replication programs results in decentralized monitor data and complex configuration. However, it takes more time for a centralized monitor control server to detect and report an alert condition than a local monitor control server. Furthermore, a centralized monitor control server cannot detect problems if it loses connectivity with the remote servers.

You can use a monitor qualifier to start more than one instance of the monitor program. Starting multiple monitor programs allows you to distribute the workload among monitors or ensure that a mission-critical application has a dedicated monitor process.

When you have created a monitor control server you can begin defining alert conditions and their thresholds, and identifying contacts for any potential alerts. The following are the available alert conditions:

- Capture or Apply program is down
- Latency between commits to CD tables by a Capture program
- Capture or Apply program writes an error message
- Capture or Apply program writes a warning message
- Amount of memory used by a Capture program

- Failed processing of a subscription set
- Latency between the processing of a subscription set
- Deactivation of a subscription set due to error
- Apply performs a full refresh of target tables
- Apply rejects a transaction due to an update anywhere conflict
- Number of rows reworked
- End-to-end latency of a subscription set

In Figure 22.5, a screen from the Replication Center shows a definition of a "Capture program is down" alert condition.

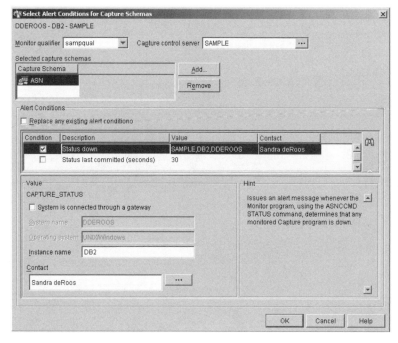

Figure 22.5
Definition of an alert condition.

Once you have defined one or more alert conditions, you can start the Replication Alert Monitor. It can be stopped at any time. If you need to change contact information or an alert condition while the Replication Alert Monitor is running, you can activate these new settings without interrupting the monitoring. Make the changes by reinitializing the Replication Alert Monitor.

Checking the Current Status of Replication Programs

Status information for the replication programs is available for fast and easy access from either the Replication Center or the DB2 command line.

From the Replication Center, you can access status information for the Capture and Apply programs. (Note that the Replication Alert Monitor program can only be monitored from the DB2 command line.) For Capture program status, select the desired Capture control server and use the Query Status tool. For Apply program status, select the desired Apply qualifier and use the Query Status tool.

From the DB2 command line, you can access status information for the Capture, Apply, and Replication Alert Monitor programs. Table 22.1 lists the command to be used for each replication program.

Table 22.1 Operating Commands for Replication Programs

Replication Program	Operating Command
Capture	`asnccmd`
Apply	`asnacmd`
Replication Alert Monitor	`asnmcmd`

To retrieve the replication program's status information, use the status keyword with the operating command. For example, the following command requests the status of a Capture program:

```
asnccmd capture_server=sample capture_schema=ASN status
```

Analyze Historical Data of Replication Programs

You can use the Replication Center to query historical data to review how your replication environment performed during a particular time interval. The following information is available:

- Messages—The error and informational messages that the Capture and Apply programs issued.
- Capture throughput—On average, the number of rows processed in the CD table for a given period of time.
- Capture latency—The most recent time when the Capture program committed data into the CD table.
- Apply throughput—On average, the number of rows that were processed in the target table for a given period of time.
- End-to-end latency—On average, the amount of time elapsed between the time when the Capture program read the changes from the DB2 log and the Apply program replicated the changes to the target tables.

Historical data for the Capture program can be accessed from the Capture control servers. Historical data for the Apply program can be accessed from the Apply qualifiers.

For each historical data report, you have the ability to isolate the data by date and time. You can further adjust the focus of the data by adjusting the interval of time to better group the results. Figure 22.6 shows an example of a report on Apply throughput data.

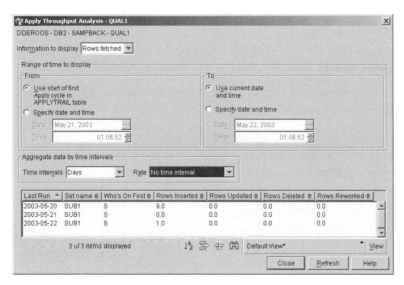

Figure 22.6
Historical analysis of Apply throughput data.

Here, all of the data is displayed (from the start of the first Apply cycle in the APPLYTRAIL table up until the current time). Because there were only 10 affected rows, the data is most meaningfully represented in day-long intervals.

GENERAL ENHANCEMENTS

Windows Process Model for Replication Programs

In Windows NT or Windows 2000, each Capture, Apply, and Replication Alert Monitor program runs as a separate service. These services are created and dropped through the Replication Center or with the commands asnscrt (create a replication service) and asnsdrop (drop a replication service).

As separate services, you can start or stop the replication programs individually. You can stop and start these services from the Windows Control Panel, under the Services section of the Administrative Tools.

Password Encryption for Replication Programs

All stored passwords (contents of the password file) are encrypted, and passwords are no longer stored in plain text. The `asnpwd` command enables you to create and maintain the password file so that the Apply program, the Replication Alert Monitor, and the Replication Analyzer can access data on remote servers.

Replicating Data Links Values

If a Data Links reference to an external file is defined with `RECOVERY YES`, then DB2 replication can ensure that the reference and external file are consistent when replicated.

DB2 Data Links Manager version 8.1 provides a replication daemon (`DLFM_ASNCOPYD`) for retrieving and storing external files managed by Data Links. As a result, the `ASNDLCOPYD` daemon is no longer required to replicate files stored in DB2 Data Links Manager.

Longer Table Names and Column Names

Source and target table names can be up to 128 characters and column names can be up to 30 characters. These limits are subject to the limits imposed by the database source, database target, or control server.

Migration Utility

A replication migration utility is included with DB2 UDB to convert existing DB2 UDB v5, v6, and v7 replication environments to DB2 UDB v8 replication. You can invoke this utility by typing `asnmig8` at the DB2 command line.

New Trace Facility

The replication trace facility logs program flow information from Capture, Apply, and Replication Alert Monitor programs. You can start or stop the trace facility without stopping and restarting any of these programs. Also, the replication trace output is compact, often resulting in smaller trace files than were generated in previous releases of DB2 UDB. The replication trace command (`asntrc`) has syntax that is modeled after the DB2 trace commands, and it provides output that is consistent with the DB2 trace format.

For details on the syntax, and for example implementations of the replication trace facility, see the *IBM DB2 Universal Database Replication Guide and Reference, Version 8*.

64-Bit Support for Replication Programs

You can replicate on platforms where DB2 offers 64-bit support. In addition to Capture and Apply, the Replication Center is also supported on 64-bit operating systems.

CAPTURE ENHANCEMENTS

Controlling the Capture Program

The Capture program is controlled by signals that you or the Apply program can store in the signal table, IBMSNAP_SIGNAL. This table, along with other replication control tables, ensures that the Capture and Apply programs communicate effectively with each other and with the Replication Alert Monitor.

Capture uses signals from IBMSNAP_SIGNAL for the following situations:

- To determine when to start capturing changes for a particular table
- To determine when to terminate
- Whether it must perform update-anywhere replication
- To provide the log sequence number for setting a precise endpoint for Apply events

The signal table also allows for precise termination of log record reading and for users to communicate with the Capture program through log records.

Changing the Capture Program's Operational Parameters

The operational parameters that govern the use of the Capture program are stored in the IBMSNAP_CAPPARMS table (formerly known as IBMSNAP_CCPPARMS). This table is read when the Capture program starts.

You can override the IBMSNAP_CAPPARMS table entries by specifying values for operational parameters when starting the Capture program. For example, the following Capture program overrides the startmode parameter so that it will cold start, regardless if any warm start information is available:

```
asncap capture_server=SAMPLE capture_schema=asn startmode=cold
```

> **NOTE**
> You can also override IBMSNAP_CAPPARMS table entries when starting the Capture program from the Replication Center.

Overridden IBMSNAP_CAPPARMS values stay in effect until the Capture process is stopped or until they are dynamically changed with the use of the chgparms parameter.

If the Capture program is already active, you can dynamically change the operational parameters. This can be done through the Replication Center, or with the chgparms keyword of the asnccmd command. For example, the following command increases the commit interval from the default of 30 seconds to 60 seconds:

```
asnccmd capture_server=SAMPLE capture_schema=asn chgparms commit_interval=60
```

Dynamic changes to operational parameters remain in effect until the Capture process is stopped or until you issue another change command.

Instead of overriding default values for operational parameters, you can create new defaults by updating the desired column values in the IBMSNAP_CAPPARMS table. For example, if you want the default commit interval to become 60 seconds, issue the following SQL statement:

```
update asn.ibmsnap_capparms set commit_interval=60
```

New Start Modes for Capture

With the addition of two new Capture start modes, you have increased control over cold starts. The two new values for the startmode operational parameter are as follows:

- warmsi—When you start the Capture program for the first time, it performs a cold start. For subsequent starts (if warm start information is available), the Capture program performs a warm start and resumes processing where it ended in its previous run. If the IBMSNAP_RESTART table is empty, the Capture program switches to cold start. The warmsi mode is the default starting mode for the Capture program.
- warmsa—If warm start information is available, the Capture program performs a warm start and resumes processing where it ended in its previous run. If the IBMSNAP _RESTART table is empty, the Capture program switches to cold start.

Capture and Apply Programs Can Be Started in Any Order

Once Capture has been cold started successfully, there is no longer a requirement to always start Capture before starting Apply, or that Capture must be running before Apply processes a new subscription.

Dynamically Updatable Replication Definitions

You can register new replication sources, update existing registrations, add new subscription sets, or update existing subscription sets at any time. If you complete any of these tasks while the Capture program is running, it does not need to be reinitialized, or stopped and restarted. However, after changing registration attributes for registered objects, you must reinitialize the Capture program.

Dynamic Addition of Columns to Replication Source Tables

You can add columns to your replication source tables (and the change data tables) at any time without having to reinitialize, or stop and restart, the Capture program. This is assuming that you do not need to replicate the data in the new columns.

If you need to replicate the data in the new columns, you need to stop the Capture program and deactivate the subscription sets. Once you make the necessary changes to the target table, change data (CD) table, and the associated subscription set members, you can reactivate the subscription sets and restart the Capture program.

Enabling Row Capture for Individual Replication Sources

When you register a table for replication, you can define a *row-capture rule* for that object. A row-capture rule stipulates that no changes from a replication source can be captured unless the change affects the columns that you have identified. The default behavior of the Capture program is to collect changes for a row whenever any column of the replication source changes. For example, if you want to register a table with 100 columns for replication, but you want to collect changes for only two of the columns and only when these two columns are updated, you would specify this as a row-capture rule when you register the table.

In previous versions of DB2 UDB, the operational parameter `chgonly` determined if the Capture program would collect all the changes in the replication sources, or only the changes in columns registered in row-capture rules. This option could not be set for individual replication sources. In DB2 UDB v8.1, the operational parameter `chgonly` is gone, and the replication source registration attribute `chgonly` is introduced. Now, you can activate or deactivate row-capture rules for individual replication sources.

Control over Recapturing Data from Replicas

With update-anywhere replication, a change made to a replica table is captured and replicated to all other tables. If you use multitier replication, or if you have replica tables that are logical partitions of the source table, you might not want changes from one replica table forwarded to all the others.

You can specify if you want changes recaptured and forwarded to other replicas, or if you want the Capture program to ignore changes that have already been collected by other replica tables.

When you are registering the master table, you can choose if it will recapture updates that originated at a replica and forward them to other replicas. To see where this can be controlled, see Figure 22.7, an example of the Register Tables window in the Replication Center. The "Capture changes from replica target table" check box located here controls this function.

When you are registering the replica table, you can choose if the replica table recaptures updates that originated at the master table and forwards them to other replicas that subscribe to this replica. This can also be controlled by the "Capture changes from replica target table" check box shown in Figure 22.7.

Preventing changes from being recaptured can increase performance and reduce storage costs.

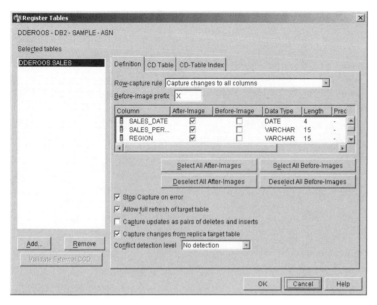

Figure 22.7
Register Replication Source Tables window.

Concurrent Capturing and Pruning of Data

In previous releases of DB2 UDB, the Capture program could not concurrently capture and prune data. This caused problems either with replication latency (if pruning was done regularly), or with inefficient data storage (if pruning was not done enough). In DB2 UDB v8.1, a separate pruning thread is initialized when the Capture program is started, and it remains active while the Capture program is running. Normal pruning and retention-limit pruning is performed by a pruning thread so that performance throughput does not suffer at the expense of keeping data storage minimized.

The Capture program prunes the UOW table, trace table (IBMSNAP_CAPTRACE), signal table (IBMSNAP_SIGNAL), monitor table (IBMSNAP_CAPMON), and the CD tables.

You can prune the Capture program tables manually by using the prune option of the asncmd command. It is, however, recommended that you rely on automatic pruning, which is enabled by default with the autoprune operational parameter.

Multiple Capture Instances

You can run multiple instances of the Capture program on a given server by creating multiple sets of Capture control tables. Each Capture program has its own schema (known as a Capture schema), control tables, and CD tables. A Capture program is uniquely defined by the combination of the source server name and the Capture schema.

You can create additional sets of Capture control tables using the Replication Center by repeating the steps you took to create the first set of Capture control tables. (An easy way to do this is to use the Launchpad, and select the first step: Create the Capture Control Tables. See Figure 22.2.) There is one additional step: You must provide a unique name for the Capture schema.

The following sections explain some benefits and potential applications of using multiple Capture instances.

Run Multiple Captures against a Single Log or Journal

You can run more than one Capture program against a single DB2 log or journal. Because each Capture program is independent of any others, different organizations can maintain their own replication environments using the same source data.

Isolate Low-Latency Tables

You can optimize performance by using multiple Capture instances to provide your important low-latency tables with their own replication plans. For example, you can assign a particular table its own Capture instance. You can then assign this table's Capture program with a different run-time priority, and set the Capture program parameters, such as pruning interval and monitor interval, to suit the nature of this table.

As with subscription sets, any tables that require transactional consistency must be handled by the same Capture.

Increase Capture Throughput

You can implement multiple Capture instances to potentially realize significant performance benefits and improve throughput. There is some additional CPU overhead due to the use of multiple log readers, so multiple capture instances would be most beneficial in a data source environment with multiple CPUs.

Replicate Multiple Non-DB2 Source Databases

By using multiple Capture instances you can replicate data from multiple non-DB2 relational source databases in the same federated database.

Capture Multi-partitioned Databases

With DB2 v8.1.2, you can replicate data from multi-partitioned databases.

When you start Capture for the first time in a multi-partitioned database, Capture creates an additional control table named IBMSNAP_PARTITIONINFO in the same table space as the IBMSNAP_RESTART table. This table enables the Capture program to restart from the earliest required log sequence number within each partition's set of log files. A row is inserted into IBMSNAP_PARTITIONINFO every time a partition is added. If you have never started the Capture program, `IBMSNAP_PARTITIONINFO` is empty, and the Capture program must perform a cold start.

APPLY ENHANCEMENTS

Transaction Commit Frequency

The Apply program can use one of two modes to commit transactions: *table mode* or *transaction mode*.

In table-mode processing, the Apply program issues a single commit after all fetched data is applied. Table-mode processing is the default. In transaction-mode processing, the Apply program commits changes in the order of commit sequence for all subscription-set members at the same time. You can specify how many transactions the Apply program processes before committing its work.

By starting the Apply program so that it commits its work in transaction mode, the user-copy and point-in-time target tables can have referential integrity.

You can enable transaction-mode processing in the Create Subscription Set window from the Set Information tab. In the "Set processing properties" section, there is a check box to "Allow Apply to use transactional processing for set members." You can then set the interval for the interim commits in the box below it.

There are some restrictions for transaction-mode processing. You must have user-copy, point-in-time, or replica target tables in a subscription set, and subscription sets cannot contain target tables with LOB data or Datalinks.

Replicating Changes to Target-Key Columns

Changes to target table primary key values can be handled without converting all captured updates to delete–insert pairs. First, when you are registering a replication source (see Figure 22.7), indicate that you want the Capture program to capture the after-image value (the value in the column after a change was made) and the before-image value (the value that was in the column before the change was made). Second, when you define a subscription set member, specify that the Apply program should use the before-image values when the Apply program builds a `WHERE` clause using the primary key columns in its predicates. Apply can use the before-image values to locate the target table row for an update. This avoids the conversion of an update to an insert.

The method used to change target table primary key values before DB2 UDB v8.1, where Capture converts all updates to delete–insert pairs, is still available and should be used if partitioning key values are subject to change. You can have Apply use delete–insert pairs for updates by selecting this option in the replication source registration. In the Replication Center, this is done in either the Register Tables window (see Figure 22.7), or the Registered Table Properties window.

REPLICATION PERFORMANCE

Fewer Joins between Replication Tables

In DB2 UDB v8.1, many joins between replication control tables have been eliminated, resulting in substantial improvements in performance. Following are the joins that have been removed:

- The column IBMSNAP_UOWID is replaced by IBMSNAP_COMMITSEQ in CD tables. The IBMSNAP_COMMITSEQ column allows the Apply program to process certain target table types without having to join the CD table with the UOW table.

- CD tables that are not involved in replica scenarios with conflict detection can be pruned without a join. In cases where a join between the CD table and the UOW table is required, the join is made using the IBMSNAP_COMMITSEQ column.

- Joins of the CD table and the UOW table are no longer required when applying changes to user copies. All the information needed for such copies is contained in the CD table. If information from the UOW table is needed for a subscription predicate or target table column, you can set a flag to tell Apply to do the join.

Faster Full Refreshes of Target Tables

The load improvements in DB2 UDB v8.1 enable faster full refreshes of target tables.

Improved ASNLOAD Exit Routine

The Apply exit routine, ASNLOAD, is shipped as a sample exit routine in both source format (C) and compiled format. If you have large source tables, you might want to use the ASNLOAD exit routine to copy the data more efficiently to the target during a full refresh. You can use the sample compiled exit routine as provided, and can influence some of its behavior by customizing the replication configuration, or you can customize the exit routine source code.

To use the ASNLOAD exit routine, activate the loadxit Apply program keyword and start the Apply program.

Apply Program Optimization for One Subscription Set

By default, the Apply program is optimized for many subscription sets. If your Apply program only has one subscription set, you can optimize the processing of the Apply program for this condition by activating the opt4one Apply program keyword.

When you optimize the Apply program for one subscription set, the Apply program uses fewer CPU resources, and you improve throughput rates. The Apply program also caches and reuses the information regarding the subscription-set members and columns.

When you activate the `opt4one` Apply program keyword and you add a member to a set or otherwise modify a set, you must stop the Apply program and start it again. This enables the Apply program to pick up the changes in the control tables.

Fewer Updates for Subscription Sets with Multiple Members

Compared to previous versions of DB2 UDB, in DB2 UDB v8.1 the Apply program makes fewer updates to control tables for subscription sets with multiple members.

CD-ROM
Installation

The accompanying CD-ROM contains a copy of DB2 UDB Personal Edition v8.1.2 for Windows. This product is provided in "Try and Buy" mode. Once the product has been installed, it will continue to operate for 180 days. To use this software past the 180-day period requires a DB2 license, which is not provided.

DB2 INSTALLATION

To install DB2 for Windows, perform the following steps:

- Insert CD-ROM.
- If the installation does not automatically start, use the file manager to execute `X:\SETUP.EXE` (where X is the drive letter of your CD drive).

If you are installing on a Windows NT/2000/XP/2003 workstation, you must be an administrator. This username must belong to the Administrators group and must comply with SQL naming standards.

DOCUMENTATION

Two sets of documentation are provided on the CD. The documentation can be found in the following directories:

- DB2-PDF
  The documentation in this directory contains the manuals in PDF (Adobe Acrobat Reader) format. The *README.TXT* file contains the titles of the documents and their corresponding file name in this directory.

To obtain the Adobe Acrobat Reader, please go to the Adobe product website:
www.adobe.com/products/acrobat/

- DB2-HTML

    The DB2-HTML directory contains all of the documentation in HTML format. To view
    the documentation you need to use either Internet Explorer or Netscape Navigator. Use
    your browser to view the file called *INDEX.HTM* and the browser will display the main
    DB2 Information Center screen:

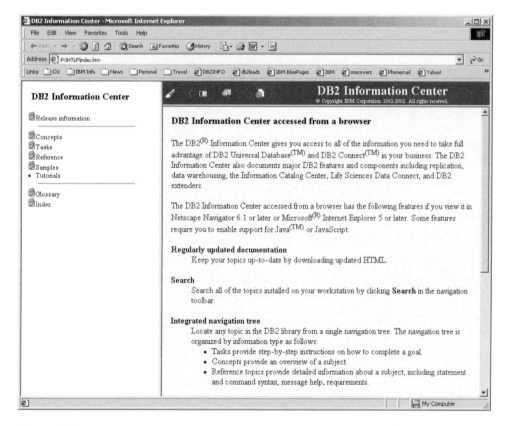

Figure A.1
Main DB2 Information Center screen.

You can access the documentation from this screen, as well as search for keywords
across all of the documentation.

DB2DEMO

The DB2DEMO program is included on the CD-ROM in the DB2DEMO directory. The DB2DEMO
program allows you to try out various features of DB2 without having to write any code.

One of the shortcuts created in the DB2DEMO folder is the DB2 UDB v8 Certification Examples icon. By clicking on this icon, you will be able to try out many of the features found within the Certification Guide. Help for this program can be found from within the product itself, or by using a browser to view the INDEX.HTM file in the DB2DEMO directory that was created as part of the installation process.

Installation File

The DB2DEMO installation program consists of only one file that contains the executable along with all of the supporting files required to run the program. The file is found in the DB2DEMO directory on the CD:

- *DB2DEMOSETUP.EXE*—Installation program for the DB2DEMO program
  Before beginning the installation, make sure that you have about 40M of disk space available (half of this is temporary space that will be released when the installation is complete).

Setup and Installation of the Program

From within the directory that you found the DB2DEMOSETUP program (either the CD-ROM or on your hard drive), you double-click your left mouse button on this file name, or execute it from a command line:

```
X:\DB2DEMO\db2demosetup.exe
```

After clicking on the DB2DEMOSETUP program, there will be some temporary messages displayed while the program unpacks some files:

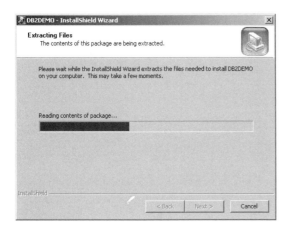

Figure A.2
InstallShield Wizard—Extracting Files screen.

When the files have been unpacked. you will be presented with the first installation screen:

Figure A.3
DB2 UDB Demonstration Program Welcome screen.

Make sure that you have exited any programs that may be currently running (just to be on the safe side) and the hit NEXT to continue on to the next step.

The next screen gives you the copyright and legal information for the program. Please read it and select YES to continue:

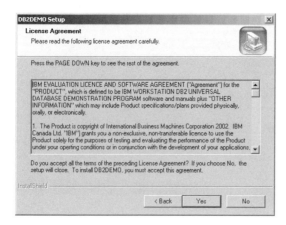

Figure A.4
DB2DEMO License Agreement screen.

The next screen that appears is the directory screen:

Figure A.5
Directory screen.

Select a drive and directory to place the DB2DEMO program into. By default, the name of the directory is called DB2DEMO and it is placed on the C: drive. Use the Drives and Directories list boxes to change the value of the field to point to the installation directory you want.

When you are ready to go, hit the NEXT button. At this point in time, the installation program will ask you for the Program Group that the DB2DEMO program will be placed into:

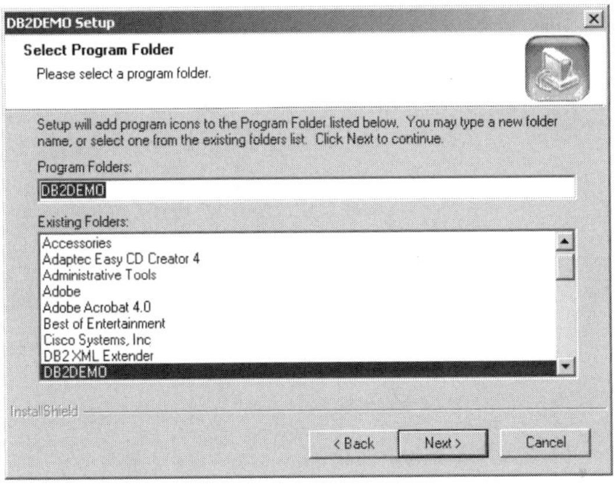

Figure A.6
Select Program Folder screen.

Once you have selected the group name, the program will confirm the installation information:

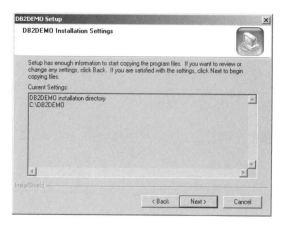

Figure A.7
Installation Settings confirmation screen.

Once you hit the continue button, the program will begin copying files:

Figure A.8
Copying program files progress screen.

When copying is complete, the final dialog box will be displayed:

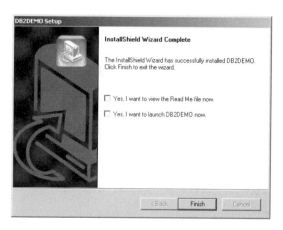

Figure A.9
Installation complete screen.

Depending on which operating system you were installing on, you may be asked to reboot the machine, or be given an option to try out the demo program or look at the additional README information that is supplied with the program. You can also start up DB2DEMO by going into the DB2DEMO group and selecting the DB2DEMO icon:

Figure A.10
DB2DEMO icon.

Advanced Installation

The SAMPLE database can be installed on any server supported by DB2 UDB. The program that creates that sample database is called db2sampl and can be found in the *sqllib\bin* directory on your server.

When you install the database on a different machine, you still need to use the DB2DEMO program on Windows 2000 or Windows XP, but the data will be on the server instead of the local machine.

In order to install this on a different server, you need to be very familiar with DB2 commands and the security of the machine you are working on. The steps required to run this demo against a different server are:

1. Install DB2 on the server operating system
2. Create a privileged userid that can administer the DB2 system
3. Create the sample database on the system
4. Create a userid on this system that can be used to connect from the remote system
5. Set up the Windows client so that the SAMPLE database has been catalogued properly. This includes installing the DB2 Client Application Enabler code on the workstation. Without this code, the demonstration program cannot run.

Once the installation is complete, you should be able to run the DB2DEMO program from the client and connect to the remote SAMPLE database.

Special Notes for Windows 98/Me Users

DB2 UDB version 8.1 supports Windows XP/2000/NT/2003 users. Earlier releases also supported Windows 95/98/Me which required special handling from a security perspective. Note that Windows 95 is no longer supported in DB2 version 8.1, but continues to be supported for DB2 version 7.2.

DB2 UDB requires that you be logged on with a username before anything can be done in the database. Usually this is not a problem with Windows NT/2000/XP since you must logon before getting to your desktop. The situation is not that straightforward in Windows 95/98/Me. You might have a logon panel if you are connecting to a network. You can bypass this logon however, and still get your desktop! What this means is that for some of you have never identified yourself with a userid to the system.

When DB2 starts up, either with a DB2START command or any of the other system commands, it first determines if you have identified yourself to the system. If not, it will look at the DB2LOGON information to determine what your userID should be. In the majority of cases, you will have not issued a DB2LOGON, and so the commands will fail. If you find that commands are failing, you may want to issue the DB2LOGON command and enter a userID and password before issuing any DB2 commands. The userID and password can be any value you like, as long as DB2 has something to work with.

The DB2DEMO program looks to see if you are logged on as a user. If you are not logged on, the program will create a default logon with a userID of DB2DEMO and with a password of DB2DEMO. You can see if this has occurred after the program has started by looking at the system variables by issuing a %DUMPVARS command. This will display all of the variables in the system, and USERID and PASSWORD should be displayed in this list.

If you find yourself outside of the demonstration program having problems using DB2, you may want to issue the DB2LOGON command. The db2logon command simulates a user logon. The format of the db2logon command is:

```
db2logon userid /p:password
```

The userID that is specified for the command must meet the DB2 naming requirements:

- It can be a maximum of 30 characters (bytes) in length.
- It cannot be any of the following: USERS, ADMINS, GUESTS, PUBLIC, LOCAL, or any SQL reserved word that is listed in the SQL Reference.
- It cannot begin with: SQL, SYS or IBM
- Characters can include:
  - A through Z (Windows 95 and Windows 98 support case-sensitive user IDs)
  - 0 through 9
  - @, #, or $

Uninstalling the Demonstration

To uninstall the DB2DEMO program, use the Add/Delete panel within the Services group to delete the application:

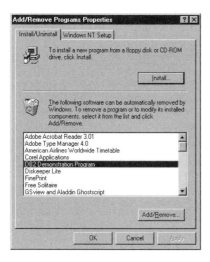

Figure A.11
Uninstalling the demonstration.

Select the DB2 Demonstration program and the various files will be deleted. The directory may not be deleted if you have personalized any of the files.

Support

We've tried to think of everything, but occasionally things go wrong. If you have a problem with the demonstration code, please send us a note with your email address, name, and a description of the problem. We can be reached at baklarz@yahoo.com.

Index

A

Administration notification log, 163–164
AIX and DB2 UDB, 4
AIX5.2B support, 172
ALLOW READ ACCESS, 103–104
ALTER TABLESPACE statement, 141, 142f
    and rebalancer, 162
ANDing, 40–42
APIs (administrative application programming inter-
        faces), 149
    snapshot functions, 191–194
Apply enhancements
    program optimization, 343–344
    target-key columns (replicating changes), 342
    transaction commit frequency, 342
ARAM (Automatic Relationship and Association),
        94
ASNLOAD exit routine, 343

B

BCP (Bulk Copy Program)/Sybase text file format
        and data movement utilities, 169
BERNOULLI sampling, 209–211
BI (business intelligence), 3
    IBM's direction, 8
    see also DB2 UDB Data Warehouse Edition
BID (Block ID), 30
BIND command, 260
Bit-filters selection, 95
Block-based buffer pools, 92–93

Buffer pools see Dynamic memory allocation/online
        reconfiguration

C

CA (Configuration Assistant), 115–118
CALL statement, 200–201
Capture enhancements
    concurrent, 340
    multiple instances, 340–342
    operational parameters overrides, 337–338
    program control, 337
    pruning data, 340
    recapturing control from replicas, 339
    replication definitions/source tables and col-
            umns dynamic update, 338–339
    row capture (individual replication sources),
            339
    start modes, 338
CIM (Common Information Model), 298
Clustering index, 24
Compression, 57–58
    COMPRESS SYSTEM DEFAULT option, 58
    example, 60–63
    identification of, 65
    NULL, 57
    row record format, 59–60
    savings estimation, 66
    supported data types, 64
    VALUE COMPRESSION, 58–59
Configuration see DB2 database project/project con-
        figuration and properties

Connection concentrator, 6
   activation, 76
   and connection management, 75–76
   `max_connections`, 76
   `max_coordagents`, 76
   `num_poolagents`, 76
   operation, 76–77
Consistency token, 259
Container operations, 141
   adding containers/no rebalancing, 145–146
   dropping containers from DMS table space,
      143–144
   size reduction in DMS table space, 144–145
   table space maps, 141–143
`CREATE INDEX` statement, 52–54
`CREATE/ALTER TABLE` commands, 33, 58–59, 70,
   80, 173
CRM (customer relationship management), 3
Cube Views, 10–11
`CURSOR` file type, 109

D

DADX (Document Access Definition Extension)
   files, 320, 322
   SQL operations, 320
   XML operations, 321
DAS (DB2 Administration Server), configuration
   parameters (online), 150
Data Connections folder *see* DB2 Data Connections
   folder
Data movement utilities, and OEM products, 169
Database monitoring, 83
   collection of timestamps issues, 83
   and Control Center performance monitor capa-
      bility, 89
   `CREATE EVENT MONITOR` statement, 84–85
   deadlock monitoring, 84
   SQL access to event monitor data, 84–85
   SQL access to snapshot monitor data, 86–88
Database project *see* DB2 database project
`DATABASE_MEMORY` (dynamic memory allocation/
   online reconfiguration), 148
DB2 Connect ASE (DB2 Connect Application Server Edition), 12
DB2 Data Connections folder, 270–271
   procedures and functions, 272
      and `ADO.NET` code, 272–273

   tables and views folder, 271
      and `ADO.NET` code, 272
DB2 database project, 268–269, 282, 296–297
   adding a database project, 283
   advanced scripting/script options, 290
      data grid output options, 291
      ignoring error options, 291
      platform restriction option, 292
      scripts and database transactions, 290
      statement separator option, 292
      test scripts, 290
   build order, 296
      project items build order, 296
   DB2 project scripts, 284–285
      procedure scripts, 285
   DB2 reference section for a project, 283–284
   function scripts, 287–289
   generic scripts, 289–290
   project configuration and properties, 292–293
      file extensions, 294
      item properties, 294
      persisting properties, 294–295
      project properties, 293
   project dependencies, 295–296
   script template files, 269
      procedure script templates, 286
   script wizards, 269–270
      procedure script wizard, 287
DB2 UDB Data Warehouse Edition, 8
   BI platform, 8
   EE and SE editions, 11
   infrastructure, 9–10
   see also Cube Views; MOLAP
DB2 UDB Enterprise Server Edition, 8
   Connect component, 12–13
DB2 UDB Express, 5–6
   capabilities and benefits, 6–7
DB2 UDB Personal Edition, 5
DB2 UDB V8.1.2, 3
   extensibility features changes, 14
      DB2 Information Integrator (II), 15–16
      Query Patroller, 16–17
      Spatial Extender, 15
      text searching extenders, 14
      XML Extender, 14
   licensing and packaging changes, 5, 6f, 12,
      13–14, 17
   operating systems, 4, 4t–5t
   release-specific data, 4

see also Container operations; Development Center; Dynamic memory allocation/online reconfiguration; Information Integrator; Package version identifiers; Replication enhancements; Tools; Utilities (online); Web services

DB2 UDB Workgroup Server/Workgroup Server Unlimited Editions, 7

db2fm, 139

db2Inspect API *see* INSPECT

db2stop, 138

DEADLOCKS, 84

Debugging/testing *see* Development Center

DECLARE GLOBAL TEMPORARY TABLE statement, 51

DECLARE statement, 55

Deferred binding, 259

Development Center, 217–218
    areas, 234–235
    debugging/testing, 236–238
        Java stored procedures, 239–240
        SQL PL debugging, 239
    launching, 218–219
        Project View, 219–224
    object creation/manipulation, 235–236
    stored procedure creation, 231
        steps, 232–234
    UDF creation, 224–225
        definition panel, 226–228
        function name panel, 225
        options panel, 229–230
        parameters panel, 228–229
        return value panel, 228
        summary panel, 230–231
    see also SQL Assist tool

DGTT (declared global temporary table), 51–52
    creating a temporary index, 53–54
    default logging for rollback support, 54–55
    index restrictions, 52–53
    index support, 52
    statistics support, 55

Distributed catalog cache, 91–92

DMTF (Desktop Management Task Force), 298

DPF (database partitioning feature), *see* DB2 UDB Enterprise Server Edition

DROP utility, 80

DSD (Dynamic System Domain) support, 172–173

Dynamic memory allocation/online reconfiguration, 147
    configuration parameters (online), 149–150
    CREATE/ALTER BUFFERPOOL statement, 147–148
    memory customization, 148–149

E

ERP (enterprise resource planning), 3

F

Fault Monitor facility, 138–139

Federated Data Server, 307

Federated systems enhancements
    Control Center administration of federated objects, 310, 311f
    data manipulation (on data sources), 308
    MQTs for data sources, 310
    supported federated server platforms, 311
    table manipulation (on data sources), 308
        altering tables, 309–310
        dropping tables, 310
        table creation, 308–309
        transparent DDL transaction restrictions, 310
    see also WebSphere MQ integration enhancements

FLUSH PACKAGE CACHE, 261

FMC (fault monitor coordinator), 138

G

GRANT package privilege, 260

H

Health Center, 118–119
    health indicator thresholds, 119–119
        recommended actions, 123t–124t
        recommended actions/example, 121–122
    health monitor, 119
    health snapshots, 194–196

High-water mark, 143

HISTORY command, 173–174

HP-UX and DB2 UDB, 4

I

IBM.Data.DB2, 278
Identity column support, 196
    identity column, 196–198
    sequences, 198–199
    uniqueness considerations, 199–200
Impact policy, 162
IMPORT utility, 80
Index reorganization, 153
    renaming existing indexes, 153
    see also Clustering index; MDC tables/and in-
        dexes
Indoubt Transaction Manager, 135
    actions available, 137
    container, 136–137
    user interface, 135–136
Information Integrator, 307–308
    data sources available, 311–312
    see also Federated systems enhancements
Informational constraints, 67, 70
    and complex queries, 70
    considerations, 73
    example, 70–72
    redundancies, 69
    Star Schema, 68–69
    usage, 67–68
INSERT operator, with UNION ALL, 177–180
INSPECT, 153–154
    authority requirements, 154
    and customized error reporting, 155
    example, 155–156
    syntax, 154
INSTANCE_MEMORY (dynamic memory allocation/
    online reconfiguration), 148
INSTEAD OF triggers, 183–185

J

Java
    debugging/testing Java stored procedures,
        239–240
    enhancements, 257–258
    Java-based routines/multithreading, 93–94
JDBC Universal Driver, 257–258
    and Type 2 connectivity, 258
    and Type 4 connectivity, 258
Join variations (new), 95

L

Linux, LDAP (Lightweight Directory Access Proto-
    col) support, 171–172
Linux and DB2 UDB, 4
Load functions
    data loading from cursor, 109
    data loading into partitioned databases,
        106–108
    LOAD IN PROGRESS table state, 105
    LOAD QUERY command, 106
    LOAD utility, 80
        online load, 103–104
    Load wizard, 109–114
LOCK WITH FORCE, 105
Logging, 99
    diagnostic (improvements in), 102
    log chaining, 173
    transactional (improvements in), 99
        infinite active log space, 99–100
        log space, 99
        log space consumption, 100
        mirroring, 101
        performance improvements, 100
        transaction blocking (full logs), 101–102
    see also Administration notification log
LPAR/DLPAR (dynamic) support, 172

M

MDC (multidimensional clustering) tables, 21–22,
    31–33, 32f, 48–49
    benefits, 22
    creation, 33–34
    and DELETE operations, 46–47
    dimensions, 22
        selection of, 47–48
    and indexes, 35
        ANDing, 40–42
        composite block indexes, 38–40
        dimension block indexes, 35, 36f, 37–38
        operations, 40
        ORing, 42
    and INSERT operations, 44–46
    organization, 24–25, 25f
    and query SELECT operations, 43–44
    terminology, 26, 27f
        block, 29
        Block ID (BID), 30

block index, 29–30
block size/blocking factor, 29
cell, 28, 29f
dimension, 26, 28f
generated column, 30–31
MDC table, 26
montonicity, 31
and OLAP, 22
slice, 26, 28, 28f
vs. traditional tables, 23–26
and UPDATE operations, 46
utilities, 48
Memory Tracker, 127–128
Memory Visualizer, 124–125
history view, 127
tree view, 126–127
MERGE SQL, 201–203
authorization, 208–209
error conditions, 207–208
IGNORING records, 206
MERGE syntax, 203–205
WHEN MATCHED logic, 205–206
Microsoft environment and DB2, 4, 263–264, 303;
Windows process model for replication
enhancements, 335
ADO.NET sample code, 279
DB2 managed provider ADO.NET objects, 278
DB2 managed provider tools, 280
Command text editor, 281–282
Data Adapter Configuration Wizard,
280–281
Data Connection editor, 280
native managed .NET providers, 278
Visual Studio .NET, 265–266, 278
DB2 objects, 278–279
development overview, 267–268
development tools customization, 275–276
dynamic help, 274
launch (development and administrative
tools), 276–277
output views, 274–275
product availability, 266
registering Add-Ins, 266–267
Server Explorer, 270–273
Solution Explorer, 268–270
SQL editor, 273
Windows 2003 support, 264–265
see also DB2 Data Connections folder; DB2
database project; WMI; XA interface

MIGRATE DATABASE command, 323
MOLAP (multidimensional online analytical processing), 9–10, 21
see also MDC tables
Monotonicity, 31
Moore's law, 21
MQT (materialized query table), 79, 156
creation, 80
for data sources, 310
incremental refresh, 157–159
performance considerations, 81
populating, 80
restrictions, 79–80
see also Summary table

N

Nicknames, 308
NOT LOGGED, 54–55
NULL compression see Compression

O

Object creation/manipulation see Development Center
OLE DB Provider, 301
enhancements, 301–302
restrictions, 302
ORDER BY enhancements, 186
FETCH FIRST clause, 186, 187–188
ORDER BY ORDER OF clause, 186–187
ORing, 42

P

Package version identifiers, 259
FLUSH PACKAGE CACHE, 261
package overview, 259
package privileges, 260
VERSION example, 260
Page cleaner I/O improvements, 93
PARTITIONED DB CONFIG, 107–108
Performance enhancements, 91
prefetching see Block-based buffer pools
see also ARAM; Bit-filters selection; Distributed catalog cache; Java-based rou-
tines/multithreading; Join variations
(new); Page cleaner I/O improvements; 64-bit support

PLM (planning and logistics management), 3
Pool relative addressing, 141
PRECOMPILE command, 260

Q

QUIESCE command, 166–167

R

READ ACCESS table state, 105–106
Rebalancing, 143
Reconfiguration *see* Dynamic memory allocation/
    online reconfiguration
REFRESH TABLE statement, 79
Relational databases
    and complex queries, 209
    multidimension issues, 21
    and SQL, 177
    see also MDC tables; MOLAP
REORG INDEXES command, 151
REORG TABLE command, 151
REORGCHK utility, 151
REPEATABLE sampling, 214–215
Replication enhancements, 329
    64-bit support, 336
    and data links values, 336
    migration utility, 336
    monitoring, 332
        current status (replication programs),
            333–334
        historical data analysis (replication pro-
            grams), 334–335
        Replication Alert Monitor, 332–333
    name length extension, 336
    password encryption, 336
    performance, 343
    Replication Center, 329
        Launchpad, 330
        Operations folder, 331
        Replication Definitions folder, 330, 331f
        starting, 329–330
    Replication Server, 307
    trace facility, 336
    Windows process model, 335
    see also Apply enhancements; Capture en-
        hancements
REVOKE package privilege, 260

ROLLFORWARD DATABASE command, 168
RUNCMD command, 173–174
RUNSTATS, 55
    enhancements, 167–168
RUNSTATS utility, 151

S

SELECT statement, TABLESAMPLE clause, 209–215
SIGNAL command, 207–208
64-bit support, 94
Snapshot API functions, 191, 192t–193t
    general form, 193–194
Snapshot monitor, 86
    DB2_SNAPSHOT_NOAUTH registry variable, 88
    SNAPSHOT_FILEW file capture, 87–88
    SNAPSHOT_FILEW request types, 86–87
SOAP (Simple Object Access Protocol), 315
    UDF installation, 316
    UDF signatures, 316–317
    UDF tasks, 316
    UDF usage examples, 317–319
Solaris and DB2 UDB, 4
SQL Assist tool, 240, 257
    sample session, 246–257
    start points, 240–241
    structure, 241, 242f
        details area, 243–245
        outline view, 242–243
        panel buttons, 246
        SQL Code window, 245–246
SQL (Structured Query Language), 177, 215–216
    editor (Microsoft environment), 273
    functions, 188–189
    health snapshots, 194–196
    INSTEAD OF triggers, 183–185
    MERGE SQL, 201–203
        authorization, 208–209
        error conditions, 207–208
        IGNORING records, 206
        MERGE syntax, 203–205
        WHEN MATCHED logic, 205–206
    operations, 320
    ORDER BY enhancements, 186–188
    sampling, 209, 215
        BERNOULLI sampling, 209–211
        REPEATABLE sampling, 214–215
        SYSTEM sampling, 211–213

and snapshot API functions, 191, 192t–193t
    general format, 193–194
stored procedure debugging, 239
UNION ALL (insert), 177–180
and XML publishing functions, 190–191, 190t
    see also CALL statement; Identity column support
        port
Star Schema, 68–69
Storage Management tool, 128
    Storage Management view, 128, 132–133
        columns, 133–135
        Specify Threshold Settings notebook,
            128–132
Stored procedure creation see Development Center
Stripe, 141
    stripe set, 145
Summary table, 156–157
    example (with incremental refresh), 157–159
SYSCAT.INDEXES, queries, 152
SYSCAT.TABLES, queries, 152
SYSTABLES, 91
SYSTEM sampling, 211–213

T

Table reorganization, 151
    determination of need, 151–152
    and type-2 indexes, 152–153
    see also Index reorganization
Table space
    adding containers/no rebalancing, 145–146
    ALTER TABLESPACE statement, 141, 142f
    dropping containers from, 143–144
    history file change, 164–166
    maps, 141–143
    rebalancing, 143
    size reduction, 144–145
    with UNION ALL, 180–182
Table states, 105–106
Tables, traditional vs. MDC, 23–26
TABLESAMPLE clause (SELECT statement), 209–215
Throttling utilities, 161–162
TIMESTAMP, 83
    TIMESTAMP_FORMAT function, 188–189
Tivoli focused options, 171
Tools
    Configuration Assistant (CA), 115–118
    Fault Monitor facility, 138–139
    Health Center, 118–124

Indoubt Transaction Manager, 135–137
    Memory Tracker, 127–128
    Memory Visualizer, 124–127
    Storage Management, 128–133
    see also SQL Assist tool
Trace facility enhancements, 169–170
Transaction log space usage, 173
Transaction support, 297–298
Type-2 indexes, 152–153

U

UDF creation see Development Center
UNION ALL, 177–180
    and table spaces, 180–182
UNION query, 67–68
Universal Driver see JDBC Universal Driver
UNIX, and multiple service level install, 170
User-maintained summary tables see MQT (materialized query table)
util_impact_lim, 162
Utilities (online), 151
    database inspection tool, 153–156
    index reorganization, 153
    table reorganization, 151–153

V

VARCHAR_FORMAT function, 188–189
VARGRAPHIC, 173
VERSION example, 260
Visual Studio .NET see Microsoft environment and
        DB2

W

WBEM (Web-Based Enterprise Management), 298
Web services, 315
    application server, 322
    DB2 as consumer, 315–319
    DB2 as provider, 319
        architecture, 319–320
        DADX files, 320–322
    Web Tools, 322
    see also XML enhancements
WebSphere MQ integration enhancements, 312
    asynchronous MQ listener utility, 312–313

message queues (transactional support), 313
   nontransactional MQ functions, 314
   single-phase commit transactional MQ
      functions, 313–314
Windows and DB2 UDB *see* Microsoft environment
   and DB2
WMI (Microsoft) Windows Management Instrumentation, 298–299
   architecture, 299
   benefits, 300–301
   WMI SDK (Software Development Kit), 300
WORF (Web Object Runtime Framework), 319–320
   installation/configuration, 322
WSDL (Web Service Definition Language) file, 315

X

XA interface, 297–298
XBSA (X/Open Backup Services API) support, 168
XML enhancements
   migrating XML-enabled databases, 323
   new UDFs, 324–325
   timestamp normalization, 325
   validating XML documents, 323–324
   XML extender, 322–323
      in partitioned database environments, 325
   XML MQ stored procedures, 327t
   XML MQ UDFs, 326, 326t

About the CD-ROM

The CD-ROM included with *DB2 Version 8: The Official Guide* contains a copy of DB2 UDB Personal Edition v8.1.2 for Windows. This product is provided in "Try and Buy" mode. Once the product has been installed, it will continue to operate for 180 days. To use this software past the 180-day period requires a DB2 license, which is not provided. For further information, please refer to Appendix A.

LICENSE AGREEMENT

Use of the software accompanying *DB2 Version 8: The Official Guide* is subject to the terms of the License Agreement and Limited Warranty, found on the previous two pages.

TECHNICAL SUPPORT

If the CD-ROM is damaged, you may obtain a replacement copy by sending an email that describes the problem to: *disc_exchange@prenhall.com.*

If you are having problems with this software, call (800) 677-6337 between 8:00 a.m. and 5:00 p.m. CST, Monday through Friday. You can also get support by filling out the web form located at http://247.prenhall.com/mediaform.